PRIVACY MATTERS

Navigating the Data Protection Maze

Ketan Modh, PhD

INDIA • SINGAPORE • MALAYSIA

ISBN
Paperback 979-8-89632-306-8
Hardcase 979-8-89699-459-6

To my home city of Mumbai,
where privacy is fleeting but worth its weight in gold

Table of Contents

Part 3

Corporate Strategies for Data Protection Compliance

Table of Contents

Foreword: The country inches forward, but the biggest reforms are yet to come

17.8% of the world's population lives in India[1]. At the time of writing, standing at 1.429 billion, India is the world's largest country in terms of population. It is also the world's largest democracy with the potential to be playing a leading role in Asia[2], leveraging its geographical position in South Asia to inspire other countries in the region to deploy best practices in the protection of privacy and other fundamental human rights.

Over the past twenty years or so, I have had the pleasure of visiting various parts of India on a number of occasions, sometimes for work, sometimes for pleasure. It is impossible to visit India without being

1. 17.5% of the world's population lives in China
2. Only two countries taken together, out of the UN's 193 member states, India and China, account for more than 35% of the world's population, which is a sobering thought when one reflects on what happens if either of these two, let alone both of them, makes mistakes when protecting the fundamental right to privacy. To put things in perspective, all 46 member states of the Council of Europe (i.e. all of Europe minus Russia, which disgraced itself and was subsequently kicked out of the Council of Europe following the 2022 full-scale invasion of Ukraine) group 673 million inhabitants. Which means that even if all European countries get privacy right (and they don't all do so) this only represents just over 8.23% out of the world's population estimated to be somewhere around 8.2 billion at the end of 2024. Moral of the story: the world desperately needs many more countries to get things right when it comes to protecting fundamental human rights like privacy for as large a number of the world's population as possible.

awestruck by the diversity and richness of its culture, its peoples and their history. Some of India's beauty may be out in the open, some of it may be quite hidden but all of it makes me appreciate how much more India has to offer to the rest of the world…and to its own people. There have been many occasions, during the past forty years which I have dedicated to the protection of the fundamental human right to privacy, when I have paused to reflect about India and its citizens. How many of those 1.429 billion Indians know about their fundamental right to Privacy? How many of them are aware that India is a signatory to and has ratified the International Covenant on Civil and Political Rights (ICCPR) of 1966 in which India has committed itself to protect the privacy of each and every person on its territories? Even if they know, how many of them have a realistic expectation that this fundamental right will be protected by their very own governments?

Arriving as it does, barely a year after the India Digital Personal Data Protection Act 2023 (DPDPA) came into effect on September 1, 2023, Ketan Modh's book is a useful and timely guide to readers wishing to navigate the latest privacy law that India has recently adopted. As Dr. Modh explains, this new law follows the landmark *Puttaswamy* judgement of India's highest court which, in 2017, finally confirmed an interpretation of India's constitution which includes the fundamental right to privacy. It is perhaps therefore useful to ask - *and* attempt to answer - the question: do *Puttaswamy* and the DPDPA mean that concerns about the right to privacy in India are now over? The answer must be a resounding NO. At the end of 2024 and at the dawn of 2025, we are not even approaching the end of the beginning of a comprehensive and effective approach to the protection of privacy in India, let alone the beginning of the end part of the implementation of a holistic approach to providing adequate safeguards and remedies to Indian citizens concerned about their privacy.

This cautious assessment of the situation in India at end 2024 is not because of the visible defects of what the DPDPA sets out to cover but rather that which it does not cover and which it was never intended to provide for. As it stands, the DPDPA sets out to cover the use of personal data in much the same way and to an extent which is comparable to the EU's GDPR. The main cause for concern are therefore those areas of law which the GDPR never intended to cover but which are provided for by other areas of European law or US or Australian law and which have a significant impact on the level of protection that is afforded to citizens of those other major democracies. Dr. Modh's book assists the reader in understanding how personal data is now protected by the DPDPA when such data is used by commercial corporations, individuals and most government departments. It understandably does not delve into those areas which the DPDPA does not seek to regulate and chief amongst these one must note the reluctance of India's Government to transparently subject the personal data processing activities of its police and intelligence agencies. In accordance with the intent of the legislator in India, the DPDPA does not apply to personal data that is processed for law enforcement or national security purposes. This exception should be one of grave concern for India's citizens. To put things bluntly, how is the right to privacy of a person living in India protected from unlawful breach by police or secret services working in pursuit of a law enforcement or security mandate?

It is impossible to speak of rule of law in such cases because, quite literally, save for what comes out of *Puttaswamy*, there IS no law. The main point I'd like to make in this foreword is that there SHOULD be a law and, the sooner, the better. The second main point being made here is "not just any law", especially not a half-hearted one which only partially addresses the issues, but a law which, in the words of a leading Indian privacy lawyer, entrenches "comprehensive privacy for all Indians"[3] A carefully-thought out and well-discussed law which should strive to learn from the efforts and mistakes made in other countries. What, then, should this law consist of?

While mine is a voice which has cared deeply for India for many years, it is time for Indian Governments to listen to Indian voices which have rightly raised serious concerns over a span of more than two decades. Let those Indian voices be the ones which indicate much of what India lacks and what the next pertinent law in India should provide for. For, firstly, the protection of Indian citizens from the actions of their own regional or federal governments is nothing new. It is an issue which has been brewing since India's independence and which has been the subject of public debate for at least fifty years: "In 1975, during the infamous Emergency of Indira Gandhi, the RAW was accused[4] of being a private agency of the Prime Minister rather than the nation's external intelligence agency. In the 1990's then Prime Minister PV Narasimha Rao used the Intelligence Bureau to spy on his own MPs.[5] Indeed, back in 2016, Vinay Sitapati reminded his readers that "ALMOST 25 years ago, in

---

3. Vrinda Bhandari, *The Pegasus Case Must be Used to Press for Change in Surveillance Laws*, 05 August 2021, The India Forum, last accessed on 22 December 2021
4. For the in-depth story reported in September 1977 and updated in April 2015, see Dilip Bobb and A.R.Shree , *Home Minister Charan Singh determined to cut RAW down to size,* India Today, Sep 15, 1977 | UPDATED: Apr 1, 2015 16:28 IST, last accessed on 22 December 2024 at https://www.indiatoday.in/magazine/special-report/story/19770915-home-minister-charan-singh-determined-to-cut-raw-down-to-size-823884-2014-09-04
5. Edmund ROY, *India: A very colonial hangover*, The Interpreter, 28 July 2021, Last accessed on 19 December 2024 at https://www.lowyinstitute.org/the-interpreter/india-very-colonial-hangover

late 1991, Narasimha Rao asked for a telling report from the Intelligence Bureau (IB). He wanted to know which of his Congress MPs were against which specific economic reform. The IB replied with a detailed note listing the four major kinds of economic reforms that the Rao government had unveiled: "i. Liberalization of trade and commerce, decontrol of industry.; ii. liberal entry of multinationals, foreign investment. iii. Privatization/dilution of public sector. iv. Reduction of fertilizer subsidy and agricultural policy."[6]

If Indira Gandhi was accused of using a national Indian intelligence service for narrow political ends, she was not alone in doing so. "In 1988, the chief minister of Karnataka Ramakrishna Hedge quit after allegations that he ordered phone taps on at least 50 of his colleagues and rivals. In 1990, Chandra Shekhar, who later briefly became prime minister, alleged that the then government was illegally tapping phones of 27 politicians, including his own. In 2010, 100 tapes of phone conversations between corporate lobbyist Niira Radia and leading politicians, industrialists and journalists recorded by tax investigators were leaked to the media. The then main opposition leader LK Advani remarked that the recordings reminded him of the Watergate scandal. "What has now changed is the scale, speed and discreteness with which electronic surveillance is being done on those who dissent," Rohini Lakshane, technologist and public policy researcher, said."[7]

---

6. Vinay Sitapati, *IB gave Narasimha Rao list of Congmen, ministers against 1991 reforms*, The Indian Express, 15 June 2016, last accessed on 22 December 2024 at https://indianexpress.com/article/india/india-news-india/intelligence-bureau-ib-narasimha-rao-congress-manmohan-singh-sonia-gandhi-2874380/
7. Soutik Biswas, *Pegasus: Why unchecked snooping threatens India's democracy*, BBC, 20 July 2021, last accessed on 21 December 2024 at https://www.bbc.com/news/world-asia-india-57887300

"In 2010, India's former vice President Hamid Ansari called for independent oversight and accountability to address executive domination over and "*misuse*" of the intelligence agencies.

In 2011, Manish Tewari, a former Minister of Information and Broadcasting, advanced a private member's Bill, seemingly in response. It was poorly drafted. It appeared to be making radical changes when, in fact, it did little more than maintain the status quo.[8]

The IDSA Task Force Report[9] of 2012, edited and authored by S.R. Banerjee remained largely unheeded as did other calls for reform in 2014[10]. Rather unsurprisingly but "More worrying in light of this history is the fact that so far there's been a complete lack of political will to change the status quo. Every federal government in independent India from the Congress to the BJP has been comfortable with carrying on an unaccountable and immune system set in place by the British Raj."[11] Being somebody born a subject of Her Majesty Queen Elizabeth II back when Malta was still a British colony and, also having studied the history not only of my birthplace but also of dozens of other British colonies, it is easy to agree with Edmund Roy that India is still suffering from "A very colonial hangover"[12]. "Like the British colonial police force, modern India's intelligence services operate with no legal

8. Ravi Nair, *Post Nijjar and Pannun fiascos, can India continue without parliamentary oversight for intelligence services?,* The Leaflet, last accessed om 21 December 2021 at https://theleaflet.in/explainer/post-nijjar-and-pannun-fiascos-can-india-continue-without-parliamentary-oversight-for-intelligence-services
9. A Case for Intelligence Reforms in India, IDSA Task Force Report, ISBN: 978-93-82169-03-1, India, 2012
10. Shashank Joshi, *India's intelligence agencies need fresh scrutiny,* The Interpreter, 16 January 2014, last accessed on 21 December 2021 at https://www.lowyinstitute.org/the-interpreter/india-s-intelligence-agencies-need-fresh-scrutiny
11. Edmund ROY, *India: A very colonial hangover*, The Interpreter, 28 July 2021, op.cit.
12. Ibid.

regulation or democratic oversight. That has led to a succession of scandals over the years, with India's spies standing accused of illegal espionage conducted at the behest of the political leadership. This is a real threat to democracy, which the country needs to address."[13]

Tracing the roots of the problem to India's colonial past has also been the subject of editorial opinion concerning one of the oldest intelligence agencies in the world, India's Intelligence Bureau (IB) "Take the case of IB. It was set up in 1887 through an administrative order by a British official. Today, 134 years later, there is no constitutional or statutory backing for IB, or even a formal charter, apart from a law in 1985 restricting some of its rights. There's no independent oversight or external scrutiny. It is essential to lay out an intelligence agency's remit, the range of actions permitted to the minister it reports to, and protections for the agency's director. There must be institutional safeguards to allow officials to refuse unreasonable instructions from the political executive."[14]

The allegations about the domestic interceptions of the IB remain seriously worrying: "The ability of the bureau to wiretap phones and listen in on almost all forms of communication without the need for a warrant is a cause of concern for many. While the use of sophisticated monitoring equipment has no doubt played a crucial role in enabling IB to better perform its job, the total lack of any oversight or regulations

13. "Security Code:-intelligence services can become enemies of india's law bring judicial legislative oversight", podbean, 25 March 2024, Last accessed on 19 December 2024 at https://theprint.podbean.com/e/security-code-intelligence-services-can-become-enemies-of-india-s-law-bring-judicial-legislative-oversight/

14. TOI Edit, *Spooky change: Intelligence agencies need parliamentary oversight. Let that be the post-Pegasus consensus,* Times of India, 25 July 2021, Last accessed on 19 December 2024 at https://timesofindia.indiatimes.com/blogs/toi-editorials/spooky-change-intelligence-agencies-need-parliamentary-oversight-let-that-be-the-post-pegasus-consensus/

makes it worrisome. IB keeps call data records, without any legal backing or cause, of select individuals for the Ministry of Home Affairs. Additionally, IB reportedly taps phone lines of every minister and prominent opposition figures. It also taps some civil servants as well journalists and other activists. This creates a situation where democracy is possibly undermined by those very individuals who are tasked to safeguard it. Furthermore, following the November 2008 Mumbai attacks, IB ordered all communications companies to discontinue the use of VoIP call service to and from the country till a way to track these calls was established. While warrantless wiretapping has been declared illegal, it is unlikely that the practice will cease to exist in the absence of strong regulatory and oversight mechanisms."[15]

"Ever since 1991, when evidence emerged that the Rajiv Gandhi government had conducted illegal wiretaps not just of its opponents but also senior ministers, similar scandals have regularly punctuated the course of India's politics. From Gujarat in 2013, to Karnataka in 2019 or Maharashtra in 2022, though, this subversion of the law and democratic institutions has passed unpunished."[16]

This is why one cannot disagree that "There is a need for specific legislation that would give India's intelligence community a statutory basis and a charter, and provide it with institutional levels of accountability."[17] In the words of Indian politician Manish Tewari,

---

15. Last accessed on 21 December 2024 at http://www.allgov.com/india/departments/ministry-of-home-affairs/intelligence-bureau?agencyid=7590
16. Praveen Swami, *Intelligence services can become enemies of India's law. Bring judicial, legislative oversight,* The Print, 17 March 2024 Last accessed on 21 December 2024 at https://theprint.in/opinion/security-code/intelligence-services-can-become-enemies-of-indias-law-bring-judicial-legislative-oversight/2003879/
17. 10Pointer, *India's Enduring Challenge of Intelligence Reforms,* 10Pointer, 19 December 2020, Last accessed on 19 December 2024 at https://www.10pointer.com/current-affairs/indias-enduring-challenge-of-intelligence-reforms

"A first step to protecting the right to privacy is to reform our intelligence agencies. No other major democracy has such a legal black hole in their intelligence and surveillance framework."[18]

The controversies during the 40 year-period 1975-2015 were not enough to convince the judges of India's highest court of the dire need to nudge the Government to legislative action. "A Public Interest Litigation filed in mid 2011 in Karnataka High Court alleges that the Intelligence Bureau operates in a "constitutional vacuum." The petition was filed by R.N. Kulkarni, a former joint assistant director of the IB who served the bureau for over three decades. The court admitted the petition in June and the hearing was adjourned on November 10, 2011. Kulkarni's petition points out that the IB was "not set up as an Act of Parliament, has no charter of duties, no framework of policies, no rules and regulations relating to personnel, recruitment, training, promotion and transfers." Another question raised is whether IB is a civilian or police organization. Moreover, Kulkarni contends that IB's broad powers, secret budget, and no accountability and transparency threatens the rights of Indian citizens and the democratic structure, thereby violating Article 21 of the Indian Constitution. In March 2012, Karnataka High Court ordered Center to explain the issue of IB's existence."[19] Yet, in 2016, one was compelled to read that "The Supreme Court today dismissed a petition that sought to make intelligence agencies like the Intelligence Bureau (IB), the Research & Analysis Wing (RAW) and the National Technical Research Organisation

18. Menash TEWARI, *To protect right to privacy, reform intel agencies first,* Deccan Chronicle, 3 April 2023, Last accessed on 19 December 2024 at https://www.deccanchronicle.com/opinion/columnists/080423/manish-tewari-to-protect-right-to-privacy-reform-intel-agencies-fir.html

19. Last accessed on 21 December 2024 at http://www.allgov.com/india/departments/ministry-of-home-affairs/intelligence-bureau?agencyid=7590

(NTRO) accountable to Parliament, saying that getting into the domain of intelligence may create a dent in national security"[20].

"We are not inclined to entertain this petition...Trying to get into the domain of intelligence may create dent in national security," a bench comprising Justices Dipak Misra and Shiva Kirti Singh said while rejecting the PIL filed by NGO Centre for Public Interest Litigation (CPIL)"[21] It is extremely difficult to understand in which bubble this particular bench of Indian judges were operating, displaying as they did a profound ignorance of the debates about privacy and surveillance raging across the world. When they arrived at this decision in February of 2016, this was over twenty years after, e.g. the establishment of the Intelligence Services Act 1994 in the UK and only a month after some freely accessible major Parliamentary discussions about topics which had been making headlines in the UK for the previous six months. In November 2016, only eight months after India's Supreme Court delivered its February 2016 decision which again condemned India to languish in the dark ages of Technology Law, the UK Parliament adopted the Investigatory Powers Act 2016. If the UK had been suffering from legislative blindness and a failure to properly oversee its intelligence services for centuries, only to wake up properly in 2016, all the available evidence suggests that in that very same year Indian legislators and judges were still suffering from a very colonial hangover and continued to embrace the inheritance of the Raj. The Supreme Court may have partially redeemed (with a substantially different bench

---

20. India TV News Desk, *No parliament oversight, CAG audit for RAW, IB, NTRO, rules Supreme court* , 23 Feb 2016, Last accessed on 21 December 2024 at https://www.indiatvnews.com/news/india/supreme-court-financial-audit-intelligence-agencies-57845.html.
21. Ibid.

of judges sitting) its failure of 2016 with the *Puttaswamy* judgement of 2017.

While the new DPDPA may have come into force last year in September 2023, controversies about surveillance in India have not let up and are continuing unabated into the winter of 2024. "Amnesty said journalists Siddharth Varadarajan of The Wire and Anand Mangnale of The Organized Crime and Corruption Reporting Project had been targeted with the spyware on their iPhones, with the latest identified case occurring in October.

In conclusion, it should be fairly obvious that you don't shake off a colonial hangover by refusing to learn from the mistakes that colonial masters make in their own homeland. On the contrary, you should study those mistakes closely in an effort not to repeat them at your own expense. For once in our lives, rather than being exploited by colonial masters, we have an opportunity of learning at their expense about mistakes that *they* made in their own homeland. Let us therefore look at some of the historical mistakes that, for example, the British have made when it comes to domestic and foreign intelligence services:

For centuries they allowed them to operate without a proper legal basis. The intelligence services were not subject to clear legal constraints nor bound by clearly defined objectives until the Intelligence Services Act 1994;

For centuries they allowed them to operate without Parliamentary scrutiny, It was only in 1994 that the Intelligence Security Committee was established in the UK.

For decades they permitted the Executive to decide exclusively whose phones or other means of communication could be placed under surveillance. It was only after the Investigatory Powers Act of 2016 that the UK introduced a system of Judicial Double Lock where decisions of the Minister responsible for Home Affairs enabling surveillance now require endorsement by independent senior Judges,

The British, like the French, like the Dutch, like the Belgians (and some other ex-colonial masters) learned that having Parliamentary oversight is not enough. They learned that, perhaps above all, the most effective oversight is that provided by an independent statutory expert agency, staffed by an adequate number of full-timers who could combine, at minimum, three different categories of skills:

Legal and Judicial knowledge and experience

Operational knowledge and preferably past experience of police and intelligence work

Information technology expertise

Introducing a package of laws which would address the above concerns would also enable India to join the club of the world's leading nations by signing and ratifying the Data Protection Convention where Articles 9[22] and 11[23] make clear provision on the derogations that may be applicable in the case of use of personal data for purposes of national security, defence and law enforcement. Effective and independent oversight is one of the key safeguards entrenched in the international gold standard provided by Convention 108+.

22. Convention 108 ETS
23. Convention 108+

The principal message in this short foreword is therefore a warning against complacency. There can be no doubt that the DPDPA explored by Dr. Modh in this book is an important step forward but it should be understood as being only that i.e. a first step. There is much more which is left to be done before once can rest assured that the fundamental right to privacy is adequately protected in India. Successive Governments in India, regardless of the party ideology to which they may have adhered to, have, for more than 70 years, been reluctant to do much to remove one of the most dubious leftovers from its colonial past i.e. the unfettered activities of a powerful intelligence service answering only, if at all, to political masters. We have seen that there is an emerging gold standard at the international level, already embraced by fifty-five other democracies. It is high time that the largest democracy on our planet, India, follow suit and implement the same standards, thus establishing itself as the major point of reference in privacy law in Asia. When it does so, it should not only look at the past and the present of other countries but also its own. Amongst other things, there is no evidence of significant effort in India to understand the evolution of privacy in its own past, in its own peoples, including all of its indigenous peoples[24]. For how can one take informed decisions about the present and the future without understanding when, how, and why certain practices and principles relevant to privacy and autonomy were born in India, when how and why they evolved and who was responsible for doing so?

On Sunday 9th June 2024 Narendra Modi was sworn in for his third consecutive term as Prime Minister, on this occasion for the first time in a power-sharing agreement as part of a coalition. While some have opined that this factor will make it more difficult for Modi to govern

24. Yet another task to add to the TO DO LIST of the conscientious legislator and minister

effectively, there is at least one area where he may be presented with a golden opportunity to secure his legacy at a relatively low risk to the possibility of achieving compromise with his coalition partners. Consensus with other parties should be easier to obtain on a measure which would reinforce the rule of law in India and here we should recall Modi's words on his most recent inauguration ""To run the government, a majority is necessary. But to run the nation, a consensus is necessary."[25]

For Modi can now bequeath to an Indian nation to whom he has dedicated a life of service, something which no other Indian Prime Minister has ever had the guts to do. He can give the lie to the naysayers, to all those who have claimed that a vote for Modi is one which puts democracy in danger by giving to the Indian nation a law which greatly strengthens democracy. Narendra Modi may well have the wisdom to introduce a package of laws which would put India's intelligence services on a proper legal basis while at the same time introducing a modern system of external oversight. The latter would not only entail the creation of a Parliamentary committee on Intelligence and Security but also a well resourced, effective and statutorily independent agency staffed with full time experts from all three major categories: judicial/ legal, operational and technological. This full-time oversight authority would, like its counterparts outside India, be responsible for oversight, both *ex-ante* as well as *ex-post*, of all forms of surveillance carried out by all of India's Intelligence services and possibly even its Police forces. Modi's longest-lasting legacy would thus include a carefully-thought out mechanism for strengthening the rule of law by also protecting India's citizens and residents from abuse of power and breach of privacy

25. Hannah Ellis-Petersen, *Narendra Modi sworn in for third term as prime minister of India,* the Guardian, 9th June 2024 ,last accessed on 23rd December 2024 at https://www.theguardian.com/world/article/2024/jun/09/narendra-modi-sworn-in-for-third-term-as-prime-minister-of-india

by the very forces set up by the state to protect a democratic way of life. Modi's track record suggests that he has the guts to do so and the political ability to negotiate the required parliamentary consensus. Time will tell whether he also has the wisdom to bequeath such a legacy to India's citizens.

J.A.C.[26]
Tal-Qroqq
Malta
23 December 2024

26. Joe Cannataci is head of the Department of Information Policy & Governance at the Faculty of Media & Knowledge Sciences of the University of Malta. He also co-founded and continues as Co-director (on a part-time basis), of STeP, the Security, Technology & e-Privacy Research Group at the University of Groningen in the Netherlands, where he is also Full Professor, holding the Chair of European Information Policy & Technology Law. A Fellow of the British Computer Society (FBCS) and UK Chartered Information Technology Professional (CITP), his law background meets his techie side as a Senior Fellow and Associate Researcher at the CNAM Security-Defense-Intelligence Department in Paris, France as well as the Centre for Health, Law and Emerging Technologies at the University of Oxford. His past roles include Vice-Chairman/Chairman of Council of Europe's (CoE) Committee of Experts on Data Protection 1992-1998, Working Parties on: Data Protection and New technologies (1995-2000); Data Protection & Insurance (1994-1998); CoE Rapporteur on Data Protection and Police (1993; 2010; 2012); CoE Expert Consultant on Data Protection and Cybercrime (2012-2014); UNESCO Expert Consultant on Privacy & Transparency on the Internet (2015); Scientific Co-ordinator of multiple EU FP7 & H2020 research projects focussing on privacy. He has designed and led several EU-supported research projects, both as Principal Investigator and overall scientific co-ordinator, since1986. He was decorated by the Republic of France as *Officier de l'Ordre de Palmes Academiques* (2002). Cannataci received the Louis F. Brandeis Prize for Privacy in the US in 2016 and was the laureate awarded the 2024 Amnesty International Chair by the University of Ghent. He was appointed by the Council of Europe as its lead expert to guide work on the interpretation of the world's largest and only international treaty regulating privacy and data protection, Convention 108+ (2022-2023). This followed Cannataci's appointment as the UN's first-ever Special Rapporteur on the Right to Privacy from which role he stepped down in August 2021 after having served the maximum of two successive three year-terms in the post.

Preface: Navigating the Data Protection Maze

Picture this: It's a typical morning in Bangalore's bustling tech district. Arjun Patel, the newly minted Chief Information Security Officer of a fast-growing startup, is staring at his computer screen in trepidation. The headline glaring back at him? "Government Enforces the Digital Personal Data Protection Act, 2023". His phone immediately starts buzzing with messages from colleagues, each more urgent than the last. Everyone is looking to him for answers, but all he sees is a maze of legal jargon and technical challenges.

Now imagine Priya Sharma, a young professional, casually scrolling through her social media feed. She pauses on an article about a recent data breach, and a thought crosses her mind: "What happens to all the information I put online?" She starts to wonder how companies handle her data, and what rights she has over her digital footprint.

If you're anything like Arjun or Priya, you're not alone. In today's digital India, data protection is no longer an abstract concept - it's a daily reality that affects us all. Whether you're a business trying to navigate the complex web of regulations, or an individual wanting to take control of your personal information, the data protection landscape can feel like a daunting maze.

But here's the good news: You're holding the map to navigate this maze. "Privacy Matters" is your comprehensive guide to understanding the world of data protection. If you are someone interested in learning about this world, this book can guide you on the part of becoming aware of it, to acting upon it, and perhaps to even advocating for it. If you are a professional responsible for implementing data protection in your company at any level, this book will guide you from the most basic, practical strategies all the way towards wearing your company's advanced data protection readiness as a badge of honour and trust.

Why This Book, and Why Now?

Data has been the lifeblood of our digital economy for years now. From the smartphones in our pockets to the algorithms that shape our online experiences, data is at the heart of innovation and growth. But with great power comes great liability. As we've seen from high-profile breaches and privacy scandals, mishandling of personal data can lead to serious consequences - for individuals, for businesses, and for society as a whole.

This is especially true in India after the passage of the country's new data protection law, the Digital Personal Data Protection Act 2023 - a game-changer in this context. It introduces robust rights for individuals and hefty obligations for businesses. But more than that, it represents a cultural shift in how we think about personal data. It's a call to action for every Indian to become more data-aware, and for every organization to put privacy at the core of their operations.

That's where this book comes in. As someone who has worn many hats in the data protection world - as a privacy advisor at a Big 4 consulting firm, an academic researcher, a lecturer, and policy advisor - I've seen the challenges of data protection from all angles. I've grappled with the legal complexities, the technological challenges, and the ethical dilemmas, and helped companies and lawmakers work through them.

I've also seen the immense potential of getting data protection right. When individuals are empowered with knowledge and tools to manage their data, they can make informed choices and demand better practices. When businesses embrace privacy as a core value, they can build deeper trust with their customers and unlock new opportunities for innovation. And when data protection becomes a societal norm, we can harness the power of data for good while minimizing the risks of harm.

Who Am I, and Why Should You Listen to Me?

I've been fortunate to have a diverse journey in the world of data protection. It started with an academic curiosity leading from watching data protection and information security clauses get negotiated between businesses way back in 2013. Wanting to understand the theory of how law and technology intersect in the digital age led me to head to Leiden University in The Netherlands to pursue an LLM in Law and Digital Technologies and, as a Marie Curie Fellow, a double PhD from the University of Malta and the University of Groningen. There, I delved deep into the legal and ethical frameworks of data protection and identity management. Having a foundation of legal training from National Law University, Jodhpur, certainly helped.

I also had the privilege of sharing my knowledge with the next generation of privacy professionals, as a tenure-track lecturer at the University of Malta. Teaching courses on information law, data protection, and big data gave me a chance to distill complex concepts into accessible frameworks, and to learn from the diverse perspectives of my students.

Perhaps the most eye-opening experience was my work with the United Nations, where I had the honour of assisting the first UN Special Rapporteur on the Right to Privacy, Prof. Joe Cannataci, through most of his two tenures. This experience was also enhanced by having my work presented at august forums such as the European Parliament's Committee on Civil Liberties, Justice and Home Affairs (LIBE) as part of the EU's legislative process, as well as the Council of Europe. This exposed me not only to the global dimensions of data protection, but also the crucial role it plays in upholding human rights in the digital age.

But I wasn't content with just researching the issues - I wanted to apply them in the real world, and, more importantly, at home in India. That's what led me to my role as a privacy advisory professional at a Big 4 consulting firm, where I help businesses of all sizes navigate the practical challenges of data protection. From conducting risk assessments to designing privacy programs, I see firsthand how the principles of data protection translate into operational reality. In the mean time, I have continued to upgrade my learning through certifications as a privacy professional and as a lead implementer of information management systems.

Throughout this journey, one thing became clear: data protection is not just a legal or technical issue - it's a deeply human one. It's about the stories of individuals like Arjun and Priya, and the choices we make as a society about how we want our data to be used. That's the perspective I bring to this book - a commitment to making data protection relatable, actionable, and empowering for everyone.

A Call to Action

Data protection is not an optional extra or a box to be ticked. In the digital age, it's a fundamental necessity - for our individual rights, for business success, and for societal well-being.

But achieving effective data protection is not a spectator sport. It requires active participation from all of us - as individuals, as professionals, and as citizens. It requires us to ask questions, challenge assumptions, and imagine better ways of doing things.

That's the spirit in which this book is written. It's not just about imparting knowledge, but about sparking a conversation and igniting change. It's an invitation for you to become part of the solution - whether that's by exercising your own data rights, championing privacy in your organization, or advocating for better policies.

As you navigate the pages ahead, I encourage you to keep this bigger picture in mind. Every step you take, no matter how small, is a step towards a more privacy-conscious India. And every voice that joins the chorus makes the call for change that much stronger.

So let's dive in. Let's navigate this maze together, and emerge on the other side with a clearer vision for a data-protected future. The journey starts now.

Ketan Modh, PhD
January 28th, 2025

How to Use This Book

Before we dive into the heart of the matter, let's take a moment to orient ourselves. This book is designed to be your comprehensive guide to data protection in India, but it's not meant to be read in a single sitting or in a linear fashion. Here's how you can make the most of your journey through these pages.

1. Book Structure Overview

The book is divided into three main parts, each serving a distinct purpose:

- **Part 1:** Understanding Data Protection in India lays the foundation by exploring the legal, cultural, and technological landscape of data protection. It's your crash course in the key concepts, laws, and trends shaping the field.

- **Part 2:** The Individual's Guide to Data Protection is your personal roadmap to navigating data protection as an individual. From understanding your rights to taking action to protect your data, this section empowers you to take control of your digital footprint.

- **Part 3:** Corporate Strategies for Data Protection Compliance is the business professional's playbook for ensuring organizational compliance. Using a maturity-based approach, it guides you through the stages of building a robust data protection program, from assessment to continuous improvement.

While each part can stand alone, they also build upon each other. The foundational knowledge from Part 1 informs the personal strategies in Part 2, which in turn align with the corporate approaches in Part 3. For a holistic understanding, we recommend reading the parts in sequence.

2. Navigating the Content

Throughout the book, you'll encounter recurring features designed to enhance your learning experience:

- **"Data Dilemma" Boxes:** These present real-life scenarios that illustrate the data protection challenges individuals and businesses face daily. Use these as thought-starters to contextualize the concepts you're learning.
- **"Jargon Busters":** Confused by a technical term or legal phrase? Look out for these boxes that break down complex jargon into plain English.
- **"Quick Tips":** These are your actionable takeaways - brief, practical advice you can implement immediately, whether it's adjusting your privacy settings or updating your organizational policies.
- **"Deep Cuts":** In certain places, I could not resist adding additional flavour to some points of discussion. Here you will find small reflections from my journey through academia, policy work and industry that should hopefully allow you to explore further should you choose to do so.

In Part 3, you'll also find a special feature - the **Data Protection Maturity Matrix**. This is your at-a-glance guide to assessing your organization's current compliance posture and planning your way forward. Use the matrix to identify your stage and level, then dive into the corresponding chapter for detailed strategies.

3. Reading Recommendations

While we encourage everyone to read the book in its entirety, we understand that different readers have different needs and interests. Here are some suggested reading pathways:

1. If you're an **individual** primarily concerned about your personal data protection, focus on Part 2. Skim Part 1 for context, and feel free to dip into Part 3 to understand how businesses handle your data.

2. If you're a **business professional** charged with ensuring compliance, make Part 3 your core focus. Use Part 1 as your background primer, and Part 2 to understand the individual perspective you're serving.

3. If you're looking for a **comprehensive understanding** of data protection in India, read the book from cover to cover. You'll gain a 360-degree view of the field, from the legal foundations to the practical applications.

4. Interactive Elements

Learning is not a passive process, and this book is designed to engage you every step of the way. You'll find a range of interactive elements, from quizzes and checklists to self-assessment tools and exercises.

We encourage you to actively participate in these elements. Test your knowledge with the quizzes, use the checklists to track your progress, and leverage the self-assessment tools to identify areas for improvement.

In the appendices, you'll also find a treasure trove of templates and resources - sample policies, contract clauses, data subject request forms, and more. These are your practical tools to apply the book's concepts in your own context. Adapt them, customize them, and make them your own.

5. Staying Updated

Data protection is a rapidly evolving field, and no book can stay current forever. That's why we've designed this book to be your starting point, not your end point.

Throughout the book, you'll find references to online resources where you can find the latest updates, case studies, and best practices. We encourage you to use these resources to stay informed about developments in the field.

We also invite you to share your own experiences and insights. Whether it's through the companion website, social media, or professional networks, your voice is a valuable part of the data protection conversation. Share your challenges, your successes, and your lessons learned - you never know who you might help or inspire.

6. A Note on Examples and Scenarios

In this book, you'll encounter a wide range of examples and scenarios. While these are all based on real-world situations, they are not all real cases. Many of the specific scenarios, especially in the "Data Dilemma" boxes, are hypothetical, derived from my experiences with helping individuals and companies navigate their way through such scenarios - designed to illustrate a particular point or challenge.

I have chosen to use hypothetical scenarios in some cases to protect the privacy of individuals and organizations, and to allow us to adapt the facts to best serve the learning objective. Rest assured that even the hypothetical scenarios are grounded in the realities of data protection in India.

7. Final Tips

As you embark on your data protection journey, here are a few final tips to keep in mind:

- **Explore Widely:** While some sections of the book might not seem immediately relevant to you, we encourage you to at least skim them. Data protection has a way of touching every aspect of our personal and professional lives, often in unexpected ways. The more context you have, the better equipped you'll be.
- **Use the Book as a Guide:** This book is designed to be a comprehensive resource, but it's not a substitute for legal advice. If you're facing a specific data protection issue or compliance question, always consult with a qualified legal professional.
- **Keep the Conversation Going:** Data protection is not a one-and-done exercise. It's an ongoing journey that requires continuous learning, adaptation, and collaboration. Use this book as a springboard for deeper engagement with the data protection community. Attend conferences, join forums, and

participate in the policy-making process. Every voice matters in shaping our data-driven future.

With that, you're ready to dive in. Keep this guide handy as you navigate the chapters ahead, and remember - you're not alone on this journey. We're here to support you every step of the way.

Part 1: Understanding Data Protection in India

Chapter 1: Why Your Data Matters

In the humming tech hub of Bangalore, Priya Sharma swipes her smartphone to order her lunch. As she does, a complex dance of data begins - her location, order history, and payment information flow seamlessly through digital channels. Across town, Arjun Patel, Chief Information Security Officer at TechInnovate India, scrutinizes a dashboard showing the flow of customer data through his company's systems. Both Priya and Arjun are participants in a new reality - one where data has become the lifeblood of our digital economy.

Welcome to the world of data protection, where every click, swipe, and transaction leaves a digital footprint. In this chapter, we'll embark on a journey to understand why your data matters more than ever before. We'll trace the evolution of data from dusty file cabinets to cloud servers, explore the global awakening to privacy concerns, and examine India's unique path in the data protection landscape.

As we navigate this complex terrain, we'll encounter key questions:

- How has our relationship with personal information changed over time?
- What sparked the global privacy awakening, and how has it affected India?
- Why do we need data protection laws, and how are they shaping our digital future?

- What rights do you have over your personal data, and how can you exercise them?

By the end of this chapter, you'll have a clearer understanding of the data protection landscape and why it matters to you - whether you're an individual concerned about your privacy or a business leader navigating compliance challenges.

So, let's dive in and begin our exploration of the data protection maze.

The Evolution of Data: Then and Now

A Glimpse into the Past: Data in the 1970s

Picture this: It's a typical Monday morning in 1975 at the Mumbai branch of the State Bank of India. Swati Singh, a diligent bank clerk, begins her day by unlocking a massive metal filing cabinet. Inside, neatly arranged folders contain thousands of customer records - each a treasure trove of personal information.

As Swati processes a loan application, she meticulously records the applicant's details on a paper form. Name, address, employment history, and financial information - all carefully penned in black ink. Once complete, she files the form alphabetically, where it will remain, largely untouched, unless needed for future reference.

Business Perspective: Data Management Circa 1975	**Individual Impact: Personal Privacy in the Pre-Digital Era**
– Data stored primarily in physical form (paper records, microfilm)	– Limited data collection due to storage constraints

– Manual data entry and retrieval processes – Limited data sharing capabilities – Physical security measures (locked cabinets, restricted access rooms) – Data retention often based on available storage space	– Privacy often protected by practical obscurity – Difficult for unauthorized individuals to access or aggregate personal data – Limited ability to track or profile individuals across multiple data sources – Errors in records could persist unnoticed for long periods

Fast Forward: Data in the Digital Age

Now, let's leap forward to the present day. TechInnovate India, a rapidly growing fintech startup based in Bangalore, offers a mobile banking app that has gained popularity across the country. Let's follow the journey of a loan application through their modern data ecosystem:

1. **Data Collection**: Aanya, a young professional in Delhi, applies for a loan through TechInnovate's app. The app collects her personal details, financial history, and even her device's location.

2. **Data Processing**: Within milliseconds, TechInnovate's AI-powered algorithms validate Aanya's information, cross-referencing it against vast datasets of financial behaviour.

3. **Data Storage**: Aanya's application, enriched with AI-generated insights, is securely stored in TechInnovate's state-of-the-art cloud infrastructure.

4. **Data Sharing**: With Aanya's consent (hopefully), her credit score and relevant financial information are shared with partner banks through secure APIs.

5. **Data Protection**: Throughout this journey, Aanya's data is protected by layers of security:

   – End-to-end encryption shields the data in transit

   – AI-powered anomaly detection guards against unauthorized access

   – Advanced tokenization replaces sensitive data points with non-sensitive equivalents

In just a few minutes, Aanya receives multiple loan offers tailored to her financial profile. Her data's journey, while complex, is protected at every step by advanced technologies and stringent data protection practices - a far cry from the manual, paper-based processes of the 1970s.

Business Perspective: Modern Data Management	**Individual Impact: Personal Privacy in the Digital Age**
– Real-time data collection and processing – AI-powered analytics for instant decision-making – Cloud-based storage with advanced security measures	– Comprehensive digital footprints across multiple platforms – Increased control over personal data (access, correction, deletion rights) – Potential for more personalized services based on data analysis

– Seamless data sharing through secure APIs	– Greater need for digital literacy and privacy awareness
– Continuous monitoring and updating of data protection practices	– Risks of data breaches and unauthorized access balanced against robust security measures

Tech Talk: Securing Modern Data

Today's data journey is safeguarded by several advanced technologies These include end-to-end encryption, which protects data in transit; tokenization, which replaces sensitive data with non-sensitive equivalents; AI-powered anomaly detection systems, which guard against unauthorized access; and possibly even Blockchain technology, which ensures data integrity and transparent audit trails.

As we can see, the evolution of data handling from paper to pixels has brought both tremendous opportunities and significant challenges. In the following sections, we'll explore how these changes have sparked a global privacy awakening and led to the development of comprehensive data protection laws.

The Data Privacy Timeline

The journey of data privacy is marked by significant milestones that have shaped our understanding and approach to protecting personal information. Let's explore this timeline:

Year	Event	Business Impact	Individual Impact
1890	Warren and Brandeis publish "The Right to Privacy"	Set the stage for privacy as a legal right	Established the concept of a "right to be let alone"
1948	Universal Declaration of Human Rights	Businesses begin to consider privacy in their practices	Privacy recognized as a fundamental human right
1980	OECD Privacy Guidelines	First internationally agreed-upon data protection principles	Set expectations for how personal data should be handled globally
1995	EU Data Protection Directive	Harmonized data protection laws across the EU	Introduced stronger rights for individuals and restrictions on data transfers
2000	Indian IT Act	First Indian legislation addressing digital transactions and cybercrime	Limited provisions for protecting personal data in digital form
2011	Indian IT Rules for protection of sensitive personal data	Introduced specific requirements for handling sensitive data	Provided some protection for sensitive personal information
2013	Snowden revelations	Increased focus on data security and transparency	Raised global awareness about digital surveillance
2016	EU General Data Protection Regulation (GDPR) adopted	Set new global standards for data protection compliance	Significantly expanded individual rights and control over personal data
2017	Indian Supreme Court declares privacy a fundamental right	Businesses in India begin preparing for stricter data protection laws	Affirmed privacy as a constitutional right for Indian citizens

Year	Event	Business Impact	Individual Impact
2023	Indian Digital Personal Data Protection Act	Comprehensive data protection framework for India	New rights for Indian citizens over their personal data

Data Dilemma: The Aadhaar Debate

In 2009, India launched Aadhaar, the world's largest biometric ID system. While it aimed to provide a unique identity to every Indian resident, it also sparked intense debates about privacy and data protection.

- **Business Perspective**: Companies saw opportunities in Aadhaar for easier KYC processes and potential for new services.

- **Individual Perspective**: Many citizens were concerned about the mandatory nature of Aadhaar and the potential for surveillance. On the other hand, a majority of citizens handed over their personal data even though appropriate legal backing for the programme only came in 2016 with the Aadhaar Act.

The Aadhaar debate highlighted the need for a comprehensive data protection law in India, contributing to the privacy awakening in the country.

Jargon Buster: Key Terms in Data Protection

- **Personal Data**: Any information relating to an identified or identifiable individual.
- **Data Principal**: The individual to whom personal data relates (in the rest of the world, especially where laws are derived from the European General Data Protection Regulation, this is the Data Subject).

- **Data Fiduciary**: The entity that determines the purposes and means of processing personal data (in the rest of the world, especially where laws are derived from the European General Data Protection Regulation, this is the Data Controller).
- **Data Processor**: An entity that processes personal data on behalf of the controller.
- **Consent**: Freely given, specific, informed, and unambiguous indication of the data subject's agreement to the processing of their personal data.

As we reflect on this timeline, we see a clear progression from the recognition of privacy as a human right to the complex data protection landscape we navigate today. For companies like TechInnovate India, this rich history serves as a reminder of the weighty responsibility they bear as custodians of personal data.

In the next section, we'll dive deeper into how personal information transitioned from paper to digital form, and the implications of this shift for both businesses and individuals.

From Paper to Pixels: The Digitization of Personal Information

The transition from paper-based record-keeping to today's digital data landscape marks a profound shift in how we handle, store, and perceive personal information. This journey has reshaped not only business practices but also individual experiences with their personal data.

The Paper Era

In the not-so-distant past, personal information was primarily stored in physical form. Government offices, banks, hospitals, and businesses of all sizes relied on vast filing systems to manage customer and employee data.

Business Perspective: For companies, this meant:	**Individual Impact**: For individuals, the paper era meant:
– Large physical storage spaces dedicated to file cabinets	– Limited proliferation of personal data due to physical constraints
– Time-consuming manual processes for data retrieval and updating	– Privacy often protected by the sheer impracticality of accessing or collating information
– Limited ability to analyze or derive insights from collected data	– Difficulty in updating or correcting personal information across multiple organizations
– Physical security measures like locked rooms and controlled access	– Less concern about data breaches, as large-scale data theft was logistically challenging

The Dawn of Digitization

The introduction of personal computers in the 1980s and their widespread adoption in the 1990s marked the beginning of the digital transformation.

Tech Talk: From Punch Cards to PCs

The journey to digitization began with mainframe computers and punch cards in the 1960s and 70s. However, it was the personal computer revolution of the 1980s that truly democratized digital data management. Early PCs used floppy disks for storage, with capacities measured in kilobytes. Hard drives, introduced in the mid-1980s, dramatically increased storage capabilities, paving the way for more comprehensive digital record-keeping.

To illustrate this transition, let's consider a typical Indian company's digitization journey:

GlobalTech Solutions' Path to Digitization

GlobalTech Solutions, a typical mid-sized IT services company based in Pune, exemplifies the digitization journey many Indian businesses experienced:

1985: Founded as a small software development firm, GlobalTech relies entirely on paper records for client information, employee data, and project documentation.

1995: GlobalTech invests in its first computer network. Employee records are gradually transferred to spreadsheets, but client data remains largely paper-based due to security concerns.

2000: With Y2K projects boosting business, GlobalTech implements its first digital document management system. However, many employees still prefer printing documents for review and storage.

2005: GlobalTech adopts a cloud-based CRM system, marking a significant shift towards fully digital client data management. Paper usage drops dramatically.

2010: Mobile devices are integrated into GlobalTech's workflows. Field technicians begin using tablets to access and update client information in real-time.

2015: GlobalTech implements a comprehensive Enterprise Resource Planning (ERP) system, digitalizing nearly all aspects of its operations, from human resources to project management and financial records.

2020: With the Covid-19 pandemic accelerating digital transformation, GlobalTech transitions to a fully paperless office, with advanced digital signature and document verification systems in place.

This scenario illustrates the gradual but transformative journey many Indian companies experienced in their transition from paper to digital data management.

Business Impact of Digitization:	**Individual Experience in the Digital Age**:
– Improved efficiency in data retrieval and processing	– Faster service from businesses as they could access records more quickly
– Reduced physical storage needs	– Increased accuracy of personal records, with easier correction of errors
– Enhanced ability to analyze and utilize collected data	– Growing concerns about data privacy and security as digital storage became more common
– New challenges in data security and employee training	– The beginning of the "digital footprint" concept, as more aspects of life began to generate digital data

The Current Data Landscape

Today, we find ourselves in a world where data is generated, collected, and processed at an unprecedented scale.

Business Realities in the Current Data Ecosystem:	**Individual Challenges and Empowerment in the Digital Age:**
– Data has become a critical asset, driving decision-making and innovation	– Increased control over personal data through rights granted by modern privacy laws
– Advanced analytics and AI enable deeper insights from collected data	– Need for digital literacy to navigate the complex data ecosystem
– Increased regulatory pressure (e.g., GDPR, CCPA, India's DPDPA) necessitates robust data governance	– Balancing the benefits of data-driven services with privacy concerns
– Growing importance of data ethics and responsible data practices	– Growing awareness of the value of personal data and the importance of protecting it

As we reflect on this journey from paper to pixels, it's clear that the digitization of personal information has brought both tremendous opportunities and significant challenges. For businesses, the key lies in leveraging the power of digital data while upholding the highest standards of data protection and ethical use. For individuals, the digital age demands a new level of awareness and engagement with our personal data, balancing the conveniences of the digital world with the need to protect our privacy.

The Global Privacy Awakening

As digital technologies reshaped the landscape of personal information, a parallel awakening in privacy consciousness began to sweep across the globe. This shift wasn't a single, dramatic moment, but rather a series of events and revelations that gradually brought data privacy from the shadows of tech discussions into the spotlight of public discourse.

The Social Media Revolution

The dawn of social media in the early 2000s marked a turning point. Platforms like Orkut (particularly popular in India before Facebook took over), Facebook, and Twitter offered unprecedented connectivity, but also ushered in an era of voluntary sharing of personal information on a massive scale. Initially, users revelled in the ability to connect and share. However, as these platforms grew, so did concerns about the extent and use of the data they were amassing.

The Power of Data: From Arab Spring to Cambridge Analytica

In 2011, the world witnessed a stark demonstration of the power and peril of this new data landscape. The Arab Spring, while primarily a political movement, showcased how social media could be used to organize and amplify voices. Simultaneously, it highlighted the risks individuals faced when their online activities could be tracked and potentially used against them.

This realization had ripple effects across the globe, including in India. As social media usage surged in the country, with platforms like Facebook and WhatsApp gaining millions of users, discussions about digital privacy and data protection began to emerge in public discourse.

The real watershed moment, however, came in 2013 with Edward Snowden's revelations about global surveillance programs. The public was confronted with the reality that governments and corporations were collecting and analyzing personal data on an unprecedented scale.

This revelation sent shockwaves through society, catalyzing a global conversation about privacy rights in the digital age.

In India, these revelations coincided with the ongoing rollout of Aadhaar, the world's largest biometric ID system. The juxtaposition of global surveillance concerns with the collection of biometric data from millions of Indians intensified the privacy debate in the country.

The Cambridge Analytica scandal of 2018 further underscored the potential for data misuse. The revelation that personal data from millions of Facebook users had been harvested without their consent and used for political advertising sparked global outrage and led to increased scrutiny of data practices by tech giants.

Compliance Corner: Business Adaptation to Privacy Concerns

- Implementation of more transparent data policies
- Investment in robust data security measures
- Appointment of Data Protection Officers (DPOs), or the inclusion of a DPO's responsibilities in the mandate of the Chief Information Security Officer or the Chief Risk Officer
- Development of privacy-by-design principles in product development
- Regular privacy impact assessments
- Enhanced user controls for data sharing and privacy settings

The Legislative Response

As public awareness grew, so did demands for greater control over personal data. Governments and regulatory bodies began to respond, leading to the implementation of more comprehensive data protection laws. The European Union's General Data Protection Regulation (GDPR), implemented in 2018, set a new global benchmark for privacy legislation, influencing similar laws worldwide.

In India, the privacy awakening took a unique path. The Supreme Court's landmark judgment in 2017, declaring privacy a fundamental right, while far later than the rest of the world, was a pivotal moment. This decision not only affirmed the importance of privacy in the digital age but also set the stage for more robust data protection legislation in the country.

Know Your Rights: Emerging Individual Data Rights

- Right to access personal data held by companies
- Right to request correction of inaccurate data
- Right to data portability (transfer data between service providers)
- Right to be forgotten (request deletion of personal data)
- Right to object to processing of personal data
- Right to human intervention in automated decision-making

It's important to remember that not all rights are in every law around the world; some laws tend to skip some rights based on the legal or cultural reality of that country. Another thing to keep in mind: these rights are not absolute, and come with a lot of caveats.

The Indian Context

In India, the privacy awakening was further fuelled by several key events:

1. **The Aadhaar Debate**: The rollout of Aadhaar, while aimed at providing unique identification for all residents, sparked intense debates about privacy and data protection.

2. **Digital India Initiative**: As the government pushed for greater digitization, questions about data security and privacy came to the forefront.

3. **Data Localization Discussions**: Debates around where Indian citizens' data should be stored highlighted the geopolitical aspects of data protection.

4. **Rise of Indian Tech Giants**: As companies like Jio and Paytm amassed large user bases, their data practices came under increased scrutiny.

Data Dilemma: The WhatsApp Privacy Policy Controversy

In 2021, WhatsApp's announcement of a new privacy policy that would share user data with Facebook sparked a major controversy in India, its largest market. This led to a surge in downloads of alternative messaging apps and highlighted the growing privacy consciousness among Indian users.

Business Impact: Companies had to reassess their data sharing practices and communication strategies.

Individual Impact: Users became more aware of the terms of service they agree to and the extent of data sharing between apps.

Quiz: Test Your Privacy Awareness

How well do you understand the current privacy landscape? Test your knowledge with this quick quiz:

1. In which year did the EU's General Data Protection Regulation (GDPR) come into effect?

   a) 2016

   b) 2018

   c) 2020

   d) 2022

2. What right allows individuals to request the deletion of their personal data?

   a) Right to access

   b) Right to rectification

   c) Right to be forgotten

   d) Right to object

3. In India, privacy was declared a fundamental right by:

   a) The Parliament

   b) The Supreme Court

   c) The Ministry of Electronics and IT

   d) The Data Protection Authority

4. Which of these is NOT typically considered sensitive personal data?
    a) Health information
    b) Financial data
    c) Biometric data
    d) Public social media posts
5. What does the term "privacy by design" refer to?
    a) Stylish privacy policies
    b) Embedding privacy into the design of systems and processes
    c) Designing private spaces in offices
    d) A type of encryption algorithm

(*Answers:* 1-b, 2-c, 3-b, 4-d, 5-b)

This global privacy awakening has fundamentally changed how we view and value personal data. As we move forward, the challenge lies in balancing the immense potential of data-driven technologies with the fundamental right to privacy. In the next section, we'll explore how this awakening has translated into concrete data protection laws around the world and in India.

The Rise of Data Protection Laws

As the digital revolution transformed the way we handle personal information, legislators and policymakers around the world scrambled to keep pace. The rise of data protection laws reflects a growing recognition of the need to safeguard individual privacy in an increasingly data-driven world.

Global Pioneers in Data Protection

The European Union has been at the forefront of this legislative push. The Data Protection Directive of 1995 was a pioneering effort to harmonize data protection laws across EU member states. However, as technology continued to advance rapidly, it became clear that a more comprehensive and uniformly applied regulation was necessary.

Enter the General Data Protection Regulation (GDPR), implemented in 2018. The GDPR represented a seismic shift in the data protection landscape, setting a new global benchmark for privacy legislation. Its extraterritorial scope meant that any organization dealing with EU citizens' data, regardless of where the organization was based, had to comply with its stringent requirements.

Global Ripple Effects

The GDPR's influence extended far beyond Europe's borders. It inspired similar legislation around the world, including:

- The California Consumer Privacy Act (CCPA) in the United States
- Brazil's General Data Protection Law (LGPD)
- Japan's amended Act on the Protection of Personal Information
- South Africa's Protection of Personal Information Act (POPIA)

The Impact of Data Protection Laws

To understand the profound impact of these laws, let's compare the landscape before and after their implementation:

Aspect	Before	After
Data Collection	Often indiscriminate	Purpose-limited, minimized
User Consent	Frequently implied or buried in fine print	Must be explicit, informed, and freely given
Data Subject Rights	Limited or non-existent	Comprehensive (access, rectification, erasure, etc.)
Cross-border Data Transfers	Often unrestricted	Subject to adequacy requirements
Breach Notification	Typically not required	Mandatory within specific timeframes
Penalties for Non-compliance	Often minimal	Potentially severe (e.g., up to 4% of global turnover under GDPR)
Corporate Attitude to Data Protection	Often an afterthought	Board-level priority
Public Awareness	Generally low	Increasing, with growing demands for privacy

Data Dilemma: Balancing Innovation and Privacy

Consider TechInnovate, our hypothetical Indian fintech startup. They're developing an AI-powered credit scoring system that could revolutionize loan approvals for underserved populations. However, the system requires processing large amounts of personal data.

- **Business Challenge**: How can TechInnovate balance their innovative ambitions with the stringent requirements of the DPDPA? Can they leverage their compliance activities for the RBI's policies as a fintech company?

- **Individual Concern**: How can users benefit from such innovations while maintaining control over their personal data?

This dilemma illustrates the ongoing challenge of balancing technological advancement with privacy protection - a key consideration in modern data protection laws.

As we look to the future, the evolution of data protection laws shows no signs of slowing down. Emerging technologies like artificial intelligence, the Internet of Things, and blockchain continue to raise new privacy concerns, prompting ongoing legislative responses.

The rise of data protection laws marks a significant shift in how we view and value personal data. It reflects a growing consensus that in our digital age, robust privacy protections are not just desirable, they're essential. In the next section, we'll take a closer look at India's unique journey in data protection and what it means for businesses and individuals in the country.

India's Data Protection Journey: From Ancient Wisdom to Digital Age Legislation

India's relationship with privacy and data protection is as ancient as its civilization and as modern as its burgeoning tech industry. This journey, spanning millennia, reflects the unique cultural, philosophical, and technological evolution of the world's largest democracy.

Ancient Roots of Privacy in India

The concept of privacy in India can be traced back to ancient texts and traditions. The Hitopadesha, a Sanskrit text of fables and proverbs, advises in Verse 131 of Book One, The Winning of Friends: "One should not reveal one's ideas, wealth, mantra practice, conjugal life, humiliation, and charity." This ancient wisdom underscores a long-standing recognition of the importance of personal privacy.

In the Arthashastra, the ancient Indian treatise on statecraft, economics, and military strategy, Chanakya discusses the need for protecting sensitive information of the state and its citizens. While not directly addressing individual privacy as we understand it today, these concepts laid the groundwork for the idea that certain information should be protected.[1]

Colonial Era and Early Modern Period

The British colonial period introduced Western legal concepts to India, including aspects of privacy law. The Indian Penal Code of 1860 included provisions against trespassing and breach of confidentiality, indirectly addressing privacy concerns.

Post-independence, India inherited a legal system that recognized certain aspects of privacy, primarily through case law rather than specific legislation. The right to privacy was gradually developed through judicial interpretations of fundamental rights guaranteed in the Constitution of India.

India's Data Protection Journey

In India, the path to comprehensive data protection legislation has been a winding one, marked by gradual progress and pivotal moments. As the new millennium dawned, India took its first tentative steps into the digital age with the Information Technology Act of 2000. This landmark legislation acknowledged the growing importance of digital transactions and cybersecurity, but its provisions for data protection were limited, barely scratching the surface of what was to come.

For over a decade, this act stood as India's primary bulwark against digital threats. But as the country's tech industry boomed and millions of Indians came online, it became clear that more robust protections were needed. In 2011, responding to growing concerns about data privacy, the government introduced the Information Technology Rules. These rules brought more specific guidelines for protecting sensitive personal data, signalling a growing awareness of the importance of data protection in the digital age.

But the real watershed moment came in 2017. In a landmark decision that would reshape the landscape of digital rights in India, the Supreme Court recognized privacy as a fundamental right.[2] This judicial pronouncement wasn't just a legal milestone; it was a clarion call for more comprehensive data protection legislation. It set the stage for a new era in which privacy would be viewed not as a luxury, but as a basic right of every Indian citizen.

Riding the wave of this momentous decision, 2018 saw the introduction of the draft Personal Data Protection Bill. This marked India's first serious attempt at crafting comprehensive data protection legislation, aligning the country with global trends in privacy regulation. The bill sparked intense debate and discussion, as lawmakers, industry leaders, and civil society grappled with the complexities of balancing data protection with innovation in the world's largest democracy. The public consultation was followed by yet another draft of the bill released in 2019.

After years of deliberation, revision, and public discourse, India finally passed the Digital Personal Data Protection Act (DPDPA) in 2023. This pivotal piece of legislation ushered in a new era of data protection in India, establishing a robust framework for safeguarding personal data in the digital age. The DPDPA represented not just the culmination of a long legislative journey, but a bold step into a future where data protection would play a central role in India's digital growth story. It has taken more than a year for the Rules relating to the DPDPA to be released for public consultation, and the actual enforcement of the Act is still a ways away. In sum, India's journey towards having a law safeguarding personal data may - generously - be called languid.

Having said that, from the limited scope of the IT Act in 2000 to the comprehensive protections of the DPDPA in 2023, India's journey towards data protection legislation reflects the country's evolving digital landscape. It's a story of gradual awakening, judicial wisdom, and legislative action, setting the stage for a new chapter in India's digital future. We'll explore the DPDPA in more detail over the coming chapter.

Business Prep: Key Steps for Regulatory Compliance	**Individual Empowerment: How These Laws Protect Personal Data**
– Conduct comprehensive data audits – Implement privacy by design in all processes and products – Appoint Data Protection Officers – Establish clear procedures for handling data subject requests – Develop and maintain detailed documentation of data processing activities – Conduct regular employee training on data protection	– Right to access personal data held by organizations – Right to request correction of inaccurate data – Right to data portability – Right to be forgotten (request deletion of personal data) – Stricter requirements for obtaining consent – Mandatory breach notifications

The Road Ahead

As India continues its data protection journey, several challenges and opportunities lie ahead:

1. **Implementation**: Effectively implementing the DPDPA across a diverse and populous nation.

2. **Digital Literacy**: Enhancing digital literacy to ensure citizens can effectively exercise their data rights.

3. **Global Alignment**: Aligning India's data protection framework with global standards to facilitate international data flows.

4. **Emerging Technologies**: Addressing privacy concerns related to AI, IoT, and other emerging technologies.

India's approach to data protection reflects its unique position as both an ancient civilization and a rapidly modernizing economy. The challenge lies in balancing traditional values of privacy with the needs of a digital economy. As we move forward, the DPDPA will play a crucial role in shaping India's digital future, affecting everyone from tech giants to individual citizens.

In our next and final section, we'll look ahead to the future of data privacy, exploring emerging trends and technologies that will shape the data protection landscape in the years to come.

The Future of Data Privacy

As we stand on the cusp of new technological revolutions, the landscape of data privacy continues to evolve. Emerging technologies promise to revolutionize how we live and work, but they also present new challenges for data protection. Let's explore some of these technologies and their implications for privacy in India and beyond.

Emerging Technologies and Privacy Challenges

1. **Artificial Intelligence and Machine Learning**

   AI and ML technologies are becoming increasingly prevalent, from chatbots to predictive analytics. While they offer immense benefits, they also raise concerns about algorithmic bias and the privacy implications of the vast amounts of data they require.

   Indian Context: As India positions itself as an AI powerhouse, balancing innovation with privacy protection will be crucial.

2. **Internet of Things (IoT)**

   The proliferation of connected devices is generating unprecedented amounts of personal data. From smart homes to wearable health devices, IoT presents new privacy risks.

   Indian Context: With initiatives like Smart Cities Mission, India is rapidly adopting IoT technologies, necessitating robust privacy safeguards.

3. **5G and Beyond**

   The rollout of 5G networks promises faster speeds and more connected devices, but also raises concerns about increased data collection and potential surveillance.

   Indian Context: As India prepares for widespread 5G adoption, privacy considerations will need to be at the forefront of implementation strategies.

Part 1

4. **Blockchain and Decentralized Technologies**

   While blockchain offers potential privacy benefits through decentralization, it also presents challenges, particularly around the right to be forgotten.

   Indian Context: India's exploration of blockchain for land records and digital currencies will need to address these privacy considerations.

5. **Quantum Computing**

   The advent of quantum computing could render current encryption methods obsolete, necessitating new approaches to data protection.

   Indian Context: India's National Quantum Mission will need to consider the privacy implications of this groundbreaking technology.

Privacy-Enhancing Technologies (PETs)

As privacy challenges evolve, so do the technologies designed to protect privacy:

- **Homomorphic Encryption**: Allows computation on encrypted data without decrypting it.
- **Differential Privacy**: Enables data analysis while protecting individual privacy.
- **Zero-Knowledge Proofs**: Allows verification of information without revealing the information itself.

Future-Proofing Your Business	**Tomorrow's Privacy Skills**
– Stay informed about emerging technologies and their privacy implications	– Develop a basic understanding of how AI and other emerging technologies handle data

– Invest in privacy-enhancing technologies – Adopt a privacy-by-design approach in all new initiatives – Regularly update privacy impact assessments to account for new technologies – Foster a culture of continuous learning about privacy and data protection	– Learn to read and understand privacy policies and terms of service – Stay informed about your rights under evolving data protection laws – Practice good digital hygiene (e.g., strong passwords, regular privacy check-ups) – Be mindful of the data you generate and share, especially with IoT devices

Interactive Scenario: Data Dilemmas of Tomorrow

Imagine it's 2030 and a world war has not occurred. You're using a new AI-powered health app that continuously monitors your vital signs through a wearable device and provides personalized health recommendations. The app can predict potential health issues with high accuracy, but it requires access to your complete medical history, real-time location data, and even your grocery purchases.

Questions to consider:

1. Would you use such an app? Why or why not?
2. What privacy safeguards would you expect to be in place?
3. How might the benefits of such technology be balanced against privacy concerns?

4. How could Indian regulators approach the governance of such technologies?

This scenario illustrates the complex privacy decisions we may face in the near future, balancing the benefits of data-driven technologies with the need to protect personal privacy.

The Path Forward

As we look to the future, the evolution of data privacy is likely to be shaped by several key trends. We can anticipate a landscape characterized by increased regulation, with more comprehensive and nuanced privacy laws emerging both globally and in India. This regulatory shift will likely be accompanied by a growing recognition of privacy as a competitive advantage, with companies that prioritize data protection gaining consumer trust and market share. Technological advancements will play a crucial role, particularly in the development of privacy-aware AI systems that are inherently designed to protect personal information.

Alongside these developments, we're likely to see a broader shift towards data minimization, with organizations moving away from collecting vast amounts of data and instead focusing on retaining only what is essential. Finally, user empowerment is set to become a central theme, with more tools and educational resources becoming available to help individuals take control of their digital privacy. Together, these trends point towards a future where privacy considerations are deeply integrated into both technological development and business practices.

The future of data privacy in India and globally will require a delicate balance between harnessing the power of data-driven technologies and protecting individual rights. It will demand collaboration between policymakers, technologists, businesses, and citizens to create a digital ecosystem that respects privacy while fostering innovation.

As we conclude this chapter, remember that the future of privacy is not predetermined. It will be shaped by the choices we make as individuals, businesses, and society. Stay informed, be proactive, and let's work together to build a privacy-respecting digital future.

Chapter Summary: Key Takeaways

As we conclude this chapter on why your data matters, let's recap the key points we've covered:

1. The evolution of data handling has transformed from paper-based systems to complex digital ecosystems.
2. A global privacy awakening has been sparked by events like the Snowden revelations and the Cambridge Analytica scandal.
3. Data protection laws have risen globally, with the GDPR setting a new benchmark.
4. India's data protection journey has culminated in the Digital Personal Data Protection Act (DPDPA) 2023.
5. The future of data privacy will be shaped by emerging technologies like AI, IoT, and quantum computing.

Action Items for Businesses checklist:

- [ ] Conduct a comprehensive data audit
- [ ] Implement privacy by design principles in all processes

- [ ] Appoint a Data Protection Officer (if required)
- [ ] Develop clear procedures for handling data subject requests
- [ ] Regularly train employees on data protection practices
- [ ] Stay informed about emerging technologies and their privacy implications

Personal Privacy Checklist for individuals:

- [ ] Review privacy settings on all your digital accounts
- [ ] Learn to read and understand privacy policies
- [ ] Be mindful of the data you share online
- [ ] Use strong, unique passwords and enable two-factor authentication where possible
- [ ] Stay informed about your rights under data protection laws
- [ ] Consider using privacy-enhancing tools like VPNs and encrypted messaging apps

Bridging the Gap: How Business Practices and Individual Rights Intersect

As we've seen throughout this chapter, data protection is not just about compliance for businesses or personal habits for individuals. It's a shared responsibility that requires understanding and action from both sides.

Businesses need to recognize that respecting individual privacy rights is not just a legal obligation, but a way to build trust and create value. By implementing robust data protection practices, companies can differentiate themselves in the market and build stronger relationships with their customers.

Individuals, on the other hand, need to be aware of their rights and actively engage in protecting their privacy. This means being informed consumers, asking questions about data practices, and making conscious choices about data sharing.

By working together, businesses and individuals can create a data ecosystem that respects privacy, fosters innovation, and builds trust in the digital age.

Deep Dive Resources

For those who want to explore these topics further, here are some valuable resources:

Essential Further Reading

1. "The Right to Privacy" by Samuel Warren and Louis Brandeis (Harvard Law Review, 1890)
2. "Data and Goliath" by Bruce Schneier
3. "The Age of Surveillance Capitalism" by Shoshana Zuboff
4. "Privacy's Blueprint: The Battle to Control the Design of New Technologies" by Woodrow Hartzog

Government and Regulatory Resources

1. Digital Personal Data Protection Act, 2023 (Official text)
2. Ministry of Electronics and Information Technology (MeitY) website

3. Data Protection Board of India (which has, hopefully, been established by the time you read this)

Non-Governmental Organizations Focused on Digital Rights in India

1. Internet Freedom Foundation
2. Centre for Internet and Society
3. Software Freedom Law Center, India

Online Courses

1. "Introduction to General Data Protection Regulation (GDPR)" on Coursera
2. "Data Privacy Fundamentals" on edX

Useful Tools and Apps for Personal Data Protection

1. Privacy Badger (browser extension for blocking trackers)
2. Signal (encrypted messaging app)
3. DuckDuckGo (privacy-focused search engine)
4. Bitwarden (open-source password manager)

Check the author's website for these additional resources:	
Business Toolkit	**Individual's Privacy Guide**
1. Template for Data Protection Impact Assessment (DPIA)	1. Template for Data Subject Access Request
2. Sample Data Breach Response Plan	2. Guide to Understanding Privacy Policies

3. Checklist for DPDPA Compliance	3. Checklist for Personal Data Security
4. Guide to Implementing Privacy by Design	4. Resources for Digital Literacy and Privacy Education

Remember, data protection is an ongoing journey. Stay curious, stay informed, and keep prioritizing privacy in your personal and professional life.

Chapter 2: The Digital Personal Data Protection Act 2023 - An Overview

Imagine waking up one day to find that the rules of the digital world have changed. The apps on your phone, the websites you visit, and the companies you interact with online are all buzzing about something called "DPDPA 2023". Welcome to the new era of data protection in India.

As we explored in Chapter 1, India's journey to comprehensive data protection legislation has been a long and winding road. From the limited scope of the IT Act in 2000 to the landmark Supreme Court judgment declaring privacy a fundamental right in 2017, each step has led us to this moment. The Digital Personal Data Protection Act (DPDPA) 2023 is not just another piece of legislation; it's a paradigm shift in how India views and values personal data in the digital age.

But what exactly is the DPDPA, and why should you care? Whether you're a college student sharing memes on social media, a small business owner managing customer databases, or a tech enthusiast excited about India's digital future, this Act will impact your digital life in ways both big and small.

In this chapter, we'll take a bird's-eye view of the DPDPA 2023. We'll explore its key features, unpack its core principles, and understand how it's set to reshape India's digital landscape. Don't worry – you won't be bogged down with legal jargon or technical details. Instead, think of this as your friendly guide to navigating the new rules of the digital road.

So, fasten your seatbelts as we embark on a journey through the DPDPA 2023. By the end of this chapter, you'll have a clear picture of what this groundbreaking law means for you, your data, and your digital future. Let's dive in!

DPDPA 2023: Key Features and Innovations

So, what makes the DPDPA 2023 stand out in the crowded landscape of global privacy laws? Let's break it down.

A Made-in-India Approach

Unlike its predecessors, the DPDPA isn't just a carbon copy of international laws like the EU's GDPR. It's tailored to India's unique digital ecosystem, balancing the need for robust data protection, the relative lack of readiness for such data protection, and the country's ambitions as a digital powerhouse.

For instance, while the DPDPA borrows concepts like data fiduciaries (entities that decide the purpose and means of processing personal data) from global standards, it adapts them to the Indian context. It recognizes the role of 'consent managers' – a novel concept that could revolutionize how Indians manage their data permissions across multiple platforms.

Simplicity is Key

One of the DPDPA's most refreshing features is its emphasis on simplicity and clarity. Gone are the days of 50-page privacy policies filled with legalese. The Act mandates that privacy notices be clear, concise, and easily understandable. It's a win for both individuals who want to understand their rights and businesses aiming for transparent communication with their users.

Data Localization: A Balanced Approach

Unlike earlier drafts that proposed strict data localization requirements, the DPDPA 2023 takes a more nuanced stance. It allows for cross-border data flows to every country except for certain notified countries and territories, striking a balance between data sovereignty, data protection and the needs of a globally connected digital economy.

Core Principles of the DPDPA 2023

At its heart, the DPDPA is built on several key principles:

1. **Lawful Processing**: Personal data can only be processed for lawful purposes and, in most cases, with the consent of the individual.

2. **Purpose Limitation**: Data should be collected only for specified purposes and not used for any other reason without consent.

3. **Data Minimization**: Only necessary data should be collected, and it should be deleted once the purpose is fulfilled.

4. **Accuracy**: Data fiduciaries must ensure the accuracy and completeness of the personal data they process.

5. **Security Safeguards**: Reasonable and appropriate measures must be taken to prevent misuse, unauthorized access, modification, or disclosure of personal data.

Let's see how these principles might play out in real life:

Data Dilemma: The Overzealous App

Imagine you've just downloaded "SuperFit", a trendy new fitness app. During setup, it asks for access to your location, contacts, and photo gallery. You pause, wondering why a fitness app needs all this information.

Under DPDPA 2023, SuperFit would need to:

- Clearly explain why it needs each type of data
- Only collect data necessary for its core functions (data minimization)
- Allow you to use the app even if you deny access to non-essential data
- Provide an easy way to withdraw your consent later

This scenario illustrates how DPDPA's principles of purpose limitation and data minimization protect you from unnecessary data collection while still allowing innovative apps to thrive.

The DPDPA 2023 isn't just another privacy law – it's a blueprint for a more transparent, consent-driven digital India. In the next section, we'll dive into the essential rights and obligations it establishes for individuals and businesses. Buckle up – your digital life is about to get an upgrade!

The Essentials of DPDPA 2023

Now that we've got a bird's-eye view of the DPDPA 2023, let's zoom in on its core components. Think of this section as your quick-start guide to the new data protection landscape in India.

Rights and Obligations at a Glance

The DPDPA 2023 is all about balance – it gives individuals (called "Data Principals" in the Act) new rights over their personal data while placing corresponding obligations on businesses and organizations (termed "Data Fiduciaries").

Your New Digital Rights

As a Data Principal, the DPDPA 2023 arms you with a set of powerful rights:

1. **Right to Access Information**: You can ask companies what personal data they have about you and how they're using it.

2. **Right to Correction**: Spot an error in your data? You have the right to get it corrected.

3. **Right to Erasure**: Done with a service? You can ask for your data to be deleted.

4. **Right to Grievance Redressal**: If a company isn't respecting your data rights, you have a clear path to lodge a complaint.

5. **Right to Nominate**: Prepare for the future - give control of your data and the ability to exercise your rights on your behalf to someone else in case of your death or disability.

Remember, we'll dive deeper into how to exercise these rights in Part 2 of this book. For now, think of these as your new superpowers in the digital world!

What Companies Must Do

On the flip side, the DPDPA 2023 sets out clear obligations for Data Fiduciaries:

1. **Lawful Processing**: They can only collect and use your data for legitimate purposes, with your consent.

2. **Privacy by Design**: Data protection should be baked into their products and services from the ground up.

3. **Transparent Communication**: No more confusing legalese – privacy policies must be clear and easily understandable.

4. **Data Security**: They must implement robust measures to keep your data safe.

We'll explore detailed compliance strategies for businesses in Part 3, but here's a quick starter guide.

Quick Guide for Businesses

- Audit your data collection practices – are you collecting only what's necessary?
- Review and simplify your privacy policies
- Implement processes for handling data access and deletion requests
- Train your staff on the new data protection requirements
- Consider appointing a Data Protection Officer if you handle large-scale data processing

The Data Protection Board: Your New Privacy Guardian

One of the DPDPA's most significant innovations is the establishment of the Data Protection Board of India. Think of it as a watchdog for your digital rights.

Key Things to Know About the Data Protection Board:

- It's an independent body tasked with enforcing the DPDPA
- It can investigate complaints, issue penalties, and block non-compliant digital platforms
- It aims to be a tech-savvy regulator, capable of understanding and addressing modern data protection challenges

The Board's existence means that your data rights aren't just on paper – there's a dedicated authority working to ensure they're respected in practice.

Jargon Buster: Data Fiduciary vs. Data Processor
- **Data Fiduciary**: The entity that determines the purpose and means of processing personal data (e.g., the company whose app you're using)
- **Data Processor**: An entity that processes data on behalf of a Data Fiduciary (e.g., a cloud storage provider used by the app company)
Understanding these roles is crucial because the DPDPA places different obligations on each, including the obligation to have a valid contract for the sharing of personal data.

As we wrap up this overview of DPDPA's essentials, remember that this is just the tip of the iceberg. In the coming sections, we'll explore how these new rights and obligations translate into real-world changes for your digital life. Get ready – the way you interact with apps, websites, and digital services is about to undergo a significant transformation!

Implications for Everyday Digital Life

Now that we've covered the what and why of DPDPA 2023, let's tackle the all-important question: How will this actually change your day-to-day digital life? Buckle up as we take a journey through a typical day in the life of Priya, both before and after the DPDPA.

A Day in the Digital Life: Before and After DPDPA

Before DPDPA:	After DPDPA:
7:00 AM: Priya wakes up and checks her favorite news app. It asks for her location to provide local news, which she accepts without much thought.	**7:00 AM:** Priya's news app now clearly explains why it needs her location and offers local news even if she declines.
9:00 AM: At work, she signs up for a new productivity tool, quickly scrolling through the 20-page terms and conditions before clicking "I Agree".	**9:00 AM:** The productivity tool presents a concise, easy-to-understand privacy notice. It only asks for necessary permissions and explains how her data will be used.
1:00 PM: During lunch, she uses a food delivery app. It requires access to her contacts to "enhance her experience", which she reluctantly grants to complete her order.	**1:00 PM:** The food delivery app cannot demand access to her contacts for an unrelated service. It must explain why it needs any data it collects.

Before DPDPA:	After DPDPA:
6:00 PM: Back home, she tries to delete her old social media account but can't find a clear way to do so on the platform.	**6:00 PM:** Priya easily finds the option to delete her old social media account, and the platform complies with her request promptly.

Key Changes to Expect

As you navigate the digital landscape under the DPDPA 2023, you'll notice some refreshing changes in how your personal data is handled. Gone are the days of opaque privacy policies and hidden data practices. Instead, you'll find yourself with more control at your fingertips, able to manage your data permissions across apps and services with greater ease and clarity.

Transparency is set to become the new norm. Those lengthy, jargon-filled privacy policies? They're on their way out. In their place, you can expect concise, clear, and informative policies that actually tell you what you need to know about how your data is being used.

Remember those times when you felt forced to share unnecessary data just to use a service? That's about to change. Companies can no longer bury important data practices in fine print or strong-arm you into sharing more information than they actually need. Your consent will truly matter, and you'll have the power to make informed decisions about your data.

Managing your digital footprint is also getting a much-needed upgrade. Whether you want to access, correct, or delete your personal data, the process will become more straightforward. No more jumping through hoops or navigating complex systems - your data, your rules.

Perhaps most importantly, there's a new sheriff in town: the Data Protection Board of India. With this watchdog in place, companies will be held more accountable for their data practices. It's not just about following rules on paper anymore; organizations will need to demonstrate real, tangible respect for your data privacy.

These changes mark a significant shift in India's digital ecosystem, putting you, the user, back in the driver's seat when it comes to your personal data. It's an exciting time to be digitally active in India, as we move towards a more transparent, respectful, and user-centric approach to data protection.

Protecting Your Data: Quick Tips

As we venture into this new era of data protection, it's important to equip yourself with practical strategies to safeguard your personal information. The digital landscape may be changing, but your role in protecting your data remains crucial.

First and foremost, take advantage of the clearer privacy notices. Those days of blindly clicking "I Agree" are behind us. Now, when you encounter a privacy notice, pause for a moment. Take the time to actually read and understand what you're consenting to. It might seem tedious, but this small act can go a long way in maintaining control over your digital footprint.

Remember, you're in the driver's seat when it comes to app permissions. Just because an app is asking for access to your location, contacts, or camera doesn't mean you have to grant it. Be selective and think critically - does this app truly need that data to function? If not, don't be afraid to deny permission. Your data is valuable, so be mindful of who you're sharing it with.

Make regular privacy check-ups a part of your digital routine. Just as you might schedule a health check-up, set aside time to review your privacy settings on key accounts. Social media platforms, email services, and other frequently used apps often update their privacy features. Staying on top of these changes ensures you're always in control of your data.

Knowledge is power, especially when it comes to data protection. The DPDPA grants you new rights, and it's in your best interest to familiarize yourself with them. Don't worry if it seems overwhelming - we'll dive deep into these rights in Part 2 of this book, giving you a comprehensive understanding of your new data protection arsenal.

Lastly, don't be a silent bystander if you notice potential violations. If you suspect a company isn't adhering to DPDPA rules, speak up. Raising a complaint isn't just about addressing your individual concern - it contributes to a broader culture of accountability and respect for data privacy. Your voice matters in shaping how organizations handle our data.

By incorporating these practices into your digital life, you're not just protecting your own data - you're contributing to a more privacy-conscious digital India. It's an exciting time to be a digital citizen, so embrace your role in this new data protection landscape.

> **Quick Tip**: Create a reminder on your phone for a quarterly "Digital Clean-up Day" where you review your app permissions, unsubscribe from unnecessary services, and update your privacy settings.

Remember, the DPDPA isn't just about restrictions – it's about creating a digital environment where you can confidently share your data, knowing that it's protected by law. As you go about your digital day, keep an eye out for these changes. You might be surprised at how quickly they become the new normal!

Navigating the New Data Protection Landscape

As we've seen, the DPDPA 2023 brings significant changes to India's digital ecosystem. Whether you're an individual concerned about your personal data or a business adapting to new compliance requirements, here are some key points to keep in mind:

For Businesses	**For Individuals**
1. Start Early: Don't wait for the enforcement date. Start adapting your data practices now. (Part 3 will provide detailed strategies) 2. Embrace Transparency: Clear, honest communication about your data practices can build trust with your customers. 3. View Compliance as an Opportunity: Rather than seeing the DPDPA as a burden, consider it a chance to differentiate your business through strong data protection practices.	1. Stay Informed: Keep an eye out for updates from your favorite apps and services about their data practices. 2. Exercise Your Rights: Don't be shy about asking companies what data they have about you or requesting corrections or deletions. (We'll cover how to do this effectively in Part 2) 3. Be Proactive: Rather than waiting for problems to arise, take charge of your data. Regularly review and update your privacy settings across platforms.

Let's test your understanding with a quick quiz:

Test Your DPDPA Basics

1. Under DPDPA, companies must:
   a) Collect as much data as possible
   b) Only collect data necessary for specified purposes
   c) Share data freely with third parties
2. The Data Protection Board of India is responsible for:
   a) Creating apps and websites
   b) Enforcing the DPDPA
   c) Collecting personal data
3. As a Data Principal, you have the right to:
   a) Access and correct your personal data
   b) Demand that companies never collect any data
   c) Use any service without providing any information

(*Answers*: 1-b, 2-b, 3-a)

Chapter Summary

As we wrap up our overview of the DPDPA 2023, let's recap the key points:

1. The DPDPA 2023 is India's comprehensive data protection law, designed to protect individual privacy while fostering digital innovation.

2. It grants new rights to individuals (Data Principals) and places obligations on businesses (Data Fiduciaries) regarding the collection and use of personal data.

3. Key principles include lawful processing, purpose limitation, data minimization, and transparency.

4. The Act establishes the Data Protection Board of India as an independent body to enforce the law and address grievances.

5. DPDPA 2023 will bring noticeable changes to everyday digital interactions, giving individuals more control over their personal data.

6. Both individuals and businesses have important roles to play in navigating this new data protection landscape.

The DPDPA 2023 marks a new chapter in India's digital story. It's not just a law – it's a shift in how we think about and value personal data. As we move forward, remember that data protection is a shared responsibility. By understanding your rights and obligations, you're not just protecting your own data, but contributing to a safer, more transparent digital India.

In the coming chapters, we'll dive deeper into specific aspects of the DPDPA. For individuals, we'll explore practical ways to exercise your new rights and take control of your digital footprint. For businesses, we'll discuss strategies for compliance and how to turn data protection into a competitive advantage.

Additional Resources

To help you on your DPDPA journey, here are some key terms and resources:

Essential Glossary

1. **Data Principal**: The individual to whom the personal data relates (that's you!)
2. **Data Fiduciary**: The entity that determines the purpose and means of processing personal data (typically, the companies you interact with)
3. **Data Processor:** An entity that processes data on behalf of a Data Fiduciary
4. **Consent Manager**: A new entity introduced by DPDPA to help individuals manage their data sharing preferences across services

Where to Learn More

- For the full text of the DPDPA 2023, visit the official website of the Ministry of Electronics and Information Technology (MeitY)
- Keep an eye on the upcoming Data Protection Board of India website for guidelines and updates
- For a deeper dive into individual rights, check out Chapter 6 in Part 2 of this book
- For business compliance strategies, refer to Chapters 10-13 in Part 3

Remember, the journey to data protection is ongoing. Stay curious, stay informed, and don't hesitate to ask questions. Your data is valuable – treat it that way!

Chapter 3: Navigating Global Data Protection - An Indian Perspective

Picture this: Aarav, a software engineer in Pune, wakes up and checks his smartphone. In those first few minutes of his day, his data embarks on a whirlwind tour around the globe. His weather app, developed by a Korean company, pings servers in Seoul. As he scrolls through his American social media feed, his likes and comments are processed in data centres spanning from California to Ireland. He books a ride through a homegrown Indian app, but the data is backed up on Australian cloud servers. Finally, he makes a quick video call to his sister studying in Canada, with the call data bouncing through nodes across continents.

Welcome to the interconnected world of global data flows, where your personal information knows no borders. In this digital age, data is the new oil, and it flows just as freely across national boundaries. But here's the million-dollar question: As your data globe-trots, who's looking out for its safety?

Understanding global data protection isn't just an academic exercise for policy wonks or multinational corporations. For every Indian netizen, it's increasingly becoming a crucial life skill. Why? Because in today's digital ecosystem, your data is likely to cross international borders multiple times a day, each journey presenting both opportunities and risks.

Think about it: When you use a global service like Google or Facebook, your data is subject to not just Indian laws, but potentially to the laws of every country where that company operates or stores data. When you shop on international e-commerce platforms or use offshore cloud storage, your personal information is embarking on its own foreign adventure.

But it's not all about risks and challenges. Understanding global data protection also opens up a world of opportunities. For Indian professionals working in global teams, knowledge of international data norms can be a career differentiator. For budding entrepreneurs, it's the key to tapping into global markets while staying compliant.

As India positions itself as a digital superpower, with initiatives like Digital India and a booming IT sector, navigating the global data protection landscape becomes even more crucial. It's not just about protecting our data; it's about shaping the future of the digital world.

In this chapter, we'll embark on a journey across the global data protection landscape. We'll explore how laws from Europe to California impact your digital life in India. We'll unpack the complexities of cross-border data flows and see how global tech giants handle your information. Most importantly, we'll equip you with practical knowledge to protect your data in this interconnected world.

So, fasten your seatbelts and get ready for a globe-trotting adventure in the world of data protection. By the end of this chapter, you'll not only understand how your data travels the world but also how to be its best protection officer. Let's dive in!

Global Privacy Laws: What They Mean for You

In today's interconnected world, privacy laws from across the globe can have a surprising impact on your digital life in India. Let's explore some of the most influential regulations and what they mean for you.

A. The GDPR Effect

The General Data Protection Regulation (GDPR) of the European Union has become a global benchmark for data protection. But you might wonder, "I'm in India, why should I care about a European law?" The answer lies in the far-reaching impact of the GDPR.

GDPR Impact on India

Indian Users	Indian Businesses	Global Standards
Stronger rights with EU services	GDPR compliance for EU	Influencing Indian Laws
More transparent practices	Stricter data handling	Raising privacy awareness
Better data control	Risk of heavy fines	Promoting best practices
Improved breach notifications	Privacy as competitive edge	Shaping the future of digital privacy

This infographic illustrates how the GDPR affects both Indian users and businesses, as well as its role in setting global standards for data protection.

Did You Know? The GDPR can fine companies up to €20 million or 4% of their global annual turnover, whichever is higher, for severe violations. This has made even tech giants sit up and take notice!

B. A World Tour of Data Rights

While the GDPR has set a high bar, other countries have their own approaches to data protection. Let's take a whirlwind tour of data rights around the world and see how they compare to India's DPDPA.

Right	India (DPDPA)	EU (GDPR)	USA (CCPA)	Brazil (LGPD)
Right to Access	✓	✓	✓	✓
Right to Rectification	✓	✓	✓	✓
Right to Erasure	✓	✓	✓	✓
Right to Data Portability	✓	✓	✓	✓
Right to Object to Processing	Limited	✓	Limited	✓
Right to Restrict Processing	Limited	✓	Limited	✓
Automated Decision-Making Rights	Limited	✓	Limited	✓
Right to Withdraw Consent	✓	✓	✓	✓
Note: This table provides a simplified overview. Actual rights may have nuances and exceptions under each law.				

This comparison shows that while India's DPDPA aligns with global standards in many areas, there are some differences, particularly in the rights related to objecting to processing and automated decision-making.

Global Data Dilemma

Imagine you're an Indian student using a U.S.-based education platform that has users worldwide. You want to exercise your "right to be forgotten" and have your data erased. The platform agrees but informs you that due to legal requirements in other countries, some of your data might still be retained in their global databases.

This scenario highlights the complexities of navigating different privacy rules in our interconnected digital world. It underscores the importance of understanding not just Indian laws, but also the global data protection landscape.

C. Lessons for India

As India continues to refine its data protection framework, there's much to learn from global best practices. The DPDPA incorporates several international standards while also addressing unique Indian contexts.

Some practical takeaways from global practices that are relevant for India include:

1. Emphasis on consent and transparency
2. The concept of privacy by design
3. Strict penalties for non-compliance
4. The establishment of an independent data protection authority

When compared to international standards, the DPDPA stands out in a few ways:

- It introduces the concept of "consent managers," which is a novel approach to help individuals manage their data sharing preferences across services.
- It takes a more flexible approach to data localization compared to some other countries.

- It balances data protection with the need to foster innovation in India's growing digital economy.

As we navigate this global landscape, remember that data protection is an evolving field. Staying informed about international trends can help you better protect your data and understand your rights in our increasingly connected world.

Imagine a company named GlobalTech Solutions which has recently conducted a manual data discovery exercise on one of their processing operations. This is the data flow that they've found:

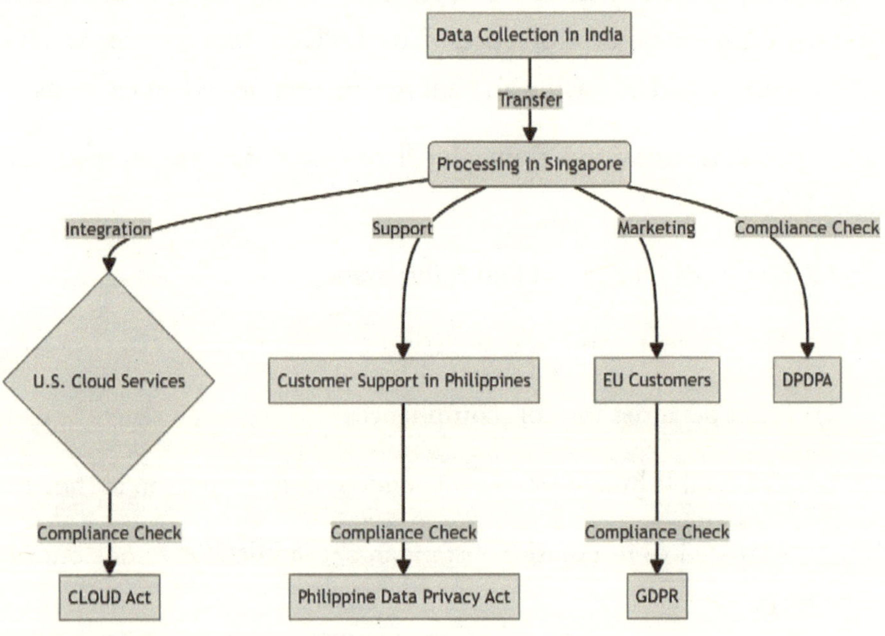

This flowchart demonstrates the complex journey of data across borders and the various compliance checkpoints it must pass through.

For GlobalTech Solutions, ensuring compliance at each of these checkpoints is crucial. They would need to consider:

1. Data transfer agreements with their Singapore server provider
2. GDPR compliance for EU customers
3. Vetting the data protection practices of their Philippine customer support team
4. Understanding the implications of using U.S.-based cloud services

B. How Global Giants Handle Your Data

Global tech companies have a significant presence in India, but how do they handle data from Indian users? Let's look at some key policies:

1. **Google**: Stores some data from Indian users in its U.S. data centers, but is investing in an Indian cloud region.
2. **Facebook**: Primarily processes Indian user data in the U.S., but faces ongoing discussions about data localization.
3. **Amazon**: Operates data centres in India for its Indian customers, aligning with data localization trends.

Tech Talk: Data Localization Explained

Data localization refers to the practice of keeping data within the country where it was generated. In India, there's been ongoing debate about data localization requirements.

Proponents argue it enhances data security and sovereignty, while critics worry it could hamper innovation and increase costs. The DPDPA takes a balanced approach, allowing cross-border transfers to certain approved countries while retaining the power to specify localization for critical data.

C. Protecting Your Data Globally

As an Indian user of international services, how can you ensure your data is protected as it travels the world? Here are some practical tips:

1. **Read privacy policies**: Pay attention to sections about international data transfers.
2. **Use strong, unique passwords**: This is your first line of defense, regardless of where your data is stored.
3. **Enable two-factor authentication**: This adds an extra layer of security to your accounts.
4. **Be cautious with public Wi-Fi**: Use a VPN when accessing sensitive information on public networks.
5. **Know your rights**: Familiarize yourself with the DPDPA and understand how it protects you when using international services.

Quick Guide: Questions to Ask About Your Data's International Journey

When using an international service, consider asking:

1. [ ] Where is my data stored?
2. [ ] Which countries does my data pass through?
3. [ ] How is my data protected during international transfers?
4. [ ] What laws govern my data in different countries?
5. [ ] Can I request my data to be stored only in certain countries?

6. [ ] How can I access or delete my data if it's stored internationally?
7. [ ] What happens to my data if the company is acquired by an entity in another country?
8. [ ] Are there any international agreements that affect how my data is handled?

Remember: If a company can't or won't answer these questions clearly, it might be a red flag about their data protection practices.

By asking these questions and staying informed about global data protection practices, you can take control of your data's international journey and make informed decisions about the services you use.

As we continue to navigate the global data protection landscape, it's crucial to understand India's unique position in the global data economy. In the next section, we'll explore how India is balancing its role as an IT powerhouse with the need for robust data protection, and the potential for India to become a leader in privacy innovation.

India in the Global Data Economy

As we've explored the global data protection landscape, it's time to focus on India's unique position. How does the world's largest democracy, with its booming IT sector and rapidly digitalizing economy, fit into this complex puzzle? Let's dive in.

A. India's Unique Position

India stands at a fascinating crossroads in the global data economy. On one hand, it's an IT powerhouse, providing services to companies worldwide. On the other, it's home to the world's second-largest internet user base, generating vast amounts of data daily. This dual role presents both opportunities and challenges.

Strengths	**Weaknesses**
– Large pool of skilled IT professionals	– Digital divide and uneven internet access
– Robust IT services sector	– Nascent data protection regulatory framework
– Huge domestic market of internet users	– Limited domestic cloud infrastructure
– Government push for digital transformation	– Low digital literacy in some segments
Opportunities	**Threats**
– Potential to become a global data processing hub	– Global competition in IT services
– Growing demand for data localization services	– Cyber security risks and data breaches
– Innovation in privacy-enhancing technologies	– Brain drain of top tech talent
– Leadership in frugal innovation for data protection	– Rapid technological changes outpacing regulation

This SWOT analysis highlights India's potential to leverage its strengths and opportunities while addressing its weaknesses and threats in the global data economy.

B. From Brain Drain to Data Drain?

Historically, India has grappled with the concept of "brain drain" - the exodus of skilled professionals to other countries. In the digital age, we face a new challenge: potential "data drain". This refers to the flow of valuable data generated by Indian users to servers and companies based outside the country.

The importance of data sovereignty - a nation's ability to control and regulate data generated within its borders - has become a key focus. Here's how India is working to keep data (and talent) local:

1. **Data Localization Efforts**: The Reserve Bank of India has mandated that all payment system data be stored in India. While the DPDPA takes a more flexible approach, it still emphasizes the importance of data sovereignty.

2. **Incentivizing Local Data Centers**: The government is offering incentives for companies to set up data centers in India, aiming to create a robust local cloud infrastructure.

3. **Skill Development Initiatives**: Programs like Digital India and Skill India aim to create a large pool of skilled professionals in data science, AI, and cybersecurity, reducing reliance on foreign expertise.

4. **Promoting Indigenous Technologies**: Initiatives like Atmanirbhar Bharat (Self-Reliant India) encourage the development of homegrown technologies, including in the data protection space.

C. India's Potential Leadership Role

India isn't just playing catch-up in the global data protection landscape - it has the potential to lead and innovate. Let's look at some areas where India is making strides:

As India continues to carve its niche in the global tech landscape, it's not just following trends – it's setting them. The country's unique blend of technological prowess, diverse challenges, and innovative spirit is giving rise to groundbreaking approaches in data protection.

Take, for instance, the burgeoning field of privacy tech. Indian startups are not just participating; they're leading the charge. Startups are turning heads with their innovative tools for privacy-aware coding and the use of artificial intelligence in understanding risks. They're weaving privacy into the very fabric of software development, potentially revolutionizing how we approach data protection from the ground up.

But India's potential for leadership doesn't stop at startups. The country has already demonstrated its capability to implement digital solutions on a massive scale with the Aadhaar system. While Aadhaar has had its fair share of controversies, those very challenges and debates have provided invaluable lessons in balancing convenience with privacy in large-scale digital identity systems. It's a goldmine of insights that could shape global practices in this delicate balancing act.

Then there's India's secret weapon of *jugaad*. This uniquely Indian concept of frugal innovation may be a game-changer in the world of data protection. It's not just a pipe dream – it's a very real possibility that could revolutionize data protection practices in emerging markets worldwide.

Perhaps India's most significant contribution could come from its experience in providing digital services to incredibly diverse populations. From bustling metropolises to remote villages, India has had to innovate to reach everyone. This experience could be the key to pioneering data protection approaches that work even in low-bandwidth, low-literacy contexts. It's about making privacy accessible to all, not just those with the latest tech or highest digital literacy.

As we stand at this juncture, one thing is clear: India's potential to lead in privacy innovation is not just about technology. It's about leveraging the country's unique experiences, challenges, and ingenuity to create solutions that are not only effective but also inclusive and adaptable. In doing so, India could well become the torchbearer for privacy innovation in the digital age.

As we wrap up this exploration of India's role in the global data economy, it's clear that the country stands at a pivotal moment. The choices made now - by policymakers, businesses, and individuals - will shape not just India's digital future, but potentially the global approach to data protection.

In our next and final section, we'll look at practical steps you can take to protect your data in this global context, and how Indian businesses can navigate the international data protection landscape.

Taking Action: Global Awareness, Local Impact

As we've journeyed through the global data protection landscape, you might be wondering: "What does all this mean for me?" Whether you're an individual concerned about your personal data or a business navigating international regulations, there are practical steps you can take to protect data in our interconnected world.

For Individuals: Protecting Your Data Globally

1. **Stay Informed**: Keep up with global privacy news. Changes in regulations like the GDPR can affect your rights, even as an Indian citizen.

2. **Read Privacy Policies**: Pay special attention to sections about international data transfers when using global services.

3. **Use Privacy-Enhancing Tools**: Consider using VPNs, encrypted messaging apps, and privacy-focused browsers.
4. **Be Cautious with Data Sharing**: Think twice before sharing personal information, especially on platforms that operate internationally.
5. **Exercise Your Rights**: Familiarize yourself with the rights granted by the DPDPA and don't hesitate to exercise them, even with international companies.

For Businesses: Navigating International Data Protection

1. **Conduct a Global Data Audit**: Understand where your data comes from and where it goes, across all international operations.
2. **Implement Privacy by Design**: Build data protection into your products and services from the ground up, considering global best practices.
3. **Stay Compliant with Multiple Regulations**: If you handle data from different regions, ensure compliance with relevant laws (GDPR, CCPA, etc.) in addition to the DPDPA.
4. **Train Your Team**: Ensure your staff understands the global implications of data protection, especially if you operate internationally.
5. **Plan for Cross-Border Data Transfers**: Develop clear protocols for how data is transferred and protected when it crosses borders.

Global Data Awareness Action Plan

For Individuals:

– [ ] Review privacy settings on all international platforms you use

- [ ] Research the data protection laws of countries where your favorite services are based
- [ ] Set up alerts for privacy news related to services you use frequently
- [ ] Learn about international data subject rights (e.g., GDPR rights)
- [ ] Practice using privacy-enhancing technologies (e.g., VPNs, encrypted messaging)

For Businesses:

- [ ] Map your data flows across international borders
- [ ] Assess compliance with relevant international data protection laws
- [ ] Develop a cross-border data transfer policy
- [ ] Appoint a team member to monitor global data protection developments
- [ ] Conduct regular training on international data protection best practices
- [ ] Review and update privacy policies to reflect global data handling practices
- [ ] Implement mechanisms for honoring international data subject rights requests

For Both:

- [ ] Stay informed about India's evolving role in the global data economy

- [ ] Engage in discussions about data protection (forums, social media, local meetups)
- [ ] Consider the privacy implications before adopting new international digital services
- [ ] Advocate for responsible data practices in your personal and professional networks

Remember: Global data awareness is an ongoing process. Regularly revisit and update your approach as the landscape evolves.

These checklists provides a practical starting point for both individuals and businesses to enhance their global data awareness and take concrete steps towards better data protection practices.

The Balancing Act: Innovation and Protection

As we navigate this complex landscape, it's crucial to remember that data protection isn't about stopping the flow of data – it's about ensuring that flow is secure, ethical, and beneficial to all parties involved. For India to thrive in the global digital economy, we need to strike a balance between fostering innovation and ensuring robust data protection.

Data Dilemma: The Global Startup

Imagine you're the founder of a promising Indian startup developing an AI-powered health app. You're excited about the potential to improve healthcare globally, but you're also aware of the sensitive nature of health data and the complex web of international regulations.

How do you balance your global ambitions with the need to protect user data across different jurisdictions? This is the kind of challenge that many Indian entrepreneurs face in the global digital economy.

The key lies in viewing data protection not as a hindrance, but as a feature. By building strong data protection practices from the ground up, you can turn privacy into a competitive advantage, earning user trust and easing entry into privacy-conscious markets.

As we conclude this chapter, remember that in today's interconnected world, thinking globally about data protection isn't just for multinational corporations – it's essential for every digital citizen and business. By staying informed, taking proactive steps, and engaging with the global privacy conversation, you can navigate the complex world of international data flows with confidence.

In our next chapter, we'll dive deeper into the practical aspects of implementing data protection in your daily life and business operations. But for now, let's recap what we've learned about navigating the global data protection landscape.

Chapter Summary: Think Global, Act Local

As we conclude our journey through the global data protection landscape, let's recap the key takeaways:

1. **Global Impact of Data Protection Laws**: Regulations like the GDPR have far-reaching effects, influencing data practices worldwide and setting new global standards.

2. **Cross-Border Data Flows**: In our interconnected world, data regularly crosses borders, subject to various national and international regulations.

3. **India's Unique Position**: As both an IT powerhouse and a massive data generator, India faces unique challenges and opportunities in the global data economy.

4. **Data Localization and Sovereignty**: The balance between global data flows and data sovereignty is a key issue, with implications for both businesses and individual privacy.

5. **Future of Privacy Innovation**: India has the potential to become a global leader in privacy innovation, leveraging its technological expertise and diverse digital landscape.

6. **Individual and Business Responsibilities**: Both individuals and businesses have important roles to play in navigating the global data protection landscape, from staying informed to implementing robust data practices.

As we look to the future, it's clear that data protection will continue to be a critical issue in our increasingly digital world. By thinking globally and acting locally, we can contribute to a safer, more ethical digital ecosystem while harnessing the benefits of our interconnected world.

"Test Your Global Privacy Street Smarts" Quiz

Let's test your understanding of the global data protection landscape with a quick quiz:

Test Your Global Privacy Street Smarts

Circle the letter of the correct answer for each question. Answers are provided at the end of the quiz.

1. Which law has had the most significant global impact on data protection practices?
   a) CCPA
   b) GDPR
   c) PIPEDA
   d) APPI
2. What does 'data localization' refer to?
   a) Translating data into local languages
   b) Storing data within the country where it was generated
   c) Using local servers for data processing
   d) Hiring local data protection officers
3. How does the DPDPA approach cross-border data transfers?
   a) It prohibits all cross-border transfers
   b) It allows transfers only to EU countries
   c) It takes a balanced approach, allowing transfers to approved countries
   d) It has no provisions for cross-border transfers
4. What is a potential advantage for India in the global data economy?
   a) Its large population of internet users
   b) Its strict data localization laws

c) Its isolation from global data flows

d) Its low digital literacy rates

5. Which of the following is NOT typically considered a data subject right under global privacy laws?

   a) Right to access personal data

   b) Right to be forgotten

   c) Right to sell personal data

   d) Right to data portability

6. In the context of global data protection, what does "adequacy" often refer to?

   a) The quality of data collected

   b) A country's data protection standards being deemed sufficient by another jurisdiction

   c) The speed of data processing

   d) The quantity of data a company can handle

7. What is a key challenge for multinational companies in complying with global data protection laws?

   a) Hiring data protection officers in every country

   b) Translating privacy policies into all languages

   c) Navigating varying and sometimes conflicting requirements across jurisdictions

d) Paying fines in different currencies

Answers: 1-b, 2-b, 3-c, 4-a, 5-c, 6-b, 7-c

Score yourself:

6-7 correct: Global Privacy Expert

4-5 correct: Privacy Savvy

2-3 correct: Privacy Aware

0-1 correct: Time to brush up on global privacy!

Remember, the world of global data protection is complex and ever-changing. Keep learning and staying informed to protect your data in our interconnected world.

As you reflect on your quiz results, remember that understanding global data protection is an ongoing journey. The digital landscape is constantly evolving, and so are the laws and practices that govern it. By staying informed, thinking critically, and acting responsibly, you can navigate this complex terrain with confidence.

In our next chapter, we'll dive deeper into the practical aspects of implementing data protection in your daily life and business operations. We'll explore specific strategies and tools you can use to safeguard your data in an increasingly interconnected world.

Chapter 4: Navigating the Indian Data Protection Landscape

Imagine a typical day in the life of Roshni, a young professional living in the bustling city of Pune. As she wakes up, her smart speaker cheerfully announces the weather forecast. She checks her phone, scrolling through social media and responding to messages. On her way to work, she uses a ride-sharing app, then stops at a local café, paying with her UPI-enabled mobile wallet.

At each step, Roshni's data is moving, being collected, processed, and stored by various entities. Her location, preferences, financial transactions - all leave a digital trail. But where does this data go? Who has access to it? And most importantly, how is it protected?

Welcome to the complex, vibrant, and rapidly evolving world of data protection in India. In a nation of over 1.3 billion people, with more than 700 million internet users, the flow of data is as diverse and dynamic as the country itself. From the narrow lanes of ancient cities to the gleaming tech parks of modern metropolises, data courses through the veins of Digital India.

But this digital revolution brings with it unique challenges and opportunities. How do we balance the push for technological advancement with the need for robust data protection? How does a country with such diversity in literacy, digital access, and technological awareness ensure the privacy rights of all its citizens?

In this chapter, we'll embark on a journey through India's data protection landscape. We'll meet the key players shaping this ecosystem, explore real-world stories of data protection successes and failures, and uncover the distinctive challenges and opportunities that make India's data protection journey unlike any other in the world.

So, let's dive in and discover how your data navigates the vibrant tapestry of Digital India!

The Indian Data Protection Ecosystem: Key Players and Their Impact

As Roshni goes about her day, her data interacts with a complex ecosystem of entities, each playing a crucial role in shaping India's data protection landscape. Let's take a closer look at these key players and how they impact the average Indian's digital life.

A. Government Bodies: Guardians of Your Data

Picture a massive control room, screens flickering with streams of data, where vigilant officials work tirelessly to protect the digital rights of millions. While not quite as dramatic in reality, this image isn't far from the intended role of India's data protection authorities.

At the heart of this system is the Data Protection Board of India (DPBI) which, hopefully by the time you are reading this, has been established under the Digital Personal Data Protection Act (DPDPA). Think of the DPBI as a digital traffic cop, ensuring that companies and organizations follow the rules of the road when it comes to handling your personal data.

Data Protection Board of India

STRUCTURE

- Chairperson
- Experts (in law, tech and data protection)
- Support staff and technical teams

KEY RESPONSIBILITIES

Enforce compliance with the DPDPA

Investigate personal data breaches

Impose penalties for non-compliance

Adjudicate disputes under the DPDPA

IMPACT ON CITIZENS

Protects personal data rights

Provides redressal mechanism for data breaches and misuse of personal data

But the DPBI isn't alone in this mission. The Reserve Bank of India (RBI) plays a crucial role in protecting your financial data. Remember when Priya used her UPI app for that morning coffee? The RBI's guidelines ensure that her transaction data is handled with utmost care.

Quick Tip: If you suspect your data has been misused, you can file a complaint with the DPBI through their online portal. Keep an eye out for this feature once the Board is fully operational!

B. Industry Initiatives: When Businesses Take the Lead

While government bodies set the rules, it's often businesses that are at the forefront of implementing data protection measures. Many Indian companies are going beyond mere compliance, seeing robust data protection as a competitive advantage by implementing privacy by design.

> **Jargon Buster**: "Privacy by Design" means considering privacy at every stage of product development, not just as an afterthought.

C. Privacy Advocates: Your Digital Rights Champions

As Roshni navigates her digital day, there's a group of dedicated individuals and organizations working tirelessly to protect her rights - often without her even knowing it.

Meet Aisha Verma, a privacy advocate with the Digital Rights Foundation of India (a fictional organization representative of real advocacy groups). Aisha's day might involve scrutinizing new tech policies, educating the public about their digital rights, or lobbying for stronger privacy protections.

Aisha's main challenge would be that many Indians don't realize the extent of their digital rights. The Foundation's job would be to bridge that knowledge gap and ensure that in the rush towards a digital future, companies don't leave privacy behind.

> **Global Connection**: Indian privacy advocacy groups often collaborate with international organizations, sharing knowledge and strategies. For instance, when Europe implemented GDPR, Indian advocates used it as a benchmark to push for stronger protections in India.

As we can see, India's data protection ecosystem is a complex interplay of government regulators, forward-thinking businesses, and passionate advocates. Each plays a crucial role in ensuring that as India races towards its digital future, the privacy rights of its citizens are not left behind.

In the next section, we'll explore how this ecosystem works in practice, through real-world stories of data protection successes and failures in Digital India.

Data Protection in Action: Stories from Digital India

As you may imagine, there have already been several cases of Indian personal data being left vulnerable to cybersecurity attacks and breaches. Here are some examples.

Case Study: The NPCI Security Audit - A Wake-Up Call for India's Digital Payments Infrastructure

Imagine you're responsible for safeguarding the financial data of millions of Indians. Now, imagine discovering that this data might be more vulnerable than you thought. This isn't the plot of a techno-thriller - it's the real-life scenario that unfolded at the National Payments Corporation of India (NPCI) in 2019.[3]

Let's set the stage. The NPCI isn't just any organization - it's the backbone of India's digital payments system. It processes billions of dollars daily and operates the RuPay card network, a point of national pride championed by Prime Minister Narendra Modi himself. So when a government audit found over 40 security vulnerabilities in its systems, it wasn't just a technical issue - it was a matter of national importance.

The audit, conducted over four months leading up to February 2019, painted a concerning picture. Among the "critical" and "high" risk vulnerabilities was a startling discovery: personal data, including

16-digit card numbers, customer names, account numbers, and even national identity numbers, were stored in "plain text" in some databases. In layman's terms, this sensitive information was left unencrypted, potentially exposed if the system were breached.

Now, you might be thinking, "Surely, an organization handling such sensitive data would have better safeguards in place?" And you'd be right to ask that question. It's a stark reminder that even organizations at the heart of our financial infrastructure can have significant security gaps.

But the story doesn't end there. The audit also highlighted other issues:

- Unencrypted RuPay card numbers visible in server logs
- "Buffer overflow" vulnerabilities in RuPay and other NPCI applications
- Outdated operating systems
- Inadequate anti-malware functionality on a mail server

These findings underscore a crucial point in data protection: security is only as strong as its weakest link. A single vulnerability can potentially compromise an entire system.

The NPCI's response to these findings is worth noting. They stated that they are regularly audited and that senior management reviews all findings, which are then "remediated to the satisfaction of the auditors." They also emphasized their compliance with standards set by the PCI Security Standards Council.

However, this case study raises some important questions for all organizations handling sensitive data:

- How often are you conducting thorough security audits?
- Are you encrypting all sensitive data, both in storage and in transit?
- Are your systems and software kept up-to-date with the latest security patches?
- How quickly do you address vulnerabilities when they're discovered?

The NPCI case serves as a wake-up call not just for financial institutions, but for any organization handling personal data. It highlights the ongoing challenges in data security and the need for constant vigilance.

Case Study: The 815 Million Indian Citizens Data Breach - A Digital Security Nightmare

Imagine waking up one day to find out that your most personal information - your Aadhaar number, passport details, even your voter ID - is up for sale on the dark web. Now multiply that by 815 million. That's the staggering reality that India faced in October 2023, in what could be one of the largest data breaches in history.

Let's break this down, shall we?

On October 15, 2023, Resecurity, an American cybersecurity company, dropped a bombshell. They reported that the personally identifiable information (PII) of 815 million Indian citizens was being hawked on the dark web for a cool $80,000. We're talking Aadhaar numbers, passport details - the works. And here's the kicker: the data was found to be valid.

Now, you might be wondering, "How on earth did this happen?" Well, that's the million-dollar question (or in this case, the 80,000-dollar question). The threat actors claimed the data came from the Indian Council of Medical Research (ICMR). Given that ICMR reported 6,000 cyber-attack attempts last year alone, it's not hard to see how they might have been a target.

But here's where it gets even more interesting. Another threat actor, going by the name "Lucius," claimed to have an even bigger treasure trove - 1.8 terabytes of data, including voter IDs and driving license records. They claimed it came from an "India internal law enforcement agency."

So, what are the implications? This isn't just about privacy - it's about national security, financial fraud, and most importantly, identity theft. Imagine the havoc a malicious actor could wreak with this information. It's enough to keep any cybersecurity expert up at night.

So, what can we learn from this nightmare scenario?

- **Data protection is an ongoing process:** The government's admission that they're still moving data to safe storage shows that data protection isn't a one-and-done deal. It's a constant, evolving challenge.

- **Legacy systems are vulnerable:** Old data, stored in outdated systems, can be a goldmine for hackers. Modernizing data storage and protection should be a top priority for any organization.

- **Third-party risk is real:** While the source of the breach isn't confirmed, the possibility that it came from a third-party aggregator highlights the importance of vetting all partners who handle sensitive data.

- **Scale matters:** In a country of over a billion people, even a small percentage of compromised data can affect millions. This underscores the need for robust, scalable security solutions.
- **Transparency is crucial:** The government's response, while prompt, left many questions unanswered. In the wake of a data breach, clear, honest communication is key to maintaining public trust.

For individuals, this case study is a wake-up call. It's a reminder to be vigilant, to use strong, unique passwords, to enable two-factor authentication wherever possible, and to be cautious about sharing personal information online.

For organizations, it's a stark reminder of the responsibility that comes with handling personal data. It underscores the need for robust security measures, regular audits, and a proactive approach to addressing vulnerabilities.

As we navigate the complex landscape of data protection in India, cases like these remind us of the high stakes involved. They underscore the importance of robust security measures, regular audits, and a proactive approach to addressing vulnerabilities.

Remember, in the world of data protection, it's not just about complying with regulations - it's about fostering a culture of security that permeates every level of an organization. As we continue to build India's digital future, let's take these lessons to heart and strive for the highest standards of data protection.

Data Dilemma: The Compromised Password

Imagine you're an employee at one of these companies that hoards massive treasure troves of personal data. You've just learned about the data breach and realize you've been using the same password for your work account and personal email. What should you do?

a) Change only your work password

b) Change both passwords immediately

c) Wait for IT to force a password change

d) Ignore it, as changing passwords is too much hassle

(We'll discuss the best course of action later in this chapter!)

B. Sector Spotlight: Your Data Across Industries

As we've seen with the case studies above, different sectors face unique challenges in protecting your data. Let's explore how various industries in India are tackling data protection.

1. **Financial Services: Banking on Privacy**

   The financial sector is at the forefront of data protection efforts. The rise of UPI and digital payments has created new challenges and opportunities. According to a report by the National Payments Corporation of India (NPCI), UPI transactions crossed 8 billion in volume in January 2023, representing a massive amount of sensitive financial data being processed daily.[4]

   The Reserve Bank of India (RBI) has taken proactive steps to ensure data protection in this rapidly growing sector. In 2018, the RBI mandated that all payment system data must be stored only in India, ensuring easier oversight and data sovereignty.[5]

2. Healthcare: Balancing Privacy and Innovation

In the wake of the COVID-19 pandemic, India's healthcare sector has seen a rapid digital transformation. The National Digital Health Mission, or Ayushman Bharat, launched in 2020, aims to create a unified health ID for every Indian citizen, raising both opportunities and concerns about health data privacy.[6]

The Ministry of Health and Family Welfare has issued telemedicine practical guidelines[7] that include provisions for data protection, emphasizing the importance of maintaining confidentiality and obtaining informed consent for telemedicine consultations.

3. E-commerce and Telecom: The Price of Convenience

India's e-commerce sector has experienced explosive growth, with the market size projected to reach US$ 325 billion by 2030, according to IBEF (India Brand Equity Foundation).[8] This growth brings with it significant data protection challenges.

E-commerce and telecom platforms collect vast amounts of data for personalization and targeted advertising. The Competition Commission of India (CCI) has recognized the potential privacy implications of this data collection. In both their 2020 market study on the e-commerce industry[9] and their 2021 study on the telecom industry,[10] the CCI noted the need for transparent data collection practices and the importance of user consent.

> **Quick Tip**: Before sharing data with any service, ask yourself: Is this information necessary for the service I'm using? Am I comfortable with how this data might be used?

C. Privacy Champions: Indian Companies Leading the Way

While data breaches make headlines, there are also success stories of Indian companies setting new standards in data protection.

For instance, Zeotap, an Indian-origin customer intelligence platform, has made significant strides in privacy-preserving technologies. They've developed a system that allows data analysis without exposing individual user data, a concept known as "data clean rooms." This technology has gained traction globally, showcasing India's potential to lead in privacy tech.[11]

Another example is Airtel, one of India's largest telecom providers. In response to growing privacy concerns, Airtel implemented a blockchain-based 'Secure Internet' solution in 2021.[12] This system allows users to block malware and surveillance attacks, adding an extra layer of privacy protection for their customers.

Global Connection: Indian innovations in privacy tech are gaining recognition worldwide. For example, the World Economic Forum's Centre for the Fourth Industrial Revolution has partnered with Indian state governments to develop privacy-preserving AI frameworks, demonstrating India's growing influence in global privacy discussions.

As we've seen through these real-world examples, data protection in India is a dynamic, evolving landscape. From major policy initiatives to technological innovations, each development shapes how we approach privacy in our digital lives.

In the next section, we'll explore some of the unique challenges and opportunities that make India's data protection journey unlike any other in the world.

Unique Challenges and Opportunities in India's Data Landscape

India's journey towards robust data protection is as diverse and complex as the nation itself. From the bustling tech hubs of Bangalore to the remote villages of Rajasthan, the country faces a unique set of challenges and opportunities in safeguarding personal data.

A. The Aadhaar Conundrum

At the heart of India's data protection debate lies Aadhaar, the world's largest biometric ID system. Launched in 2009, Aadhaar aimed to provide a unique identity to every Indian resident. However, it has become a lightning rod for privacy concerns.

The Aadhaar system presents a classic data protection dilemma. On one hand, it has enabled easier access to government services and has been instrumental in reducing benefit fraud. On the other, it has raised serious concerns about privacy and the potential for mass surveillance.

In a landmark judgment in 2018, the Supreme Court of India upheld the constitutional validity of Aadhaar but placed significant restrictions on its use. The court ruled that while Aadhaar could be mandatory for welfare schemes and filing taxes, it couldn't be required for bank accounts, mobile phone connections, or school admissions.

This ruling highlighted the delicate balance India must strike between leveraging technology for development and protecting individual privacy rights.

Aadhaar: India's Biometric ID System

Scale

- Over 1.3 billion Aadhaar numbers issued
- World's largest biometric ID system
- Covers 99% of adult Indian population

Data Collected

- Demographic data (name, address, DoB)
- Biometric data (fingerprints, iris scan)
- Optional: mobile number, email

Privacy Concerns

- Potential for surveillance
- Risk of data breaches
- Function creep (use beyond original purpose)
- Exclusion issues

Benefits

- Easier access to government services
- Reduction in benefit fraud
- Financial inclusion
- Simplified KYC for businesses

Data Dilemma: To Link or Not to Link?

Many Indians face a common dilemma: should they link their Aadhaar to various services for convenience, or keep it separate to maintain privacy? The answer often depends on individual circumstances and risk assessment.

B. Digital Literacy and Data Protection

India's rapid digital transformation has created a unique challenge: a vast population of first-time internet users who may not be fully aware of digital privacy concepts.

According to the Digital Empowerment Foundation, despite India's large internet user base, digital literacy rates remain low, especially in rural areas.[13] This digital divide poses significant challenges for implementing effective data protection measures.

Initiatives like the Pradhan Mantri Gramin Digital Saksharta Abhiyan (PMGDISHA) aim to bridge this gap by providing digital literacy training to 60 million rural households.[14] However, integrating data protection awareness into these programs remains a crucial task.

Quick Tip: If you're helping someone new to the internet, take a moment to explain basic privacy concepts, like the importance of strong passwords and being cautious about sharing personal information online.

C. Data Localization: Keeping Indian Data in India

The debate around data localization – the practice of storing data on servers physically located within national borders – has been particularly heated in India.

Proponents argue that data localization is essential for national security and easier law enforcement access. Critics, however, warn that it could stifle innovation and increase costs for businesses.

The Reserve Bank of India (RBI) took a strong stance on this issue in 2018, mandating that all payment system data must be stored only in India. This move affected global giants like Mastercard and Visa, highlighting the potential impact of data localization policies on international business.

Jargon Buster: "Data Sovereignty" refers to the idea that data is subject to the laws and governance structures of the nation where it is collected. Data localization is one way countries try to ensure data sovereignty.

As India continues to refine its approach to data protection, these unique challenges – Aadhaar, digital literacy, and data localization – will play a crucial role in shaping policies and practices. They represent the complex balancing act India must perform: leveraging data for development while protecting individual privacy rights.

In our next section, we'll look towards the future, exploring emerging trends that will shape India's data protection landscape in the years to come.

Emerging Trends: The Future of Data Protection in India

As we stand at the cusp of a new era in digital India, several emerging trends are set to reshape the data protection landscape. These developments not only present new challenges but also offer exciting opportunities for innovation and leadership on the global stage.

A. AI and Privacy: The Next Frontier

Artificial Intelligence (AI) is rapidly transforming industries across India, from healthcare to finance. However, AI's appetite for data raises significant privacy concerns.

AI and Privacy in India: Challenges and Solutions

Challenges

- AI's need for large datasets
- Potential for re-identification of anonymized data
- Algorithmic bias and discrimination
- Lack of transparency in AI decision-making
- Difficulty in obtaining meaningful consent

Potential Solutions

- Federated Learning
- Differential Privacy
- Homomorphic Encryption
- Explainable AI (XAI)
- Privacy-preserving Machine Learning

Indian Initiatives

- NITI Aayog's National Strategy for AI
- Responsible AI for Youth program
- AI research hubs in IITs and IIITs
- AI-focused startups in privacy tech

India's approach to AI governance is still evolving. In 2018, NITI Aayog, the government's think tank, released a national strategy for AI, emphasizing the need for privacy-preserving techniques in AI development. The strategy highlighted technologies like federated learning and differential privacy as potential solutions to balance innovation with data protection.

B. Privacy in the Age of 5G and IoT

The rollout of 5G networks and the proliferation of Internet of Things (IoT) devices are set to revolutionize India's digital landscape. However, they also present new privacy challenges.

According to a report by GSMA, India has had a compound annual growth rate of 4% in terms of unique mobile subscribers from 2015 to 2022, with a penetration of 55% of the Indian population.[15] This explosive growth in connectivity will generate vast amounts of data, much of it personal and sensitive.

The government has recognized these challenges. In 2018, the Department of Telecommunications (DoT) released a National Digital Communications Policy that emphasizes the need for robust data protection measures in the 5G and IoT era.

> **Global Connection**: India's approach to privacy in 5G and IoT could have global implications. As one of the world's largest and fastest-growing digital markets, India's policies and innovations in this space could serve as a model for other developing nations.

C. India's Potential as a Global Privacy Leader

Despite the challenges, India is well-positioned to become a global leader in privacy innovation. The country's unique combination of a large tech-savvy workforce, a vibrant startup ecosystem, and complex societal needs creates a fertile ground for privacy-enhancing technologies.

For instance, Indian startups are at the forefront of developing privacy-preserving AI solutions. These startups are working on homomorphic encryption techniques that allow data to be processed while remaining encrypted, potentially revolutionizing data protection in cloud computing.

Moreover, India's experience in implementing large-scale digital projects like Aadhaar and UPI provides valuable insights for balancing innovation with privacy protection. These learnings could inform global best practices in digital identity and financial technology.

The government is also taking steps to position India as a thought leader in digital ethics and privacy. In 2020, India joined the Global Partnership on Artificial Intelligence (GPAI) as a founding member, committing to the responsible development and use of AI.

As we look to the future, it's clear that data protection will remain a critical issue in India's digital journey. The challenges are significant, but so are the opportunities. By fostering a culture of privacy awareness, encouraging innovation in privacy tech, and participating actively in global discussions on data ethics, India has the potential to not just protect its citizens' data, but to shape the future of global data protection.

In our final section, we'll recap the key points of this chapter and provide some actionable steps for navigating India's evolving data protection landscape.

Chapter Summary: Navigating Your Data Future

As we've journeyed through India's data protection landscape, we've seen a complex tapestry of challenges, innovations, and opportunities. Let's recap the key takeaways:

1. India's data protection ecosystem is shaped by multiple stakeholders, including government bodies like the Data Protection Board of India, industry initiatives, and privacy advocates.

2. Different sectors, from finance to healthcare, face unique data protection challenges and are developing sector-specific solutions.

3. India grapples with unique challenges such as the Aadhaar system, digital literacy gaps, and debates around data localization.

4. Emerging technologies like AI, 5G, and IoT are reshaping the data protection landscape, presenting both new risks and opportunities for innovation.

5. India has the potential to become a global leader in privacy innovation, leveraging its tech expertise and experience with large-scale digital projects.

Now, let's translate this knowledge into action. Here's a practical "Data Protection Action Plan" for navigating your digital future in India:

Your Data Protection Action Plan

For Individuals:

1. [ ] Stay Informed:
   - Follow updates from the Data Protection Board of India
   - Subscribe to privacy news from reliable sources
2. [ ] Manage Your Digital Footprint:
   - Regularly review and update privacy settings on all your accounts
   - Be cautious about the information you share online
3. [ ] Practice Safe Data Habits:
   - Use strong, unique passwords for each account
   - Enable two-factor authentication where available
   - Be wary of phishing attempts and unsolicited requests for personal information
4. [ ] Understand Your Rights:
   - Familiarize yourself with the rights granted under the DPDPA
   - Don't hesitate to exercise these rights with companies holding your data
5. [ ] Spread Awareness:
   - Help friends and family understand the importance of data protection

– Share privacy tips and best practices within your community

For Businesses:

1. [] Implement Privacy by Design:
   – Integrate data protection principles into all aspects of your operations
   – Conduct regular privacy impact assessments
2. [] Stay Compliant:
   – Keep up-to-date with the latest DPDPA requirements
   – Develop and maintain clear data protection policies
3. [] Invest in Security:
   – Implement robust cybersecurity measures
   – Regularly train staff on data protection best practices
4. [] Be Transparent:
   – Clearly communicate your data practices to customers
   – Provide easy-to-understand privacy notices
5. [] Prepare for the Future:
   – Stay informed about emerging technologies and their privacy implications
   – Explore privacy-enhancing technologies relevant to your industry

Remember: Data protection is an ongoing process. Regularly revisit and update your practices to stay ahead in India's evolving digital landscape.

By following this action plan, you'll be well-equipped to navigate India's data protection landscape, whether as an individual safeguarding your personal information or as a business ensuring compliance and building trust.

"Test Your Indian Data Protection Street Smarts" Quiz

To reinforce what we've learned, let's conclude with a quick quiz. This will help you gauge your understanding of India's data protection landscape and identify areas where you might want to dive deeper.

1. Under the DPDPA, the body responsible for enforcing data protection rules in India is:

   a) The Supreme Court

   b) The Data Protection Board of India

   c) The Ministry of Electronics and Information Technology

   d) The Reserve Bank of India

2. Which of the following is NOT a key challenge in India's data protection landscape?

   a) Digital literacy gaps

   b) The Aadhaar system's privacy implications

   c) Data localization debates

   d) Excessive regulation of the tech industry

3. In the context of AI and privacy in India, which of the following is being explored as a potential solution?
   a) Banning AI altogether
   b) Federated learning
   c) Collecting more data
   d) Ignoring privacy concerns
4. The RBI's 2018 directive on payment system data requires:
   a) All payment data to be stored only in India
   b) All payment data to be made public
   c) Payment companies to stop collecting data
   d) Payment data to be stored for at least 10 years
5. India's potential as a global privacy leader is supported by:
   a) Its large tech-savvy workforce
   b) Experience with large-scale digital projects
   c) A vibrant startup ecosystem
   d) All of the above

(*Answers:* 1-b, 2-d, 3-b, 4-a, 5-d)

As we conclude this chapter, remember that understanding India's data protection landscape is not just about compliance or avoiding risks. It's about actively participating in shaping a digital future that respects privacy, fosters innovation, and creates value for all. Whether you're an individual navigating the digital world or a business leveraging data for growth, your actions and choices play a crucial role in building a privacy-respecting digital India.

In the next Part of this book, we'll dive deeper into practical strategies for implementing robust data protection practices in your personal life and business operations. Stay tuned!

Part 2: The Individual's Guide to Data Protection

As the warm Pune sun peeks through her curtains, Priya reaches for her smartphone. In those first few moments of her day, she's already generating data: her wake-up time, the news articles she skims, the messages she sends to friends and family. Like millions of Indians embracing the digital age, Priya's everyday actions create a rich tapestry of personal information. But who's collecting this data? How is it being used? And most importantly, how can Priya - and you - protect it?

Welcome to Part 2 of our journey through India's data protection landscape. Here, we'll equip you with the knowledge and tools to navigate the complex world of personal data in the digital age. Whether you're a tech-savvy professional like Priya or someone just starting to explore the online world, this guide is your compass in the data protection maze.

Why Your Data Matters More Than Ever

In India's rapidly evolving digital ecosystem, personal data has become a valuable currency. From the convenience of UPI payments to the personalized recommendations on your favourite streaming service, data drives many of the services we've come to rely on. However, this convenience comes with potential risks:

- Identity theft and financial fraud
- Manipulation of your choices through targeted advertising
- Unauthorized sharing of your personal information
- Potential discrimination based on data profiles

As Indians, we often find ourselves in a delicate balance. Our culture values sharing and community, which can sometimes extend to how freely we share our personal information. At the same time, we're becoming increasingly aware of the need for digital privacy. This guide will help you navigate this cultural tightrope, showing you how to enjoy the benefits of the digital world while protecting your personal information.

The Awareness, Action, and Advocacy Framework

Throughout this part of the book, we'll follow a three-pronged approach to personal data protection:

1. **Awareness**: Understanding the what, why, and how of personal data protection.

2. **Action**: Practical steps you can take to safeguard your information.

3. **Advocacy**: How to promote better data protection practices in your community and beyond.

By focusing on these three areas, you'll not only protect yourself but also contribute to building a more privacy-conscious digital India.

Meet Priya: Your Guide Through the Data Protection Landscape

To illustrate the concepts and challenges we'll explore, we'll follow Priya's journey. As a software engineer in Pune, Priya represents the tech-savvy youth of India, navigating the opportunities and pitfalls of the digital age. Through her experiences, we'll see how data protection principles apply in real-world situations.

A Day in Priya's Digital Life

Data Generated Throughout the Day

7:00 AM
Checks smartphone
Data: Wake-up time, app usage

1:00 PM
Uses UPI for lunch payment
Data: Transaction details, location

7:00 PM
Streams movie online
Data: Viewing preferences, device info

8:00 AM
Orders cab via app
Data: Location, payment info

3:00 PM
Shares photos on social media
Data: Images, location tags, interactio

10:00 PM
Sets alarm on smartphone
Data: Sleep schedule, app usage

Continuous Flow of Personal Data

Smartphone

Apps

Social Media

Location Services

Payment Systems

Streaming Services

Priya, like many Indians, interacts with various digital services throughout her day, each interaction generating different types of personal data.

What to Expect in This Section

In the following chapters, we'll explore:

- Chapter 5. Understanding Your Digital Footprint
- Chapter 6. Your Rights Under the DPDPA 2023
- Chapter 7. Decoding Privacy Policies and Terms of Service
- Chapter 8. Building Your Personal Data Protection Toolkit
- Chapter 9. Navigating Privacy in Emerging Technologies
- Chapter 10. From Awareness to Action

Each chapter will provide practical insights, actionable tips, and thought-provoking scenarios to help you better protect your personal data.

A Call to Action

As we embark on this journey, remember that data protection is not just about safeguarding your own information. It's about fostering a culture of privacy and respect for personal data in our communities. In India, where we often share our lives openly with friends and family, it's crucial to find a balance between our cultural values and the need for digital privacy.

By the end of this section, you'll be equipped to make informed decisions about your personal data, protect yourself in the digital world, and advocate for better data protection practices. You'll learn when it's beneficial to share your data and when it's wiser to hold back. Most importantly, you'll understand how to use other people's data responsibly, respecting their privacy as you would want yours respected.

Let's begin our journey through the data protection maze. Together, we'll navigate the complexities of personal data in the digital age, emerging more informed, more secure, and better prepared for the future of Digital India.

Chapter 5: Understanding Your Digital Footprint

In the age of Digital India, our online presence has become an integral part of our identity. But how much do we really know about the trails we leave in cyberspace?

Imagine your digital footprint as a vast, intricate *rangoli* pattern, with each online action adding a new colour or design. Some parts of this pattern we create consciously – our social media posts, online purchases, or digital transactions. Others are formed without our active participation – the websites we visit, the ads we view, or the data collected by our smart devices.

This chapter will take you on a journey through the complex landscape of digital footprints in India. We'll explore:

- The invisible ways our data is collected and used in everyday Indian contexts
- The potential risks and benefits of our digital trails
- Tools and techniques to map and manage your online presence
- How to become an advocate for responsible data practices in your community

As we navigate this terrain, we'll move beyond mere awareness to actionable strategies for taking control of your digital identity. Whether you're a tech-savvy professional or just beginning to explore the online world, understanding your digital footprint is crucial in today's data-driven society.

Are you ready to uncover the hidden dimensions of your online life and learn how to shape your digital legacy? Let's embark on this important exploration together.

A. Awareness: The Trails We Leave Behind

As Priya settles into her favorite chai shop in Pune, she pulls out her smartphone to check her social media. In those few moments - liking a friend's post, searching for a nearby restaurant, checking her bank balance - she's leaving digital footprints across the cyber landscape. But what exactly is a digital footprint, and why should Priya - and you - care about it?

Your digital footprint is the trail of data you create while using the internet. It includes the websites you visit, the emails you send, the photos you upload, and even the devices you use to go online. In India's rapidly digitalizing landscape, understanding your digital footprint is more crucial than ever.

Types of Personal Data Collected in Daily Life

- **Identifiable Information**: This includes your name, phone number, email address, and Aadhaar number. When Priya signs up for a new app or online service, she's often asked to provide these details.

- **Location Data**: Every time Priya uses a ride-sharing app or checks in at a restaurant on social media, she's sharing her location.

- **Financial Information**: From UPI transactions to online shopping, our financial activities create significant data trails.

- **Behavioral Data**: The websites we visit, the ads we click, and the content we engage with online all contribute to our digital footprint.

- **Health Data**: With the rise of fitness apps and online health services, even our physical well-being is becoming part of our digital profile.

Digital Footprints in the Indian Context

In India's rapidly digitalizing landscape, our digital footprints take on unique characteristics. For instance, the widespread use of UPI for digital payments means that many Indians leave significant financial digital footprints. Similarly, the popularity of WhatsApp for both personal and professional communication creates extensive data trails. In 2021, a controversy arose when WhatsApp updated its privacy policy, leading to concerns about data sharing with its parent company, Facebook.[16] This incident highlighted the importance of understanding digital footprints in the Indian context.

How Companies Use Your Data

In the bustling digital bazaar of India, data has become a precious commodity, with companies collecting and utilizing your information in myriad ways. Personalization is perhaps the most visible of these uses - you might notice, for instance, that after searching for programming tutorials, you suddenly see ads for coding bootcamps everywhere you look online.

This tailored advertising is just the tip of the iceberg. Behind the scenes, companies are constantly analyzing user data to improve their products and services, striving to create more intuitive and efficient experiences. Your online behaviour also serves as a goldmine for market research, helping businesses understand broader consumer trends and preferences.

In the financial sector, your digital footprint can have far-reaching implications, potentially influencing your creditworthiness and access to financial services. Perhaps most intriguingly, companies are increasingly employing artificial intelligence to predict your future behaviour based on your past data, attempting to anticipate your needs and desires before you even express them. This complex web of data usage underscores the immense value and power of the digital trails we leave behind in our increasingly connected world.

The Value and Risks of Personal Information

While data-driven services offer unprecedented convenience and personalization, they also bring significant risks to our digital lives. The vulnerability of personal data has been constantly highlighted with major breaches occurring every year, with even venerable institutions such as All India Institute of Medical Science (AIIMS) not being spared.[17] These incidents serve as a sobering reminder of the potential for large-scale privacy violations.

Beyond such breaches, the accumulation of personal information online opens doors for more targeted threats. Cybercriminals, armed with sufficient personal details, can engage in identity theft, impersonating individuals online for nefarious purposes. In the financial realm, compromised data can lead to unauthorized transactions, potentially causing significant monetary losses.

The long-term implications of our digital footprints extend to our reputations as well. Embarrassing or controversial online posts have the potential to resurface years later, casting shadows over both personal and professional spheres. Perhaps most insidiously, the wealth of data collected about us can be used for manipulation. Through targeted advertising and misinformation campaigns, external entities can subtly influence our decisions and beliefs, potentially shaping our worldviews without our conscious awareness. These risks underscore the importance of vigilance and informed decision-making in our increasingly data-centric world

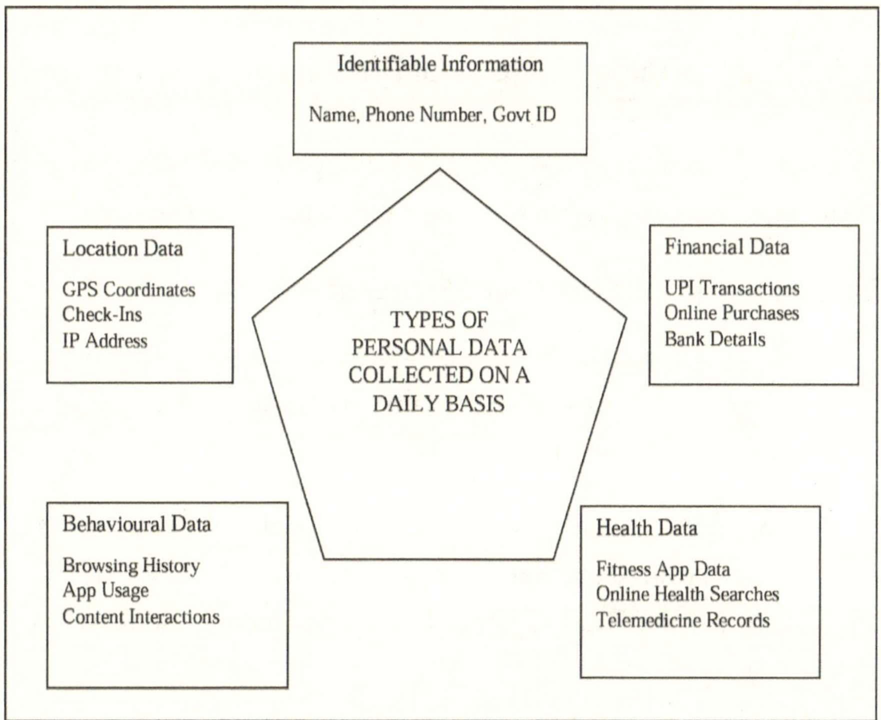

This infographic illustrates the various types of personal data collected in daily life, showing how interconnected our digital footprints can be.

Digital Footprints and the DPDPA 2023

The Digital Personal Data Protection Act (DPDPA) 2023 has significant implications for how our digital footprints are managed. While we'll explore this in detail in later chapters, it's important to note that the DPDPA gives individuals more control over their personal data. This includes the right to access, correct, and erase certain data, potentially allowing you to manage aspects of your digital footprint more effectively. As we explore tools and techniques for mapping your digital presence, keep in mind that the DPDPA may provide legal backing for many of these actions.

B. Action: Mapping Your Digital Presence

Now that we understand what a digital footprint is, let's explore how Priya - and you - can map and manage your online presence.

Tools and Techniques for Digital Footprint Analysis

- **Google Yourself**: Start with a simple Google search of your name. Priya was surprised to find old social media profiles she had forgotten about.

- **Social Media Audits**: Most social media platforms offer tools to review your data. For example, Facebook's "Download Your Information" feature provides a comprehensive look at your data.

- **Data Breach Checkers**: Websites like Have I Been Pwned can tell you if your email has been involved in known data breaches.

- **Privacy Settings Review**: Regularly check and update privacy settings on all your online accounts.

Identifying High-Risk Areas in Your Online Presence

As Priya reviews her digital footprint, she identifies several high-risk areas:

1. **Oversharing on Social Media**: Personal information like birthdate, hometown, or family details can be used for identity theft.

2. **Unsecured Wi-Fi Usage**: Using public Wi-Fi for sensitive transactions can expose your data to cybercriminals.

3. **Weak Passwords**: Using the same password across multiple sites increases vulnerability.

4. **Unnecessary App Permissions**: Many apps request more data access than they need to function.

5. **Unencrypted Communications**: Using platforms that don't offer end-to-end encryption for sensitive conversations.

This flowchart provides a systematic approach to conducting a personal data audit, helping readers understand and manage their digital footprint more effectively.

The Positive Side of Digital Footprints

While we've focused on the risks, a well-managed digital footprint can also be beneficial. In today's digital-first world, a positive online presence can enhance career prospects, facilitate networking, and even contribute to personal branding. For instance, a strong LinkedIn profile showcasing your professional achievements can open doors to new opportunities. Similarly, a carefully curated Instagram account could help budding

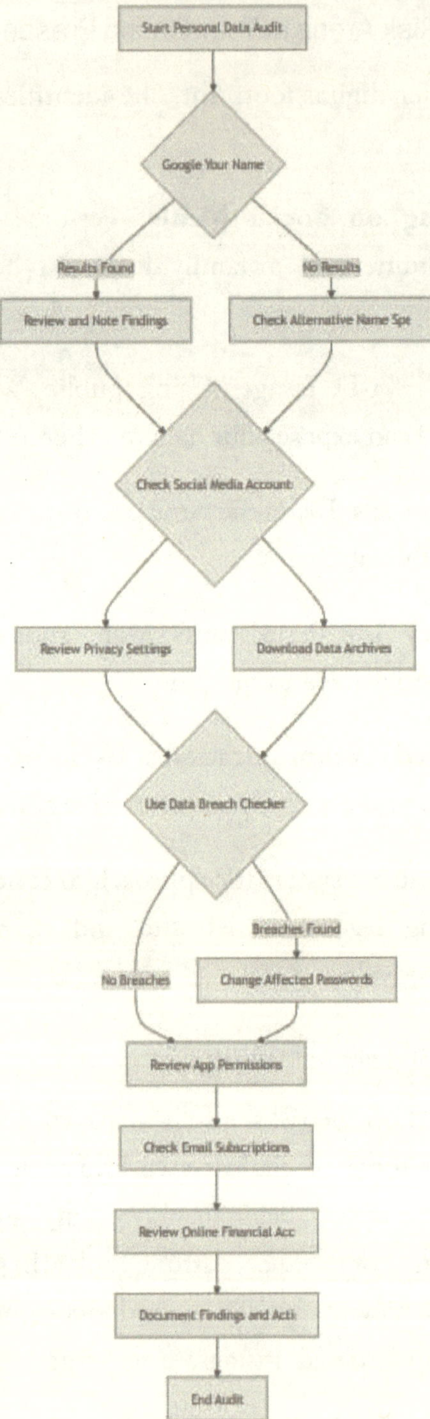
Start Personal Data Audit
Google Your Name
Results Found
No Results
Review and Note Findings
Check Alternative Name Spe
Check Social Media Account
Review Privacy Settings
Download Data Archives
Use Data Breach Checker
Breaches Found
No Breaches
Change Affected Passwords
Review App Permissions
Check Email Subscriptions
Review Online Financial Acc
Document Findings and Acti
End Audit

entrepreneurs reach potential customers. The key is to be intentional about what you share and how you present yourself online.

Global Connection: Digital Footprints Across Borders

In our interconnected world, your digital footprint isn't confined to India. When Priya applies for a scholarship to study abroad, she realizes her digital presence could be viewed by institutions in other countries. This global nature of digital footprints underscores the importance of managing our online presence responsibly.

As we've seen, understanding your digital footprint is the first step towards better data protection. In the next section, we'll explore how Priya can use this knowledge to advocate for better digital practices in her community.

C. Advocacy: Promoting Digital Awareness

As Priya becomes more conscious of her digital footprint, she realizes that many of her friends and family members are unaware of the trails they leave online. She decides to take action, not just for herself, but for her community. Let's explore how Priya - and you - can become advocates for digital awareness.

Educating Friends and Family About Digital Footprints

1. **Start Small**: Priya begins by sharing simple tips with her family WhatsApp group. She sends infographics about strong passwords and the risks of oversharing on social media.

2. **Lead by Example**: She updates her own social media privacy settings and shares the process with her friends, encouraging them to do the same.

3. **Organize Informal Workshops**: Priya hosts a "Digital Chai Time" where she invites friends to discuss their online experiences and shares what she's learned about digital footprints.

4. **Use Relatable Examples**: She explains how a seemingly harmless post about being on vacation could alert potential burglars that their home is empty.

Engaging with Online Platforms About Data Collection Practices

1. **Read and Respond**: When apps update their privacy policies, Priya actually reads them and sends feedback to the companies.

2. **Participate in Surveys**: Many platforms conduct user surveys about their services. Priya uses these opportunities to express her privacy concerns.

3. **Use Social Media Advocacy**: She tags companies in posts about data protection, encouraging public dialogue about their practices.

4. **Support Privacy-Focused Initiatives**: Priya signs and shares petitions for better data protection laws and practices in India.

Promoting Digital Literacy in Your Community

1. **Volunteer at Local Schools**: Priya offers to give talks about online safety at nearby schools, teaching students about responsible digital behaviour.

2. **Create Awareness Content**: She starts a blog sharing tips on managing digital footprints, tailored to an Indian audience.

3. **Collaborate with Local Cybercafés**: Priya works with local cybercafé owners to display posters about safe internet practices.
4. **Engage with Community Leaders**: She reaches out to community leaders to include digital awareness topics in local meetings and events.

Data Dilemma: Priya's Viral Video

Priya faces a dilemma when a funny video of her dancing at a friend's wedding goes viral without her consent. While many find it entertaining, Priya is uncomfortable with the unexpected attention.

Questions to consider:

How could Priya have prevented this situation?

What steps can she take now to manage the spread of the video?

How can she use this experience to educate others about online privacy?

This scenario highlights the importance of being cautious about what we share and what others share about us online. It's a valuable lesson in the potential far-reaching consequences of our digital footprint.

Global Connection: Digital Footprints Across Borders

In our interconnected world, digital footprints often extend beyond national boundaries. Priya realizes this when planning a trip abroad and discovers that visa officers might check her social media profiles. This global aspect of digital footprints underscores the importance of maintaining a positive and responsible online presence.

If You Only Read One Thing

Remember, your digital footprint is the trail you leave online. Be mindful of what you share, regularly review your privacy settings, and think about the long-term implications of your online actions. Encourage others to do the same, fostering a culture of digital responsibility in your community.

Self-Assessment Quiz

1. True or False: Your digital footprint only includes information you actively post online.
2. Which of the following is NOT a recommended practice for managing your digital footprint?
   a) Regularly updating privacy settings
   b) Sharing your current location on social media
   c) Using strong, unique passwords for each account
   d) Reading app permissions before granting them
3. What should you do if you find incorrect information about yourself online?
   a) Ignore it
   b) Contact the website owner to request removal or correction
   c) Post a public complaint on social media
   d) Create more online accounts to bury the incorrect information

(*Answers:* 1. False, 2. b, 3. b)

As we conclude this chapter, remember that understanding and managing your digital footprint is an ongoing process. In our next chapter, we'll explore your rights under the DPDPA 2023 and how you can exercise them to protect your personal data.

Conclusion: Your Digital Footprint, Your Responsibility

As we've journeyed with Priya through the landscape of digital footprints, we've uncovered the vast and often invisible trails we leave in our online interactions. From the morning check of social media to the evening stream of a favourite show, our digital activities paint a detailed picture of our lives, preferences, and behaviours.

Key Takeaways:

- **Awareness is Key**: Understanding the types of data you generate and how it's used is the first step in managing your digital footprint.
- **Active Management**: Regularly auditing your online presence, adjusting privacy settings, and being mindful of what you share can significantly reduce your digital vulnerability.
- **Advocacy Matters**: By educating others and engaging with platforms about their data practices, you can contribute to a more privacy-conscious digital ecosystem in India.
- **Global Implications**: Your digital footprint extends beyond national borders, potentially impacting various aspects of your life, from job opportunities to travel plans.
- **Ongoing Process**: Managing your digital footprint is not a one-time task but a continuous practice of digital hygiene.

Looking Ahead

As Priya becomes more aware of her digital footprint, she realizes that knowledge is just the first step. She wonders, "Now that I know about my digital trail, what rights do I have over my data? How can I exercise control over how it's used?"

These questions lead us to our next chapter, where we'll explore your rights under the Digital Personal Data Protection Act (DPDPA) 2023. We'll discover how this groundbreaking legislation empowers you to take control of your personal data and provides tools to protect your digital privacy.

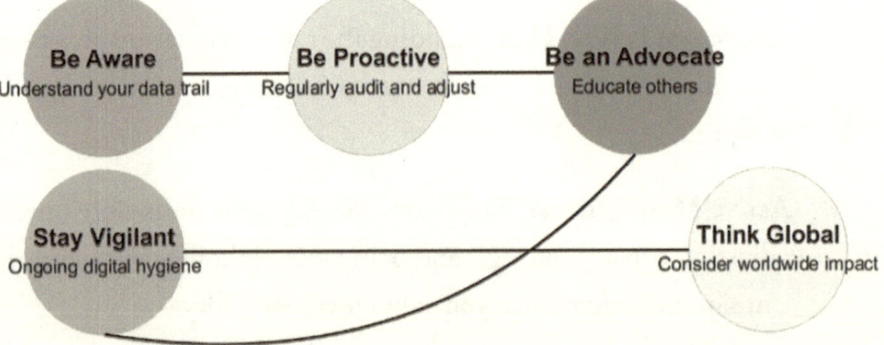

Your First Step: A 5-Minute Digital Footprint Check

Before we move on, take a moment to reflect on your own digital footprint:

Conduct a quick Google search of your name. Are you surprised by what you find?

Review the privacy settings on your most-used social media platform. Is there room for improvement?

Think about one piece of information you regularly share online. Could it pose any risks if it fell into the wrong hands?

Remember, in the vibrant digital landscape of India, where sharing is often second nature, it's crucial to find a balance between connection and protection. Your digital footprint is uniquely yours - take charge of it.

This simple exercise can be eye-opening and is a great starting point for taking control of your digital presence.

As we close this chapter, remember that understanding and managing your digital footprint is not just about protecting yourself - it's about being a responsible digital citizen in our increasingly connected world. In the next chapter, we'll empower you with knowledge about your data protection rights, giving you the tools to navigate the digital landscape with confidence.

Chapter 6: Your Rights Under the DPDPA 2023

In the bustling digital landscape of modern India, our personal data flows like an invisible river, powering everything from our morning news feed to our late-night food deliveries. But until recently, we've been mere passengers on this data stream, often unaware of where it's heading or who's accessing it. The Digital Personal Data Protection Act (DPDPA) 2023 changes this narrative dramatically. It hands you, the Indian citizen, the oars to navigate this data river. This chapter is your guide to understanding and wielding these new powers. We'll explore the rights that the DPDPA grants you - rights that, for many of us, are entirely new concepts. From accessing your data to withdrawing consent, we'll demystify these tools and show you how to use them effectively. More than just a legal explainer, this chapter is a call to action. It's about empowering you to take control of your digital footprint and, in doing so, help shape a more privacy-conscious India. So, let's embark on this journey of discovery and empowerment, as we unpack your rights under the DPDPA 2023.

A. Awareness: Understanding Your Data Protection Arsenal

Imagine Priya, our 28-year-old software engineer in Pune, scrolling through her phone one lazy Sunday morning. She comes across a news article about the Digital Personal Data Protection Act (DPDPA) 2023 and its implications for Indian citizens. As she reads, her eyes widen. "Wait a minute," she thinks, "I have rights over my personal data?"

Indeed, Priya's surprise is not uncommon. For many Indians, the DPDPA 2023 introduces a set of rights that simply didn't exist before in such a comprehensive form. It's as if we've all been handed a shiny new toolbox, filled with instruments to protect our personal data. But like any new tool, these rights are only effective if we know how to use them.

The Dawn of Data Rights in India

Before we dive into the specifics, let's take a moment to appreciate the significance of these newly minted rights. Prior to the DPDPA 2023, India's approach to data protection was fragmented at best. While certain sector-specific regulations existed, there was no comprehensive framework that empowered individuals with control over their personal data.

The DPDPA 2023 changes this landscape dramatically. It's not just a legal document; it's a paradigm shift in how we view personal data in India. For the first time, it places you, the individual, at the centre of the data ecosystem, arming you with the power to make informed decisions about your personal information.

Your DPDPA Toolbox: An Overview

Let's unpack this toolbox and examine the brand new rights you now possess:

1. **Right to Information**: You have the right to know what personal data is being collected about you and how it's being used.

2. **Right to Access**: You can request and receive a copy of your personal data that an organization holds.

3. **Right to Correction**: If you find errors in your personal data, you have the right to have them corrected.

4. **Right to Erasure**: Also known as the "right to be forgotten," you can request the deletion of your personal data under certain circumstances.

5. **Right to Withdraw Consent**: You can take back your consent for data processing at any time.

6. **Right to Grievance Redressal**: If you believe your data rights have been violated, you have the right to file a complaint and seek redress.

7. **Right to Nominate**: You can prepare for the future by nominating someone to exercise your privacy rights on your behalf in case of your death or disability.

Each of these rights is a powerful tool in your data protection arsenal. But two deserve special attention: the right to access and the right to withdraw consent.

Spotlight on Key Rights

The Right to Access: Your Data, Your Knowledge

Think of the right to access as your "data mirror." It allows you to see a reflection of all the personal information an organization holds about you. This right is crucial because it forms the foundation for exercising many of your other rights. After all, how can you correct inaccuracies or request deletion if you don't know what data is being held in the first place?

Priya, for instance, might use this right to request all the data her favourite e-commerce platform has collected about her over the years. She might be surprised to find not just her purchase history, but also records of items she's viewed, her browsing patterns, and even inferences about her preferences.

The Right to Withdraw Consent: Your Data, Your Choice

The right to withdraw consent is your "emergency brake" in the world of data processing. It empowers you to say, "Stop! I no longer want you to use my data in this way." This right acknowledges that consent isn't a one-time, irreversible decision. Your comfort level with data sharing can change over time, and the DPDPA respects that.

For example, if Priya initially agreed to share her location data with a weather app but later feels uncomfortable with this, she can withdraw her consent. The app must then stop processing her location data (although it may keep previously collected data if there's another legal basis for doing so).

How do these rights compare globally?

To truly appreciate the significance of these rights, let's take a quick world tour and see how the DPDPA stacks up against other major data protection laws.

Right	**DPDPA 2023 (India)**	**GDPR (EU)**	**CCPA (California)**	**PDPA (Singapore)**
Right to Information	✓	✓	✓	✓

Right	DPDPA 2023 (India)	GDPR (EU)	CCPA (California)	PDPA (Singapore)
Right to Access	✓	✓	✓	✓
Right to Correction	✓	✓	✓	✓
Right to Erasure	✓	✓	✓	✓
Right to Withdraw Consent	✓	✓	✓	✓
Right to Data Portability	✗	✓	✓	✓
Right to Object to Processing	✗	✓	✓ (Limited)	✓ (Limited)

Deep Cuts: The Right to be Left Alone vs Informational Self-Determination

The right to privacy seems simple enough on the surface, but gets complicated the more you look into it. The ways in which the world sees the right depends almost entirely on the history and culture of the place you come from. For example, Americans have long believed in the idea of individualism, of unlimited freedom and opportunity. Is it any wonder that they interpreted the right to privacy as "the right to be left alone"? Warren and Brandeis' article with the same title, published in the Harvard Law Review in 1890, encapsulates this philosophy perfectly.

On the other hand, German jurists saw the horrors of the second world war, and the crimes committed on people of certain backgrounds – forcing them to expose their personal information by identifying themselves in public. From this perspective, they naturally interpreted the right to privacy as the authority to determine, for oneself, the manner in which details about their private life should be communicated to others. In other words, "informational self-determination". This perspective has had a major impact on European lawmaking and can easily be seen in the European Union's General Data Protection Regulation.

The more you learn about other cultures, the more wonderfully complex the right to privacy will appear.[18]

As we can see, the DPDPA 2023 aligns closely with global standards in many areas. However, it's worth noting that some rights, such as data portability and the right to object to processing, are not explicitly included in the DPDPA. This doesn't make the DPDPA less effective, but rather reflects India's unique approach to balancing data protection with its digital growth objectives.

Global Connection: While India's DPDPA 2023 aligns with global standards in many areas, it has its unique features. For instance, unlike the EU's GDPR, it doesn't explicitly include the right to data portability. This reflects India's approach to balancing robust data protection with its digital growth objectives.

Now that we've unpacked your data rights toolbox, you might be wondering, "How do I actually use these tools?" That's exactly what we'll explore in the next section. Get ready to roll up your sleeves as we dive into the practical aspects of exercising your newfound data rights!

B. Action: Exercising Your Data Rights

Understanding your rights is one thing; putting them into practice is another. Let's walk through how you can effectively wield your data protection tools in real-life situations.

Accessing Your Personal Data: A Step-by-Step Guide

Now that we've explored your rights under the DPDPA 2023, let's roll up our sleeves and get practical. How exactly do you go about exercising these rights? Let's walk through the process, using our step-by-step guide.

Step 1. **Identify the organization**: First, determine which company or entity holds the data you want to access. Is it your favourite e-commerce platform? Your go-to food delivery app? Or perhaps your longtime telecom provider?

Step 2. **Prepare your request**: Draft a clear, concise request. Include your name, contact information, and any details that might help the organization locate your data. Be specific about what information you're seeking.

Step 3. **Submit your request**: Send your request to the organization's data protection officer or designated contact point. Many companies now have specific forms or portals for such requests. If you can't find this information, check their privacy policy or contact customer service.

Step 4. **Verify your identity**: The organization may ask you to prove your identity. This is a crucial step to ensure they're not disclosing your personal data to someone else. Be prepared to provide some form of identification.

Step 5. **Wait for the response**: Under the DPDPA, organizations should respond to your request within a reasonable timeframe. The exact timeline may be specified in the final rules, so keep an eye out for updates.

Step 6. **Review the data**: Once you receive the data, review it carefully. Look for any inaccuracies or information you weren't aware was being collected. This is your chance to understand what data is held about you and how it's being used.

Remember, this process is your right under the DPDPA. If you face any unreasonable delays or refusals, you have the right to file a complaint with the Data Protection Board of India.

Exercising Your Data Rights: A Step-by-Step Guide

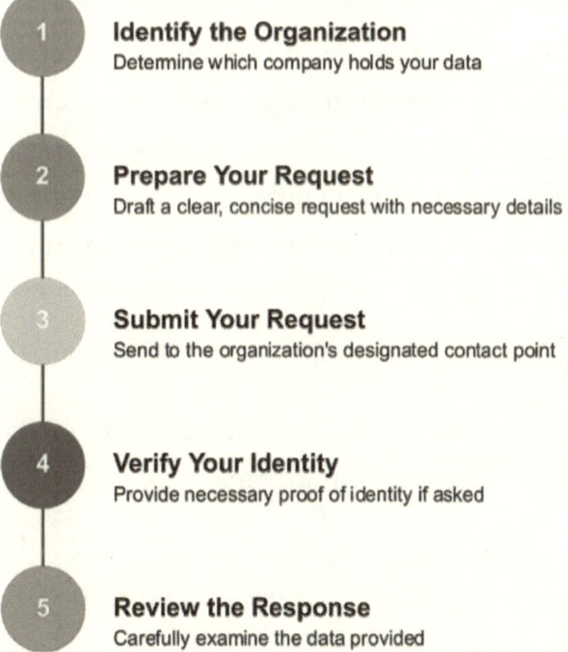

Withdrawing Consent: Hitting the Brakes on Data Processing

Now, let's say you've been using a fitness app which you initially allowed to access your location data for route mapping during runs. However, you've grown uncomfortable with the app tracking your location 24/7.

Navigate to the app's privacy settings. Look for options to manage your consent preferences. You should be able to withdraw your consent for continuous location tracking, perhaps limiting it to only when you're using the app for a run.

Be aware that changing your consent settings might affect some of the app's features. The app should inform you about these potential impacts before you confirm your decision.

> **Remember:** Withdrawing consent is not retroactive. It stops future processing but doesn't erase data that has already been processed based on your previous consent.

As you go through these processes, you might encounter some challenges. Not all companies have user-friendly processes for exercising data rights. Some may require multiple follow-ups, while others might provide data in formats that are hard to understand. Be patient but persistent, reminding yourself that these are your legal rights under the DPDPA.

In short, follow these steps:

- Step 1. **Identify the processing activity**: Determine which specific data processing activity you want to stop.
- Step 2. **Locate the withdrawal mechanism**: Check the organization's privacy policy or settings for information on how to withdraw consent.

Step 3. **Communicate your decision**: Clearly state that you're withdrawing consent for the specific processing activity.

Step 4. **Confirm the change**: Ask for confirmation that your consent has been withdrawn and the data processing has stopped.

Step 5. **Be aware of consequences**: Understand that withdrawing consent might affect the services you receive from the organization.

Data Dilemma: The Overzealous Recruiter

Priya is excited about a new job opportunity. She uploads her resume to a recruitment agency's website. However, she's taken aback when the site asks for her Aadhaar number, PAN card details, and even her parents' professions. "Do they really need all this just to match me with job openings?" she wonders.

This scenario illustrates a common issue in India: the collection of more personal data than necessary for the stated purpose. Under the DPDPA, Priya has the right to question this practice and limit the data she shares.

Here's what Priya could do:

1. **Question the necessity**: Ask the agency why they need this additional information at the application stage.

2. **Limit data sharing**: Provide only the information she's comfortable sharing and that's directly relevant to job matching (like her qualifications and work experience).

3. **Exercise her rights**: If the agency insists, Priya can remind them of her rights under the DPDPA, including the right to not provide personal data beyond what's necessary.

4. **Seek alternatives**: If the agency won't budge, Priya might consider using a different recruitment service that respects data minimization principles.

Remember, it's your right to be cautious about sharing personal data. If you're uncomfortable, it's okay to say no or seek clarification.

Practical Tips for Exercising Your Rights

Be specific: When making requests, be clear about what data you're referring to and what action you want taken.

Keep records: Document your communications with organizations about your data rights.

Be persistent: If you don't receive a satisfactory response, follow up. Remember, these are your legal rights.

Use official channels: Many companies now have dedicated data protection email addresses or forms. Use these for faster processing rather than going through a third party.

Know the exceptions: Familiarize yourself with situations where your rights might be limited (e.g., legal obligations or public interest).

By actively exercising these rights, you're not just protecting your own data – you're contributing to a culture of data respect in India. But individual action is just the start. In the next section, we'll explore how you can amplify your impact by championing data rights in your community.

C. Advocacy: Championing Data Rights in Your Community

As Priya becomes more aware of her data rights, she realizes something important: many of her friends and family members have no idea these rights exist. She decides it's time to spread the word. After all, data rights are like muscles – they grow stronger with exercise, and the more people flex them, the more robust India's data protection culture becomes.

Organizing Awareness Workshops on Data Rights

Priya decides to start small, organizing a data rights awareness session for her apartment complex. Here are the steps that she takes, and which you too can use to organize a data rights awareness session for your community.

Begin by understanding your audience - their digital literacy levels, age groups, and typical online behaviours will shape your approach. Whether you're addressing tech-savvy millennials or older adults new to smartphones, tailor your content accordingly. Make your session relatable by using everyday examples that resonate with your audience. For instance, explain how data rights apply when using popular apps or during online shopping experiences.

To keep engagement high, incorporate interactive elements like a "spot the data collection" game using familiar websites or apps. Prepare simple, clear resources for attendees to take home - a handout outlining key rights and steps to exercise them, along with contact information for relevant data protection authorities. Finally, foster an open, non-judgmental atmosphere that encourages questions and discussions about data concerns. By creating this safe space for learning and dialogue, you'll help build a more privacy-conscious community, one conversation at a time.

Remember, you don't need to be an expert to start these conversations. The goal is to raise awareness and encourage people to explore their rights further.

Engaging with Local Representatives on Data Protection Issues

Engaging with local representatives is crucial in making data protection a priority in public policy. Start by identifying key stakeholders in your area, such as your local MP, municipal officials, or consumer protection bodies. Don't hesitate to reach out to higher authorities like the PMO or Niti Aayog if the issue warrants it.

When approaching these representatives, articulate your concerns clearly and concisely, preparing a brief that outlines the data protection issues affecting your community. Strengthen your case by incorporating local examples that resonate with your audience. However, don't stop at highlighting problems – be proactive in proposing solutions. Suggest actionable steps, such as organizing community data literacy programs, that can make a tangible difference.

To amplify your voice, consider collaborating with local NGOs or consumer rights groups that share your concerns. Remember, data protection is an ongoing conversation, not a one-time effort. Stay engaged by following up regularly and keeping track of developments in this rapidly evolving field.

As you persist in these efforts, you may begin to notice subtle yet meaningful changes in your community. People might start sharing stories of successfully exercising their data rights or questioning excessive data collection practices. These small shifts in awareness and behaviour are indicators of a growing privacy consciousness, signalling the beginnings of a more data-aware society. Your consistent engagement can play a crucial role in fostering this important cultural shift towards greater data protection awareness and action.

Remember, changing deeply ingrained habits and perceptions takes time and patience. Focus on relatable, everyday examples to illustrate the importance of data rights. Consider creating a simple "Data Rights Diary" - a small booklet where people can log their experiences of exercising their DPDPA rights.

Championing data rights isn't about becoming a legal expert or a tech guru. It's about starting conversations, asking questions, and encouraging others to take small but significant steps towards protecting their digital privacy. It's about creating a culture where data protection becomes as natural as locking our doors at night.

Deep Cuts: Exercising your rights to change the world

Never think that individual contributions can't change things. Remember that Indians simply did not have the right to privacy until several citizens took it upon themselves to petition the Supreme Court. It took a nine-judge bench at the Supreme Court to finally recognize the right in 2017 – seventy years after independence!

Of course, this is not the only place where people made an impact. Edward Snowden's revelations in 2013 on global surveillance had an incredible effect on the right to privacy. People were not happy being watched without permission, and obviously found it creepy even if they claimed they "had nothing to hide". It is not a coincidence that more and more countries have passed data protection laws since then. Some examples: the European Union's General Data Protection Regulation (enacted in 2016), Brazil's General Data Protection Law (enacted in 2018), the United States' California Consumer Privacy Act (in 2018), Japan and South Korea's enhancements to their existing privacy laws in 2020, and finally, India's Digital Personal Data Protection Act (in 2023, yet to be enforced).

Data Dilemma: The Oversharing School App

Priya's nephew comes home excited about a new app his school is using. It tracks students' locations, study habits, and even eating patterns. The school claims this data helps them provide personalized education. However, Priya is concerned about the extent of data collection on minors.

This scenario highlights the need for community-wide awareness about data rights, especially when it comes to vulnerable groups like children. Here's how Priya could advocate in this situation:

1. **Educate parents**: Organize an information session for parents about children's data rights under the DPDPA.
2. **Engage with the school**: Initiate a dialogue with school administrators about data minimization and purpose limitation principles.
3. **Seek expert input**: Invite a data protection professional to speak at a parent-teacher meeting about best practices in educational technology.
4. **Propose alternatives**: Research and suggest apps that provide similar benefits with less intrusive data collection.

By taking these steps, Priya isn't just protecting her nephew – she's fostering a more privacy-conscious environment for all students.

Building a Privacy-Aware Digital India: Your Role

As we conclude this chapter, it's important to recognize that understanding and exercising your data rights is just the first step. The real challenge—and opportunity—lies in fostering a culture of data respect throughout our society.

This culture shift begins with leading by example. Be mindful of your own data practices, both in your personal life and professional role. Your actions can serve as a model for colleagues, friends, and family, subtly influencing those around you to consider their own data habits more carefully.

Initiating dialogue is another powerful tool in this cultural transformation. Incorporate discussions about data rights into your daily interactions. A simple "Did you know?" can spark valuable conversations in both casual and professional settings. These conversations, over time, help normalize the idea of data protection and make it a part of our everyday discourse.

Next, supporting privacy-focused initiatives is a tangible way to drive change. Whether it's adopting privacy-respecting services in your organization or backing data rights campaigns, your choices can influence broader trends. This support sends a clear message to the market and policymakers about the value we place on data protection.

It's also important to remember that in this rapidly evolving field, committing to ongoing learning is crucial. The landscape of data protection is constantly shifting, with new technologies, regulations, and best practices emerging regularly. Stay informed about these developments and be prepared to adapt your advocacy efforts accordingly. This commitment to learning ensures that your actions remain relevant and effective.

As you embark on this journey, remember that changing ingrained habits and organizational cultures takes time. Practice patience and persistence. Maintain your efforts to spread awareness, understanding that progress often happens incrementally. Each conversation, each policy change, each individual who becomes more privacy-conscious contributes to the larger shift.

Every time you exercise your data rights or help others understand theirs, you're contributing to a more privacy-respecting digital ecosystem in India. This is a collective journey, and each action—whether individual or organizational—plays a part in shaping our digital future. By integrating these practices into both your personal life and professional environment, you can be a catalyst for change, promoting a culture of data respect that benefits individuals and businesses alike.

As we move forward in our increasingly data-driven world, let's strive to create a digital India where privacy and innovation go hand in hand. The path may be challenging, but the potential rewards—a more transparent, trustworthy, and empowering digital ecosystem—are well worth the effort. Together, we can build a future where data protection is not just a legal requirement, but a fundamental value woven into the fabric of our digital society.

Looking Ahead: The Future of Data Rights in India

It's worth considering the broader implications of these new data rights. The DPDPA 2023 marks a significant shift in India's digital landscape, placing individuals at the centre of the data ecosystem. However, the true impact of these rights will depend on how actively citizens exercise them and how effectively they're enforced.

In the coming years, we may see further refinements to these rights as technology evolves and new challenges emerge. The rise of artificial intelligence, the Internet of Things, and other emerging technologies will likely raise new questions about data protection and privacy.

Moreover, as Indians become more data-aware, we might see a shift in how businesses approach data collection and processing. Companies that prioritize data protection and transparency could gain a competitive edge, as consumers become more discerning about their digital footprints.

Your role in shaping this future is crucial. By understanding and exercising your rights, you're not just protecting your own data – you're contributing to a culture of data respect in India. Every time you question unnecessary data collection, every time you exercise your right to access or withdraw consent, you're sending a powerful message about the value of privacy in the digital age.

Remember, data protection is not just about compliance with laws – it's about fostering a digital ecosystem where privacy is respected, transparency is the norm, and individuals have meaningful control over their personal information. The DPDPA has given you the tools; how you use them will help shape India's digital future.

If You Only Read One Thing: The DPDPA 2023 grants you unprecedented rights over your personal data in India. Understanding and exercising these rights – especially the right to access your data and withdraw consent – is crucial. But true change comes when we spread awareness and advocate for these rights in our communities. Your actions, big or small, contribute to building a privacy-aware digital India.

Now, let's test your understanding with a quick self-assessment quiz!

Self-Assessment Quiz:

1. Under the DPDPA 2023, you have the right to:
   a) Sell your personal data
   b) Access your personal data
   c) Share others' personal data
   d) Ignore data protection notices
2. The right to withdraw consent means:
   a) You can stop future processing of your data
   b) All your previously shared data will be automatically deleted
   c) Companies can never use your data again
   d) You can withdraw someone else's consent
3. When exercising your right to access, you should:
   a) Demand immediate access without verification
   b) Provide clear details about the data you're requesting

c) Threaten legal action if not responded to within 24 hours

d) Expect to receive data about other individuals as well

4. Advocating for data rights in your community can involve:

   a) Hacking into databases to prove their insecurity

   b) Organizing awareness workshops

   c) Shaming people who don't understand their rights

   d) Boycotting all digital services

5. When facing excessive data collection, like in Priya's recruitment agency scenario, you should:

   a) Provide false information

   b) Question the necessity and limit data sharing

   c) Complain on social media

   d) Share everything without question

(*Answers:* 1-b, 2-a, 3-b, 4-b, 5-b)

How did you do? Remember, understanding your rights is an ongoing process. Keep exploring, questioning, and advocating for responsible data practices. Your digital future is in your hands!

Chapter 7: Decoding Privacy Policies and Terms of Service

Priya stared at her smartphone screen, her finger hovering over the "I Agree" button. Another app, another update, another privacy policy to accept. She sighed, thinking back to all the times she'd tapped "Agree" without a second thought. But today was different. Today, she was determined to understand what she was signing up for.

Welcome to the world of privacy policies and terms of service - the digital fine print that governs our online lives. These documents, often long and laden with legal jargon, are the unsung gatekeepers of our personal information. They determine who can access our data, how it can be used, and what rights we have over it. Yet, for most of us, they remain unread and misunderstood.

In this chapter, we're going to demystify these crucial documents. We'll explore why they matter, how to decode them, and what to watch out for. Whether you're a casual internet user or a digital native, understanding these policies is essential in today's data-driven world.

Think of this chapter as your guide to becoming a savvy digital citizen. We'll equip you with the knowledge to make informed decisions about your data, the tools to manage your online privacy, and the confidence to advocate for your digital rights.

So, are you ready to peek behind the curtain of the digital world? Let's embark on this journey together, decoding the language of privacy policies and terms of service, one clause at a time. By the end of this chapter, you'll never look at that "I Agree" button the same way again.

A. Awareness: The Fine Print Matters

As Priya settled into her favourite café in Pune, sipping her masala chai and scrolling through her phone, a notification popped up. "We've updated our privacy policy," it read. Like most of us, her thumb instinctively moved to click "Accept" without a second thought. But then she paused, remembering a recent conversation with her privacy-conscious colleague. "Do you ever actually read those things?" he had asked. "You'd be surprised what you're agreeing to."

In today's digital age, we're constantly bombarded with privacy policies and terms of service. They're the digital equivalent of the fine print – often ignored, seldom read, but incredibly important. These documents are the contracts that govern our relationship with every app, website, and online service we use. They dictate what happens to our personal data, how it's used, and what rights we have (or don't have) over it.

But let's face it: these policies are often long, filled with legal jargon, and, frankly, boring. It's no wonder that several studies have found that perhaps 4 in 5 people consent to terms and conditions without reading them.[19] Yet, in an era where data is often called "the new oil," understanding these policies is crucial for protecting our digital lives.

So, how can we navigate this maze of legalese and technical terms? Let's break it down.

Deep Cuts: Negotiating terms and conditions

Over a decade ago, I used to work with contracts for a living. I negotiated with suppliers on behalf of a Fortune 50 company whenever they wanted to make purchases past a certain value. A large portion of these were software agreements – either licensing them, or customizing them for my client's specific use cases. You've most likely seen these too, before speedrunning past them and clicking on "Accept"; for individuals, these are called 'End User License Agreements'. Individually, you and I don't have any power to negotiate these terms, but large companies do so regularly – well, as long as the supplier isn't an Amazon or a Microsoft.

So, that was my job – documents that most people skip past, I would read with a magnifying glass. Negotiating these contracts surprisingly taught me very valuable skills early into my career, and the importance of paying attention to detail. It was here that I was first introduced to contractual clauses on confidentiality, data protection, intellectual property rights and information security, leading to a decade of in depth study into the laws, technologies and operations that form the foundations of these clauses.

Nowadays, people rarely license software, choosing phone or web-based apps that contain a "Privacy Policy" or a "Privacy Notice" instead. These are typically written in terms that are easier to read, but so long-winded that most people still skip past them anyway – assuming they even find them.

Key Elements to Look for in Privacy Policies

Similar to the EULAs of yesteryear, most privacy policies also follow a pretty standardized format. When you're faced with a privacy policy and are preparing to skip through it, here are the critical sections you should still make sure to focus on:

1. **Data Collection**: What personal information is being collected? This could range from basic details like your name and email to more sensitive data like your location or browsing history.

2. **Data Usage**: How is your data being used? Is it just for providing the service, or is it being used for marketing, sold to third parties, or used to train AI models?

3. **Data Sharing**: Who is your data shared with? Look for information about third-party sharing, especially if your data is being sold or shared with advertisers.

4. **Data Storage and Security**: How is your data stored and protected? Look for information about encryption and data retention periods.

5. **Your Rights**: What rights do you have over your data? Can you access it, correct it, or delete it? In India, the DPDPA 2023 grants you several rights, which should be reflected in the policy. For details on these rights, see the previous chapter.

6. **Changes to the Policy**: How will you be notified of changes to the privacy policy? Some companies might change their policies without prominently notifying users.

Red Flags and Warning Signs in Terms of Service

While privacy policies focus on data handling, terms of service (ToS) cover the broader rules of using a service. Here are some red flags to watch out for:

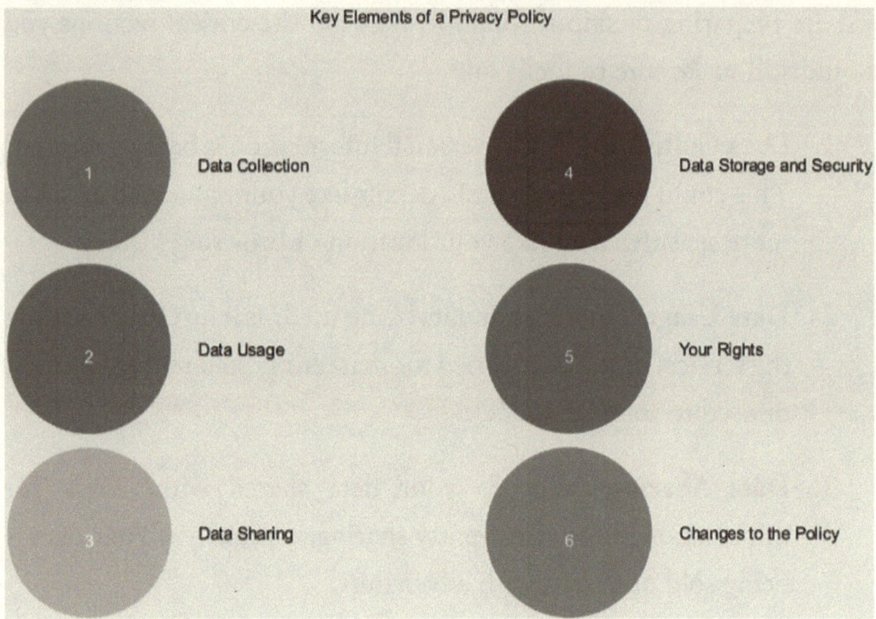

1. **Broad Rights to Your Content**: Be wary of terms that grant the company extensive rights to use, modify, or distribute content you create or upload.

2. **Mandatory Arbitration Clauses**: These clauses can limit your ability to seek legal recourse if disputes arise.

3. **Unilateral Changes**: Terms that allow the company to change the agreement without notifying you are concerning.

4. **Vague Language**: Ambiguous terms can be interpreted in ways that may not favour you as the user.

5. **Excessive Data Collection**: If the terms require you to provide more information than seems necessary for the service, it's a red flag.

Let's look at some real-world examples. While many companies have complex policies, some Indian firms are leading the way in clear communication. For instance, Vistara, the Indian airline, has a privacy policy that's notably user-friendly, clearly outlining data usage and user rights.[20] Similarly, telecom giants Airtel[21] and Reliance Jio[22] seem to have made efforts to simplify their privacy policies, making them more accessible to the average user. Whether or not these are actually implemented at these companies is, of course, anyone's guess. Or lawsuit.

It's important to note that even well-written policies can contain terms that users might find surprising or concerning. This is why it's crucial to actually read and understand these documents before agreeing to them.

In the next section, we'll explore practical strategies for evaluating these policies and making informed decisions about your data sharing. Remember, in the digital world, knowledge truly is power – and understanding these policies is your first line of defense in protecting your personal information.

B. Action: Making Informed Consent Decisions

Now that we understand the importance of privacy policies and terms of service, let's explore how to put this knowledge into action. Making informed decisions about consent is crucial in managing your digital footprint and protecting your personal information.

Strategies for Evaluating Requests for Consent

When evaluating requests for your consent to share personal data, it's crucial to approach each situation with a critical eye and a set of strategic considerations. First and foremost, context is key. Always question why a service needs the data it's requesting. For instance, if a simple flashlight app is asking for access to your contacts, it's worth pausing to consider whether this request aligns with the app's core function. Such excessive or unrelated data requests should prompt further investigation.

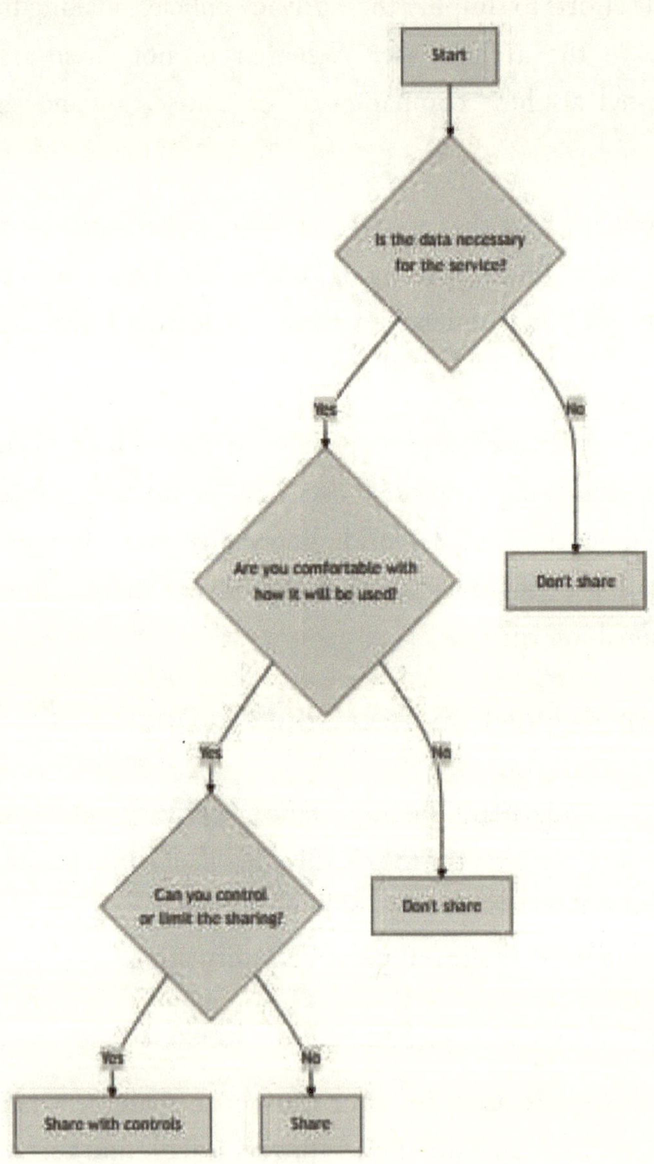

Many services now offer tiered (or "unbundled") consent options, allowing for a more nuanced approach to data sharing. This flexibility enables you to customize your privacy settings based on your comfort level. For example, you might choose to allow a food delivery app access to your location only while actively using the app, rather than granting constant access. You might also see that the app asks for your consent for several purposes, and may choose to only share personal data for some of those purposes.

It's also important to conduct a risk versus benefit analysis when considering data sharing. Weigh the convenience or value a service provides against the potential privacy risks associated with sharing your data. This thoughtful evaluation helps ensure that you're making informed decisions about your digital footprint.

While it's ideal to read a service's entire privacy policy, time constraints often make this impractical. Many companies now provide summary highlights of their privacy policies. At the very least, review these key points to get a general understanding of how your data will be handled. This practice helps you make more informed decisions about data sharing without getting bogged down in legal jargon.

By incorporating these strategies into your decision-making process, you can navigate data sharing requests more effectively, maintaining a balance between utilizing digital services and protecting your personal information.

Tools for Managing Cookie Preferences and Tracking

Cookies and tracking technologies are ubiquitous on the internet, but you're not powerless against them. Here are some tools and techniques to manage your online tracking:

1. **Browser Settings**: Most modern browsers offer built-in tools to manage cookies and tracking. For example, Chrome and Firefox allow you to block third-party cookies.

2. **Cookie Consent Managers**: Many websites now use consent management platforms that allow you to customize your cookie preferences. Take the time to adjust these settings rather than accepting all cookies.

3. **Browser Extensions**: Extensions like Privacy Badger or uBlock Origin can help block trackers and unwanted cookies.

4. **VPNs**: While primarily used for security, Virtual Private Networks can also help reduce tracking by masking your IP address.

5. **Do Not Track (DNT)**: Enable the DNT setting in your browser. While not all websites honour this, it's a good practice.

Remember, the goal isn't necessarily to block all cookies - some are essential for websites to function properly. The aim is to be selective and intentional about what data you're sharing.

Data Dilemma: Priya's Favorite App Updates Its Privacy Policy

Priya's favourite social media app just updated its privacy policy. The new policy states that the app will now use her photos to train its AI algorithms, and it will share her browsing history within the app with advertisers. The app is a big part of Priya's social life, and she uses it to stay in touch with friends and family. What should she do?

a) Accept the new policy without much thought - it's too inconvenient to stop using the app.

b) Reject the new policy and immediately delete her account.

c) Carefully review the new policy, adjust her privacy settings where possible, and make an informed decision about continued use.

d) Ignore the policy update notification and continue using the app as before.

(We'll discuss the best approach to this dilemma later in the chapter.)

In the next section, we'll explore how to advocate for clearer, more user-friendly policies, and how your individual actions can contribute to broader changes in how companies approach data protection and privacy.

C. Advocacy: Pushing for Clearer, More User-Friendly Policies

As we've seen, navigating privacy policies and terms of service can be challenging. But as users, we're not powerless. We can advocate for change and push companies to adopt more transparent, user-friendly practices. Here's how you can make a difference.

In today's data-driven business landscape, actively engaging with companies about their privacy practices is crucial for fostering transparency and accountability. Consumers and professionals alike can leverage various channels to provide feedback on privacy communications, ranging from direct company feedback mechanisms to social media platforms and app store reviews.

For more significant concerns, well-crafted emails to privacy teams or customer service can often initiate meaningful dialogues. While India currently lacks standardized privacy policy initiatives, there are ways to support and drive change. Engaging with privacy advocacy groups, participating in public consultations on data protection regulations, and educating others about digital rights can create a ripple effect of awareness.

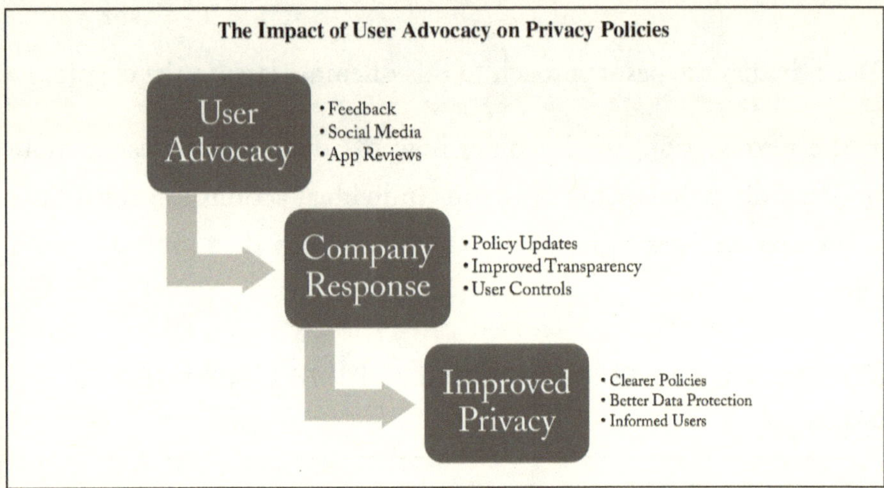

Furthermore, making conscious choices to support privacy-friendly services sends a powerful market signal, encouraging companies to prioritize user privacy and clear communication. By taking these actions, both individuals and businesses can contribute to shaping a more privacy-conscious digital ecosystem in India and beyond.

The Ripple Effect of Individual Action

As mentioned before, it's easy to feel that as an individual, your actions don't matter in the face of big tech and complex policies. But history has shown that collective individual actions can lead to significant changes. Here are some examples of how user advocacy has made a difference:

1. **WhatsApp Policy Update**: In 2021, when WhatsApp announced changes to its privacy policy, widespread user backlash in India led to the company delaying the update and launching an information campaign to clarify its policies.[23]

2. **Right to Be Forgotten**: The concept of the "right to be forgotten" gained traction largely due to individual advocacy, eventually becoming law in the EU and influencing privacy discussions worldwide, including in India.[24]

3. **App Permissions**: User concerns about excessive app permissions have led to more granular control options in both Android and iOS, allowing users to selectively grant permissions.[25]

Global Connection: The push for clearer privacy policies is a global movement. The EU's GDPR has influenced privacy discussions worldwide, including in India. By advocating for better practices in India, we're part of a global shift towards stronger data protection.

Remember, every time you make a conscious choice about your data, provide feedback, or educate others, you're contributing to a larger movement towards better data protection practices.

If You Only Read One Thing

Privacy policies and terms of service are not just legal formalities – they're the contracts that govern our digital lives. Take the time to understand key points, use tools to manage your data sharing, and don't be afraid to speak up for clearer, more user-friendly policies. Your actions, combined with those of others, can drive significant changes in how companies handle our personal data.

Self-Assessment Quiz:

1. What is the primary purpose of a privacy policy?

   a) To protect the company from lawsuits

   b) To inform users about how their data is collected, used, and protected

   c) To comply with government regulations

   d) To make the website look more professional

2. Under the DPDPA 2023, which of the following is a right granted to individuals?

   a) The right to sell their personal data

   b) The right to access their personal data

   c) The right to keep their data indefinitely stored with a company

   d) The right to share others' personal data

3. What is a "cookie consent manager"?

   a) A tool for baking cookies

   b) A platform that allows users to customize their cookie preferences on a website

   c) A person who manages cookie production

   d) A software that blocks all cookies

4. How can individual users advocate for better privacy policies?
   a) By never using digital services
   b) By providing feedback to companies and supporting privacy advocacy groups
   c) By using multiple email addresses
   d) By sharing their passwords with friends
5. What is the "right to be forgotten"?
   a) The right to delete your social media accounts
   b) The right to request the removal of personal data from internet searches and other directories
   c) The right to use a pseudonym online
   d) The right to forget your passwords

(*Answers:* 1-b, 2-b, 3-b, 4-b, 5-b)

Decoding privacy policies and terms of service is an essential skill in our digital age. By understanding these documents, making informed decisions, and advocating for clarity and user rights, we can each play a part in shaping a more privacy-respecting digital future. Remember, in the world of data protection, knowledge is indeed power – and action is impact.

Chapter Summary: Your Privacy Policy Toolkit

As we wrap up our journey through the world of privacy policies and terms of service, let's recap the key points we've covered:

1. **Awareness is Key**: Understanding the core elements of privacy policies and terms of service is crucial in protecting your digital rights. Always pay attention to data collection, usage, sharing, and your rights as a user.

2. **Make Informed Decisions**: Use strategies like context evaluation, risk-benefit analysis, and tiered consent to make smart choices about data sharing. Remember the decision tree we discussed – it can be a helpful guide in your decision-making process.

3. **Use Available Tools**: Take advantage of browser settings, cookie consent managers, and privacy-enhancing extensions to control your digital footprint.

4. **Your Voice Matters**: Don't underestimate the power of feedback and advocacy. By speaking up and supporting privacy-friendly practices, you contribute to a larger movement for better data protection.

5. **Stay Vigilant**: The digital landscape is constantly evolving. Make it a habit to review privacy policies, especially when they're updated, and reassess your privacy settings regularly.

Remember, protecting your privacy is not about completely shying away from digital services. It's about making informed choices, understanding the trade-offs, and actively participating in shaping how your data is used.

In our next chapter, "Building Your Personal Data Protection Toolkit," we'll dive deeper into practical strategies and tools you can use to safeguard your personal information across various digital platforms. We'll explore everything from secure password management to encryption basics, helping you build a robust personal data protection strategy.

Data Dilemma: Revisiting Priya's Decision

Remember Priya's dilemma with her favorite social media app's updated privacy policy? Let's revisit it:

The best approach would be option c) Carefully review the new policy, adjust her privacy settings where possible, and make an informed decision about continued use.

Here's why:

1. It allows Priya to fully understand the implications of the new policy.
2. She can potentially limit some data sharing through privacy settings.
3. It empowers her to make an informed decision based on her personal privacy threshold and the app's importance in her life.
4. If she decides to continue using the app, she does so with full awareness of how her data is being used.

5. If the new terms are unacceptable, she can explore alternatives or reduce her usage of the app.

This approach embodies the principles we've discussed throughout this chapter – awareness, informed decision-making, and taking control of your digital presence.

As we move forward, keep these lessons in mind. Each privacy policy you encounter, each terms of service you agree to, is an opportunity to exercise your data rights and contribute to a more privacy-respecting digital world.

In our increasingly connected world, your data is valuable – treat it that way. Stay informed, stay vigilant, and remember that when it comes to your personal information, you have more power than you might think.

Additional Resources

To help you further develop your skills in navigating privacy policies and terms of service, here are some valuable resources:

1. **Privacy Policy Analyzers**:

   Terms of Service; Didn't Read (https://tosdr.org/): This website provides summaries and ratings of terms of service for popular websites.

2. **Browser Extensions**:

   The EFF's Privacy Badger (https://privacybadger.org/): Blocks invisible trackersuBlock Origin (https://ublockorigin.com/): An efficient ad-blocker that can help reduce tracking

3. **Government Resources**:

   Ministry of Electronics and Information Technology (MeitY) (https://www.meity.gov.in/): Keep an eye on this website for updates on data protection regulations in India.

4. **Privacy Advocacy Organizations**:

   Internet Freedom Foundation (https://internetfreedom.in/): An Indian organization working to protect digital rights.

Electronic Frontier Foundation (https://www.eff.org/): While US-based, they provide excellent resources on digital privacy applicable globally.

Practical Exercise: Analyze a Privacy Policy

To put your new skills into practice, try this exercise:

1. Choose a digital service you use regularly (e.g., a social media platform, an e-commerce site, or a productivity app).
2. Locate and read its privacy policy.
3. As you read, answer the following questions:
   - What personal data does the service collect?
   - How is this data used?
   - Who is the data shared with?
   - What rights do you have over your data?
   - Are there any terms that concern you?

4. Based on your analysis, decide if you're comfortable with the policy. If not, what changes would you like to see?

5. Take action: Adjust your privacy settings, provide feedback to the company, or consider alternatives if necessary.

This exercise will help reinforce the concepts we've discussed and give you practical experience in analyzing privacy policies.

Chapter 8: Building Your Personal Data Protection Toolkit

Priya sighed as she scrolled through her smartphone's app permissions. "I had no idea so many apps were accessing my location data," she muttered. It was Sunday afternoon, and what had started as a quick privacy check-up had turned into a deep dive into the digital trails she'd been leaving behind. As a software engineer, Priya thought she was tech-savvy, but the more she explored, the more she realized how much she still had to learn about protecting her personal data.

In today's hyper-connected world, our personal information is constantly being collected, processed, and shared. From the apps we use to the websites we visit, our digital footprints are everywhere. But here's the good news: with the right tools and knowledge, you can take control of your digital presence and protect your personal information.

This chapter is your guide to building a robust personal data protection toolkit. We'll explore practical strategies, cutting-edge tools, and best practices that will empower you to safeguard your privacy in an increasingly data-driven world. Whether you're a tech enthusiast like Priya or someone just starting to think about online privacy, you'll find actionable advice to enhance your personal data protection.

Remember, protecting your data isn't just about avoiding risks – it's about empowering yourself to make informed choices about how your information is used and shared. By the end of this chapter, you'll have the knowledge and tools to navigate the digital landscape with confidence, making the most of technology while keeping your personal information secure.

Let's dive in and start building your personal data protection toolkit!

A. Awareness: Understanding privacy risks in various contexts

As Priya discovered, the first step in protecting your personal data is understanding where and how it might be at risk. Let's explore some of the key areas where your privacy could be vulnerable:

1. Social Media and Online Communication

Social media platforms have become an integral part of our lives, but they're also hotspots for data collection. From the posts you like to the friends you interact with, every action on these platforms contributes to a detailed profile of your interests, behaviours, and relationships.

Key Privacy Risks:

– Oversharing personal information

– Third-party access to your data through apps and quizzes

– Facial recognition technology in photo tagging

– Location tracking through check-ins and geotagged posts

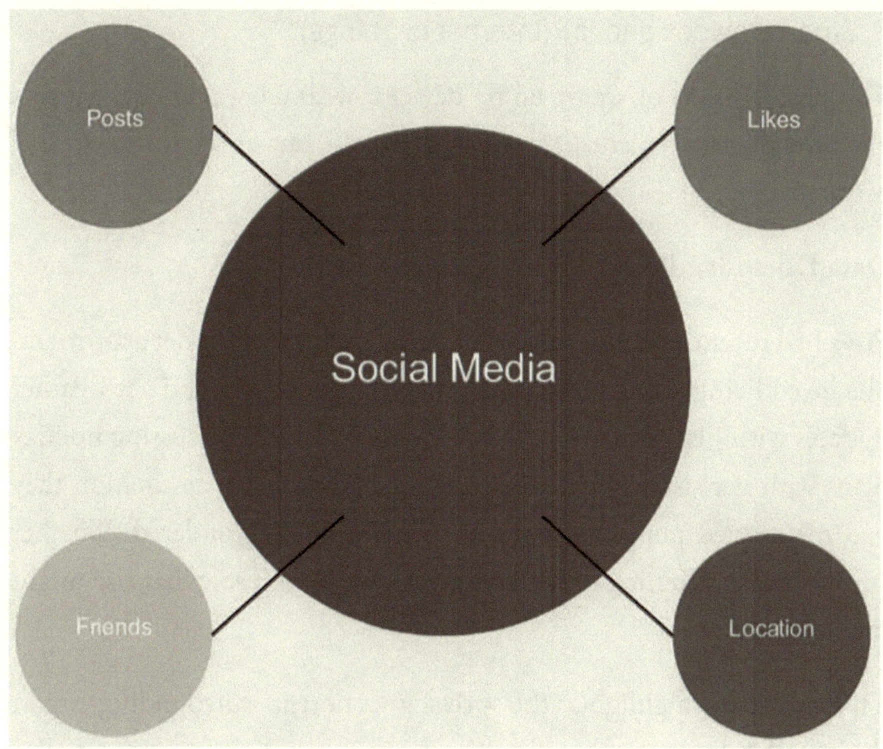

2. E-commerce and Online Banking

As online shopping and digital banking become increasingly prevalent, so do the associated privacy risks. Every purchase you make, every product you view, and every transaction you complete leaves a digital trail.

Key Privacy Risks:

- Data breaches exposing financial information
- Tracking of shopping habits and preferences
- Unauthorized access to banking details
- Phishing attempts masquerading as legitimate financial communications

3. Smart Devices and IoT (Internet of Things)

The proliferation of smart home devices, wearables, and IoT gadgets has brought convenience to our fingertips – but at what cost to our privacy?

Data Dilemma: Priya's Smart Speaker Surprise

Priya had recently purchased a popular smart speaker for her apartment. She loved being able to control her lights, play music, and get weather updates with just her voice. However, one day while discussing holiday plans with her sister, she noticed ads for flights to the destination they had mentioned popping up on her phone. Priya wondered: Was her smart speaker listening to her conversations? And if so, what else might it be recording?

This scenario highlights the privacy concerns surrounding smart devices. While they offer convenience, they also have the potential to collect vast amounts of personal data, sometimes in ways we might not expect.

Key Privacy Risks:

- Always-on microphones in smart speakers
- Location tracking through fitness wearables
- Data collection on personal habits (e.g., smart thermostats learning your schedule)
- Potential vulnerabilities in IoT devices that could be exploited by hackers

Understanding these risks is the first step in protecting your personal data. In the next section, we'll explore practical actions you can take to mitigate these risks and build a strong personal data protection strategy.

Global Connection: The privacy risks associated with smart devices have gained attention worldwide. In 2021, the European Consumer Organisation (BEUC) filed complaints against TikTok in various EU countries, citing concerns over the app's data collection practices and its failure to protect children from hidden advertising and inappropriate content.[26] This action demonstrates the growing global awareness of privacy issues in social media and smart devices, particularly concerning vulnerable users like children.

It would be remiss not to mention that India banned several Chinese apps, including Tiktok, citing similar reasons. In their press release banning these apps, the Ministry of Information Technology noted the "raging concerns on aspects relating to data security and safeguarding the privacy of 130 crore Indians" that led to the ban.[27]

As we move forward, remember that awareness is an ongoing process. Technology evolves rapidly, and with it, so do privacy risks. Stay informed about the latest developments in data collection practices and emerging privacy concerns. In the next section, we'll translate this awareness into action, exploring practical steps you can take to protect your personal data across these various contexts.

B. Action: Implementing personal data protection strategies

Now that we've explored the various contexts where your personal data might be at risk, let's dive into practical strategies you can implement to protect your information. Remember, data protection is not about completely shutting yourself off from the digital world – it's about using technology mindfully and taking steps to safeguard your privacy.

1. Essential Cybersecurity Practices for Individuals

Good cybersecurity habits are the foundation of personal data protection. Here are some essential practices everyone should adopt:

a) Strong, Unique Passwords

- Use a combination of uppercase and lowercase letters, numbers, and symbols
- Aim for at least 12 characters. Truly paranoid people aim for more than 40.
- Use a different password for each account

Remember that the longer your password is, the harder it is to crack. This is easier to do with good password managers.

b) Two-Factor Authentication (2FA)

- Enable 2FA wherever possible, especially for email and financial accounts
- Use authenticator apps rather than SMS for the second factor when available

c) Regular Software Updates

- Keep your operating system, apps, and antivirus software up to date
- Enable automatic updates when possible

d) Be Wary of Phishing Attempts

- Don't click on suspicious links or download attachments from unknown sources
- Verify the sender's email address carefully
- When in doubt, contact the purported sender through a known, trusted channel

2. Privacy-Enhancing Tools and Technologies

There are a wealth of tools designed to enhance online privacy. Here are some key categories:

a) Virtual Private Networks (VPNs)

- Encrypt your internet traffic and hide your IP address
- Choose a reputable VPN provider with a no-logs policy

b) Secure Messaging Apps

- Use end-to-end encrypted messaging apps for sensitive communications
- Examples include Signal and WhatsApp (with end-to-end encryption enabled)

c) Privacy-Focused Browsers and Extensions

- Consider using browsers with built-in privacy features like Brave or Firefox
- Add extensions like uBlock Origin for ad-blocking and Privacy Badger for tracker blocking

d) Password Managers

- Use a password manager to generate and store strong, unique passwords for all your accounts
- Popular options include 1Password and Bitwarden

> **Quick Tip**: When choosing privacy tools, it's usually best to look for open-source options that have been independently audited. This increases transparency and can provide additional assurance about the tool's security.

3. Managing Your Online Reputation

In today's digital age, your online presence can have real-world implications. Here's how you can learn to manage your digital footprint:

a) Regular Google Searches

- Periodically search for your name and check the results
- Set up Google Alerts for your name to monitor new mentions

b) Privacy Settings Audit

- Regularly review and update privacy settings on all your social media accounts
- Be mindful of what information is publicly visible on your profiles

c) Think Before You Post

- Consider the long-term implications before sharing personal information online

- Remember that even "deleted" content can sometimes be recovered

e) Right to be Forgotten

- Familiarize yourself with your rights under the DPDPA regarding data deletion

- Know how to request the removal of outdated or irrelevant information about you online

Data Dilemma: Priya's Past Post Predicament

While preparing for a job interview, Priya decided to Google herself. To her horror, she found an old blog post from her college days that contained some controversial opinions she no longer held. The post was one of the top results when searching her name.

Priya faced a dilemma: Should she try to delete the post and risk drawing more attention to it? Or should she leave it up and hope potential employers wouldn't find it? What steps could she take to manage her online reputation in this situation?

This scenario highlights the importance of managing your online presence and the potential long-term impacts of digital content. It also raises questions about the balance between personal growth, freedom of expression, and the "right to be forgotten."

As we've seen, taking action to protect your personal data involves a combination of good cybersecurity practices, leveraging privacy-enhancing tools, and actively managing your online presence. In the next section, we'll explore how you can go beyond personal action to advocate for better data protection practices in your community and beyond.

C. Advocacy: Fostering a privacy-conscious culture

As Priya delved deeper into the world of data protection, she realized that true privacy isn't just an individual effort—it's a collective one. By advocating for better privacy practices in your community and beyond, you could help create a culture where data protection is valued and prioritized. Here's how you can become a privacy advocate:

1. Initiating discussions on privacy in your workplace or school

Initiating discussions on privacy in your workplace or school is a crucial step towards fostering a culture of data protection awareness. You can start small by raising awareness in your immediate environment through various strategies. One effective approach is to organize "Lunch and Learn" sessions, hosting informal gatherings where colleagues can discuss privacy topics. These sessions can feature local experts or provide a platform for sharing insights from your own research, creating an engaging and educational atmosphere.

Another strategy is to propose privacy-focused projects within your organization. This could involve suggesting ways to incorporate privacy considerations into existing workflows or advocating for the implementation of privacy impact assessments for new initiatives. By integrating privacy into everyday processes, you can help make data protection a standard part of your organization's operations.

Sharing resources and news is also an excellent way to keep privacy topics at the forefront of your colleagues' minds. Consider circulating relevant articles, videos, or podcasts about data protection to spark interest and discussion. Creating a dedicated privacy-focused channel in your workplace communication tool can serve as a centralized hub for sharing information and encouraging ongoing dialogue about privacy issues. These efforts can collectively contribute to building a more privacy-conscious environment in your workplace or school.

Quick Tip: When initiating privacy discussions, focus on the benefits of data protection rather than just the risks. Highlight how good privacy practices can build trust, enhance reputation, and even drive innovation.

2. Supporting privacy-focused products and services

Supporting privacy-focused products and services through consumer choices can send a powerful message about the importance of data protection. By voting with your wallet, you can influence corporate practices and encourage a more privacy-conscious marketplace. One effective strategy is to choose privacy-respecting alternatives in your daily digital life. This might involve opting for services that prioritize user privacy, such as using DuckDuckGo instead of Google for web searches. Additionally, supporting companies that are transparent about their data practices reinforces the value of openness in data handling.

Providing direct feedback to companies is another impactful approach. Take the time to commend businesses that demonstrate strong privacy practices, as positive reinforcement can encourage continued commitment to data protection. Conversely, don't hesitate to express concerns to companies that fall short in their privacy measures, and offer constructive suggestions for improvement. This kind of engagement can drive positive change in corporate data practices.

Spreading the word about your experiences with privacy-focused products and services can amplify your impact. Share your insights with friends, family, and colleagues, highlighting the benefits of privacy-respecting alternatives. Consider writing reviews that specifically call attention to the privacy features of products you use. By raising awareness and influencing others' choices, you contribute to a broader shift towards valuing and demanding stronger privacy protections in the digital marketplace.

3. Engaging with policymakers and advocacy groups

To create broader change, the importance of engaging with those who shape privacy policies is necessary to consider. Here's how you can get involved:

a) Participate in public consultations

- Many government bodies seek public input on proposed privacy regulations
- Share your experiences and concerns during these consultation periods

b) Support privacy advocacy organizations

- Join or donate to groups that champion data protection rights
- Volunteer your skills to support their initiatives

c) Contact your representatives

- Write to your local politicians about privacy issues that concern you
- Attend town halls or community meetings to raise privacy-related questions

Global Connection: In 2021, Apple introduced App Tracking Transparency, requiring apps to get user permission before tracking their data across apps or websites owned by other companies.[28] This move, which gave users more control over their data, was largely driven by growing privacy concerns and advocacy from users and privacy organizations worldwide. It demonstrates how consumer advocacy can influence even the largest tech companies to adopt more privacy-friendly practices.

4. Educating others about privacy rights and best practices

Educating others about privacy rights and best practices is an essential step in fostering a more privacy-conscious society. Many of your friends and family members are interested in protecting their privacy but may not know where to begin. This is where you can make an impact.

One approach is to host community workshops. These sessions can teach fundamental privacy skills, such as password management or safe browsing techniques. The key is to tailor the content to your audience – for example, focusing on online safety for seniors or privacy strategies for parents navigating the digital world with their children.

If you're inclined towards content creation, consider starting a blog or social media account dedicated to privacy tips. This platform allows you to reach a broader audience and share concise, valuable information regularly. Developing simple infographics or short videos explaining key privacy concepts can make complex ideas more accessible and shareable, thereby expanding your reach.

For a more personalized approach, consider offering yourself as a privacy resource for your friends and family. You can guide them through the process of securing their devices and accounts, addressing specific concerns, and providing ongoing advice as new challenges arise. This one-on-one mentoring can be particularly effective in building confidence and competence in managing digital privacy. Teaching tech to the unfamiliar may be annoying, but think of it as taking one for the team since these are the folks who need such help the most.

By taking these educational initiatives, you're not only helping individuals but also contributing to a broader culture of data protection and digital responsibility. Your efforts can create a ripple effect, inspiring others to become more privacy-aware and potentially even advocates themselves. Remember, every person you educate is another step towards a more privacy-conscious community.

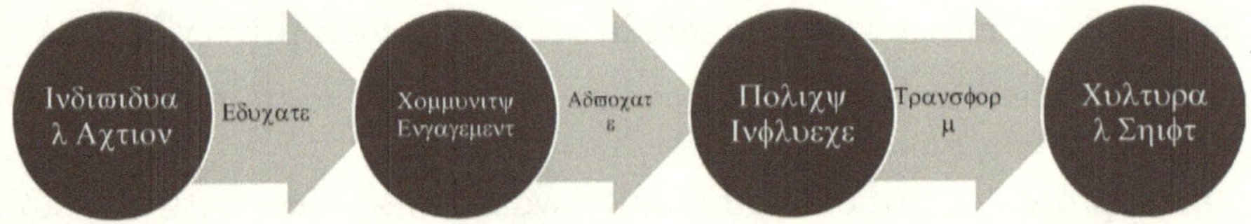

By becoming a privacy advocate, you're not just protecting your own data—you're contributing to a broader movement that values and prioritizes data protection. Remember, every conversation you start, every privacy-conscious choice you make, and every bit of knowledge you share contributes to building a more privacy-respecting digital world.

As we conclude this chapter on building your personal data protection toolkit, let's recap the key strategies we've explored:

1. Awareness: Understanding privacy risks in various digital contexts
2. Action: Implementing cybersecurity best practices and using privacy-enhancing tools

3. Advocacy: Fostering a privacy-conscious culture in your community and beyond

This approach actually ties in directly to the next part of this book. While Part 3 has been written with corporate and industry stakeholders in mind, it will give you an insider's look into how companies handle your personal data. Awareness, action and advocacy strategies are entirely relevant for each stage of a company's journey towards readiness with data protection laws. Here's a handy primer:

Compliance Stage	Corporate Strategy	Individual Engagement
Assessment and Data Mapping	- Basic: Define personal data, simple inventory - Intermediate: Leverage IT systems, conduct DPIAs - Advanced: Comprehensive data governance	- Awareness: Understand types of personal data collected - Action: Review and track personal data shared - Advocacy: Question data collection practices
Policy and SOP Development	- Basic: Essential policies and SOPs - Intermediate: Comprehensive framework - Advanced: Strategic integration	- Awareness: Understand privacy policies and rights - Action: Make informed decisions about data sharing - Advocacy: Provide feedback on policies

Compliance Stage	Corporate Strategy	Individual Engagement
Implementation	- Basic: Fundamental security measures - Intermediate: Enhanced protection - Advanced: Privacy by design	- Awareness: Recognize privacy features - Action: Use privacy settings and tools - Advocacy: Demand better privacy features
Monitoring and Improvement	- Basic: Regular compliance checks - Intermediate: Proactive management - Advanced: Continuous monitoring	- Awareness: Know about breach notifications - Action: Report issues, exercise rights - Advocacy: Participate in improving practices

Remember, protecting your personal data is an ongoing journey. Stay informed, stay vigilant, and don't hesitate to share your knowledge with others. Together, we can create a digital world where privacy is respected and protected.

If You Only Read One Thing

If you're short on time, here are the key takeaways from this chapter:

1. Understand the privacy risks in your digital life, especially on social media, e-commerce platforms, and with smart devices.

2. Implement strong cybersecurity practices: use unique, complex passwords, enable two-factor authentication, keep software updated, and be wary of phishing attempts.

3. Utilize privacy-enhancing tools like VPNs, secure messaging apps, and password managers.
4. Regularly manage your online reputation by auditing your digital footprint and being mindful of what you share online.
5. Advocate for better privacy practices in your workplace, community, and beyond. Your actions can contribute to a broader culture of data protection.

Remember: Protecting your personal data is not just about individual actions—it's about fostering a culture where privacy is valued and prioritized.

Global Connection: The Ripple Effect of Individual Privacy Actions

While we've focused on the Indian context throughout this book, it's important to recognize that personal data protection is a global concern with far-reaching implications. Let's look at how individual actions can have a global impact:

In 2018, a privacy-conscious Austrian lawyer named Max Schrems filed a complaint against Facebook's data practices. This individual action led to a landmark ruling by the European Court of Justice in 2020, known as "Schrems II." The ruling invalidated the EU-US Privacy Shield, a framework that thousands of companies relied on for transatlantic data transfers.

This case demonstrates how one individual's advocacy for privacy rights can have global repercussions, affecting international data flows and forcing companies worldwide to reassess their data protection practices.

Self-Assessment Quiz

Test your understanding of personal data protection strategies with this quick quiz:

1. Which of the following is NOT a recommended password practice?

   a) Using a combination of uppercase and lowercase letters

   b) Using the same password for multiple accounts

   c) Using a password manager

   d) Enabling two-factor authentication

2. What is the primary purpose of a Virtual Private Network (VPN)?

   a) To speed up your internet connection

   b) To block all ads

   c) To encrypt your internet traffic and hide your IP address

   d) To create a personal website

3. How often should you review and update your social media privacy settings?

   a) Never

   b) Once a year

   c) Whenever there's a platform update

   d) Regularly, at least every few months

4. Which of the following is an effective way to manage your online reputation?

   a) Never posting anything online

   b) Using a fake name on all platforms

   c) Regularly searching for your name online and monitoring the results

   d) Ignoring what appears about you online

5. How can you advocate for better privacy practices in your workplace?

   a) Demand that all employees delete their social media accounts

   b) Organize discussions or workshops about data protection

   c) Refuse to use any digital tools at work

   d) Keep your privacy concerns to yourself

   (*Answers:* 1-b, 2-c, 3-d, 4-c, 5-b)

Chapter 9: Navigating Privacy in Emerging Technologies

In today's rapidly evolving digital landscape, emerging technologies are reshaping our world at an unprecedented pace. From artificial intelligence to 5G networks, these innovations promise to make our lives more efficient and connected. However, they also bring new and complex challenges to our privacy. In India, where the digital revolution is in full swing, understanding the privacy implications of these technologies is crucial as we embrace the benefits of a tech-driven future.

Key Emerging Technologies and Their Privacy Implications

Artificial Intelligence and Machine Learning

Artificial Intelligence (AI) and Machine Learning (ML) stand at the forefront of technological innovation, offering remarkable capabilities in data analysis and prediction. In India, AI is being deployed across various sectors, from healthcare to finance, promising personalized services and improved efficiency. However, these benefits come with significant privacy concerns.

AI systems require vast amounts of data to function effectively, raising questions about the extent and nature of data collection. The implementation of deep learning algorithms, a subset of ML, often involves processing large datasets that may contain sensitive personal information. Moreover, the opacity of some AI models, particularly those using neural networks, can lead to a phenomenon known as "black box" decision-making, where the rationale behind AI-driven decisions is not easily explainable.

Jargon Buster: "Black box" in AI refers to systems where the internal workings are not transparent, making it difficult to understand how the AI arrives at its decisions.

Privacy concerns also arise from the potential for unintended biases in AI algorithms. These biases can result from skewed training data or flawed model design, potentially leading to discriminatory outcomes that infringe on individual privacy rights. For instance, an AI-powered credit scoring system might inadvertently discriminate against certain demographics due to historical biases present in its training data.

Data Dilemma: The AI-Powered Job Recruiter

An Indian tech company implements an AI-powered recruitment system to streamline its hiring process. The system analyzes candidates' resumes, social media profiles, and even facial expressions during video interviews. While it promises to reduce bias and increase efficiency, concerns arise about the system's access to personal data and the potential for inadvertent discrimination based on protected characteristics. How can the company balance the benefits of AI-driven recruitment with candidates' privacy rights and fair employment practices?

Quick Tip: When interacting with AI-powered systems, be mindful of the data you're providing. If possible, ask about the specific data points being used in decision-making processes and how long this information will be retained.

5G and Internet of Things (IoT)

The rollout of 5G networks and the proliferation of Internet of Things (IoT) devices present another frontier in the privacy landscape. As India accelerates its 5G implementation, the increased speed and connectivity will enable a vast network of smart devices, from home appliances to city infrastructure.

This hyperconnected environment, characterized by high bandwidth and low latency, will generate an unprecedented volume of data about our daily lives. While this data can lead to improved services and efficiency, it also creates new vulnerabilities. Each connected device becomes a potential entry point for data breaches, and the sheer amount of data collected could enable detailed profiling of individuals.

The concept of "edge computing," often associated with 5G and IoT, brings computation and data storage closer to the location where it is needed. While this can enhance efficiency and reduce latency, it also distributes sensitive data across a wider network, potentially increasing the attack surface for malicious actors.

Jargon Buster: "Edge computing" refers to a distributed computing paradigm that brings computation and data storage closer to the sources of data, improving response times and saving bandwidth.

Data Dilemma: The Smart City Sensor Network A major Indian city plans to implement a comprehensive IoT sensor network as part of its smart city initiative. The network will collect data on traffic patterns, air quality, and even pedestrian movements to optimize city services. However, concerns arise about the potential for this data to be used for surveillance or sold to third parties. How can the city balance the benefits of data-driven urban planning with citizens' privacy rights?

Quick Tip: For IoT devices in your home, regularly check and update their firmware, and consider setting up a separate Wi-Fi network for these devices to isolate them from your main network.

Biometrics and Facial Recognition

Biometric authentication and facial recognition technologies are gaining traction in India, being used in everything from smartphone unlocking to government identification systems. These technologies offer enhanced security and convenience but also pose unique privacy risks.

Biometric data, being intimately tied to our physical selves, is particularly sensitive. Unlike passwords or PINs, biometric identifiers such as fingerprints, facial features, or iris patterns cannot be easily changed if compromised. The widespread deployment of facial recognition, especially in public spaces, raises concerns about constant surveillance and the potential for misuse of this data.

Advanced facial recognition systems often employ machine learning algorithms to improve accuracy over time. This continuous learning process means that the systems are constantly processing and potentially storing facial data, raising questions about data retention and purpose limitation.

Data Dilemma: The Biometric Attendance System A large Indian university implements a biometric attendance system for students and staff, using fingerprint and facial recognition. The system promises to improve accuracy and eliminate proxy attendance. However, students and faculty express concerns about the collection and storage of their biometric data, and its potential misuse. How can the university balance the need for accurate attendance records with individuals' privacy concerns?

Quick Tip: When using devices or services that require biometric data, check if they offer alternative authentication methods. Also, ensure that biometric data is stored securely on your device rather than in the cloud whenever possible.

Practical Steps for Privacy Protection

Evaluating Privacy Trade-offs

When adopting new technologies, it's crucial to approach them with a critical eye. Before using a new app or device, take the time to understand its data collection practices. Scrutinize privacy policies, paying particular attention to clauses about data sharing, retention periods, and cross-border data transfers.

For AI-powered applications, be mindful of the permissions you grant. Consider the principle of data minimization – does the application really need all the data it's requesting to function effectively? For IoT devices, take the time to configure privacy settings, often buried in device menus or companion apps.

Privacy-Enhancing Technologies (PETs)

Consider employing Privacy-Enhancing Technologies to protect your data when using emerging tech. For instance, when using AI-powered services, look for those that incorporate federated learning techniques, which allow machine learning models to be trained on your device without sending raw data to central servers.

For IoT devices, consider using a Virtual Private Network (VPN) to encrypt your home network traffic. Some advanced routers now offer built-in VPN capabilities, providing an additional layer of privacy for all your connected devices.

Jargon Buster: "Federated Learning" is a machine learning technique that trains an algorithm across multiple decentralized devices or servers holding local data samples, without exchanging them.

Staying Informed and Engaged

Keeping abreast of technological developments and their privacy implications is crucial. Follow reputable tech news sources and privacy advocacy groups. Engage in public discussions about privacy, whether it's providing feedback to companies about their data practices or participating in public consultations on technology policies.

Emerging Laws and Regulations

As emerging technologies raise new privacy concerns, lawmakers around the world are responding with new regulations. Understanding these global trends can provide valuable insights for navigating the evolving privacy landscape in India.

European Union: AI Act

The European Union is in the process of finalizing the AI Act, which aims to regulate AI systems based on their level of risk. The Act proposes strict rules for "high-risk" AI applications, including those used in critical infrastructure, education, and law enforcement. It also outright bans certain AI practices, such as social scoring by governments.

United States: State-Level Biometric Privacy Laws

In the absence of federal legislation, several U.S. states have enacted biometric privacy laws. The Illinois Biometric Information Privacy Act (BIPA) is particularly notable, requiring companies to obtain explicit consent before collecting biometric data and providing individuals with a private right of action for violations.

China: Personal Information Protection Law (PIPL)

China's PIPL, which came into effect in 2021, includes specific provisions for AI and facial recognition. It requires separate consent for processing sensitive personal information, which includes biometric data, and mandates that facial recognition in public spaces be clearly indicated.

Global Connection: These international developments are likely to influence India's approach to regulating emerging technologies. The Digital Personal Data Protection Act (DPDPA) 2023 provides a foundation, but additional regulations specific to AI, IoT, and biometrics may be necessary as these technologies become more prevalent.

Quick Tip: Stay informed about international privacy regulations, especially if you use services from global tech companies. These regulations often set benchmarks that influence practices worldwide.

The Way Forward

As we navigate the complex intersection of emerging technologies and privacy, it's crucial to remain vigilant and proactive. Here are some key strategies:

1. Educate yourself about the technologies you use and their privacy implications.
2. Regularly review and adjust privacy settings on your devices and applications.
3. Support and advocate for privacy-respecting technologies and policies.
4. Participate in public discussions and consultations on technology and privacy issues.

Remember, the goal isn't to shy away from technological advancements, but to embrace them thoughtfully, ensuring that innovation doesn't come at the cost of our fundamental right to privacy.

Data Dilemma: The Privacy Advocate's Dilemma

You're a privacy advocate in India, and you've been invited to consult on a government project to implement a nationwide AI-powered healthcare system. The system promises to revolutionize healthcare delivery, especially in rural areas, but requires extensive data collection. How do you balance the potential public health benefits with the need to protect individual privacy?

This dilemma encapsulates the broader challenge we face as a society: harnessing the power of emerging technologies while safeguarding our privacy. As we move forward, it's crucial that we engage in open, informed discussions about these issues, shaping a future where technological progress and privacy protection go hand in hand.

Conclusion

As we look to the future, it's clear that the relationship between emerging technologies and privacy will continue to evolve. In India, as we stand on the cusp of a digital revolution, we have a unique opportunity to shape how these technologies are developed and deployed. By staying informed, being critical consumers of technology, and actively participating in privacy discussions, we can contribute to the development of privacy-respecting technologies. The goal isn't to shy away from technological advancements, but to embrace them thoughtfully, balancing innovation with robust privacy protections.

Chapter 10: From Awareness to Action - Charting Your Data Protection Journey

As Priya reflected on her data protection journey, she couldn't help but smile. Over the past few months, she had transformed from a casual digital user to a privacy-conscious netizen. Her smartphone, once a potential privacy liability, now felt like a fortress of personal data protection. But more than that, Priya felt empowered. She had the knowledge and tools to navigate the complex digital landscape of modern India.

This chapter marks the culmination of our journey through the individual's guide to data protection. Like Priya, you've gained valuable insights and practical skills. Now, it's time to bring it all together and chart your path forward in India's evolving data protection landscape.

Recap of Key Lessons from Priya's Journey

Priya reflected on the whirlwind of knowledge she had gained over the past few months. Her journey had begun with a startling realization about her digital footprint. She remembered the day she first truly grasped the vast amount of data she was generating daily - from her morning check of social media to her evening online shopping sprees. Each click, each like, each purchase was leaving a trail of digital breadcrumbs, painting a detailed picture of her life in data.

This awareness had led her to dive deeper into her rights under the new Digital Personal Data Protection Act 2023. Priya smiled as she recalled her initial confusion over the legal jargon, which had gradually given way to a sense of empowerment. She now understood her right to access her data, to have it corrected if inaccurate, and even to have it erased under certain circumstances. It was like discovering a new superpower she didn't know she had.

Her journey had taken an interesting turn when she started decoding privacy policies and terms of service. What once seemed like impenetrable walls of text now revealed crucial information about how companies were using her data. Priya chuckled, remembering how she had once impulsively clicked "I Agree" without a second thought. Now, she approached these documents with the keen eye of a detective, searching for clues about data collection, sharing practices, and her rights as a user.

Armed with this knowledge, Priya had set out to build her personal data protection toolkit. She had embraced essential cybersecurity practices, turning her devices into digital fortresses. From creating strong, unique passwords for each account to enabling two-factor authentication, she felt like she was leveling up in a real-life video game of digital security.

Finally, Priya had ventured into the exciting yet sometimes daunting world of emerging technologies. She had explored the privacy implications of AI, IoT, and biometrics, learning how to harness their benefits while safeguarding her personal information. It was like learning to navigate a new terrain, full of both wonders and potential pitfalls.

As she finished her chai, Priya realized how far she had come. From a casual digital user to a privacy-conscious netizen, her journey had transformed not just her online habits, but her entire perspective on the digital world. She felt prepared to face the challenges of the ever-evolving digital landscape, armed with knowledge, tools, and a newfound confidence in her ability to protect her digital self.

Each of these lessons has contributed to a comprehensive understanding of personal data protection in the Indian context.

Developing a Personalized Data Protection Strategy

Now, it's time to synthesize this knowledge into a personalized strategy. Remember, data protection isn't one-size-fits-all. Your strategy should reflect your unique digital lifestyle and privacy priorities.

Here's a framework to help you develop your strategy:

1. **Assess Your Digital Presence**: Start by mapping out your digital footprint. What devices do you use? What apps and services are part of your daily life?

2. **Identify Your Privacy Priorities**: What aspects of your digital life are most important to protect? Is it your financial data, your location information, or your social media activity?

3. **Implement Core Protections**: Ensure you have basic protections in place:

   - Use strong, unique passwords for all accounts
   - Enable two-factor authentication where possible
   - Keep your software and apps updated
   - Use a reputable VPN, especially on public Wi-Fi

4. **Customize Your Approach**: Based on your priorities, add specific protections:
   - If social media privacy is a concern, review and tighten your privacy settings
   - If you're worried about data collection by apps, regularly audit and restrict app permissions
   - If financial privacy is crucial, use secure, encrypted channels for all financial transactions
5. **Stay Informed and Adapt**: The digital landscape is always evolving. Make it a habit to stay updated on privacy news and adjust your strategy accordingly.

The Role of Individual Actions in Shaping India's Data Protection Landscape

As we've seen throughout this book, data protection isn't just about personal security—it's about shaping the future of digital India. Every time you make a privacy-conscious decision, you're contributing to a larger movement.

Consider these ways your actions can make a difference:

1. **Consumer Pressure**: When you choose privacy-respecting services and provide feedback to companies about their data practices, you're sending a powerful message to the market.
2. **Raising Awareness**: By discussing data protection with friends and family, you're helping to build a more privacy-conscious society.

3. **Civic Engagement**: Participating in public consultations on data protection policies or contacting your representatives about privacy issues can influence the regulatory landscape.

4. **Supporting Innovation**: By advocating for privacy-enhancing technologies, you're encouraging innovation in this crucial field.

Remember Priya's journey? Her individual actions—from questioning unnecessary data collection to educating her colleagues about privacy rights—rippled outward, influencing her community and beyond.

Vision for a Privacy-Conscious Digital India

Imagine a future where privacy is woven into the fabric of digital India. A future where:

- Companies compete on privacy features, not just convenience
- Children learn about data protection alongside digital literacy
- Privacy-enhancing technologies are the norm, not the exception
- Citizens are empowered to make informed choices about their personal data

This future is within our reach, but it requires collective action. Every privacy-conscious decision, every conversation about data rights, every letter to a policymaker brings us closer to this vision.

Final Self-Assessment and Next Steps

As we conclude this part of the book, take a moment to assess your progress:

1. Can you explain your key rights under the DPDPA 2023?
2. Have you implemented basic cybersecurity practices in your digital life?
3. Do you feel confident in reading and understanding privacy policies?
4. Have you started conversations about data protection in your community?

If you answered "yes" to these questions, congratulations! You've made significant strides in your data protection journey. If some answers were "no," don't worry—data protection is an ongoing process. Revisit the relevant chapters and continue to build your skills.

Here are some next steps to consider:

1. Conduct a comprehensive audit of your digital footprint
2. Create a personal data protection plan based on the framework we discussed
3. Set up a "privacy check-up" reminder to regularly review your digital privacy
4. Reach out to local privacy advocacy groups to get involved in community initiatives

Looking Ahead

As we move into Part 3 of this book, we'll shift our focus to the organizational level, exploring how businesses can implement robust data protection practices. Whether you're a professional looking to enhance your company's privacy posture or an individual interested in the broader data protection landscape, these insights will provide valuable perspective.

Remember, in the world of data protection, knowledge is power. You've equipped yourself with the tools and understanding to navigate the digital world with confidence. As you continue your journey, stay curious, stay vigilant, and keep championing the cause of privacy in digital India.

Part 3: Corporate Strategies for Data Protection Compliance

Welcome to Part 3 of our journey through India's data protection landscape! If you've been with us from the beginning, you've already gained a solid foundation in data protection principles and explored the individual's perspective. Now, it's time to flip the coin and dive into the world of corporate compliance.

But don't worry if you've just joined us – whether you're a seasoned CEO, a newly appointed Data Protection Officer, or simply curious about how businesses handle your data, this section is designed with you in mind. We'll maintain our conversational tone, so you won't get lost in a sea of corporate jargon. And when we do use technical terms, we'll have our trusty "Jargon Buster" boxes ready to translate.

Starting from Where You Are

Here's a little secret: when it comes to data protection compliance, every company in India is on a journey. Some might be taking their first steps, while others are sprinting ahead. But here's the thing – no matter where your company stands, there's always a next step to take.

Think of this part as your "choose your own adventure" guide to corporate data protection. Whether you're a small startup or a multinational corporation, we've got a path for you. And the best part? You get to choose where to begin based on your current readiness level.

Why This Matters

Let's face it – data protection laws are relatively new in India, and many businesses are scratching their heads, wondering where to start. If that's you, take a deep breath. We're here to help you climb that compliance ladder, one rung at a time.

Meet Rahul, our guide for this part of the journey. As a young IT manager at a growing e-commerce company, he's been tasked with helping his organization navigate these new data protection waters. Through his eyes, we'll explore how businesses can transform from being completely unprepared to fully compliant.

What to Expect

In the coming chapters, we'll cover everything from initial assessments and policy development to implementation strategies and continuous improvement. We'll use real-world scenarios (with a dash of imagination) to illustrate key concepts. And don't worry – we'll give you a heads-up when we're using hypothetical examples.

As we progress, you'll notice that each chapter is structured to cater to different maturity levels. Whether you're at the "Help, what's DPDPA?" stage or the "We're almost there, but how do we stay ahead?" phase, you'll find actionable advice tailored to your needs.

The Road Ahead

By the end of this section, you'll have a clear roadmap for your company's data protection journey. You'll understand how to assess your current position, develop robust policies, implement effective strategies, and continuously improve your practices.

Remember, this isn't just about ticking compliance boxes. It's about building trust with your customers, protecting your business, and contributing to a more privacy-conscious digital India.

So, are you ready to embark on this corporate adventure? Let's dive in and start navigating the data protection maze – business edition!

How to Navigate Your Data Protection Journey

As we embark on this corporate adventure in data protection compliance, it's important to recognize that every company's journey is unique. To help you make the most of this section, we've developed a matrix approach that caters to different company sizes and compliance maturity levels.

Understanding the Matrix

The compliance matrix in this book is designed to guide you through four key stages of data protection readiness:

1. Assessment and Data Mapping (Chapter 11)
2. Policy and SOP Development (Chapter 12)
3. Implementation Strategies (Chapter 13)
4. Continuous Monitoring and Improvement (Chapter 14)

For each of these stages, we provide guidance at three different maturity levels:

- **Basic**: For companies just starting their compliance journey
- **Intermediate**: For those with some measures in place but looking to enhance their approach
- **Advanced**: For organizations aiming for best-in-class data protection practices

How to Use the Matrix

1. **Identify Your Starting Point**: Before diving into the chapters, take a moment to assess your company's current data protection practices.

Which stage do you feel you're at? Are you just beginning to map your data flows, or are you looking to fine-tune existing policies?

2. **Choose Your Level**: Within each stage, determine whether you're at the Basic, Intermediate, or Advanced level. Don't worry if you're at different levels for different stages – that's completely normal!

3. **Navigate the Chapters**: Use the matrix to guide your reading. For example, if you're just starting out with policy development, focus on the "Basic" section of Chapter 12. As you progress, you can move on to the Intermediate and Advanced sections.

4. **Cross-Reference**: Remember, data protection is interconnected. While you might be advanced in one area, you may find valuable insights in the basic sections of another.

5. **Track Your Progress**: Use the matrix as a roadmap. As you implement new practices, you can visually see your company moving from Basic to Intermediate to Advanced across different stages.

Visual Matrix for Part 3 of the book:

Compliance Stage / Maturity Level	***Basic***	***Intermediate***	***Advanced***
Assessment and Data Mapping (Chapter 11)	11.A Getting Started: - Define personal data - Simple data discovery - Initial risk identification	11.B Enhancing Your Approach: - Leverage IT systems - Conduct DPIAs - Adapt security frameworks	11.C Comprehensive Governance: - Advanced discovery tools - Cross-border data mapping - Integrate with risk management

Compliance Stage / Maturity Level	*Basic*	*Intermediate*	*Advanced*
Policy and SOP Development (Chapter 12)	12.A Essential Foundations: - Basic protection policy - Key SOPs - Designate responsibilities	12.B Comprehensive Framework: - B2B vs B2C policies - Lifecycle SOPs - Establish Data Protection Office	12.C Strategic Integration: - Align with global standards - Integrate protection in all processes - Advanced governance
Implementation Strategies (Chapter 13)	13.A Fundamental Practices: - Essential staff training - Basic security measures - Key operational changes	13.B Enhanced Protection: - Role-specific training - Privacy-enhancing tech - Process re-engineering	13.C Privacy by Design: - Privacy-first culture - Advanced protection solutions - Privacy in product development
Continuous Monitoring and Improvement (Chapter 14)	14.A Essential Oversight: - Regular compliance checks - Basic incident response - Periodic policy reviews	14.B Proactive Management: - Comprehensive audit program - Robust breach management - Ongoing regulatory tracking	14.C Leading Edge Practices: - Continuous monitoring tools - Proactive risk management - Emerging tech and best practices

Remember:

- This matrix is a guide, not a strict rulebook. Feel free to jump between levels as needed.

- Data protection is a journey, not a destination. Even if you reach the "Advanced" level, there's always room for improvement and adaptation as the landscape evolves.
- Don't hesitate to revisit earlier chapters or levels as you progress. Sometimes, a fresh perspective on the basics can inspire new advanced strategies.

Now that you're equipped with this matrix, you're ready to embark on your tailored data protection compliance journey. Let's get started!

Here is a decision path you can follow to figure out where to begin:

Ultimately, the data protection readiness process flow across your organization should look like this:

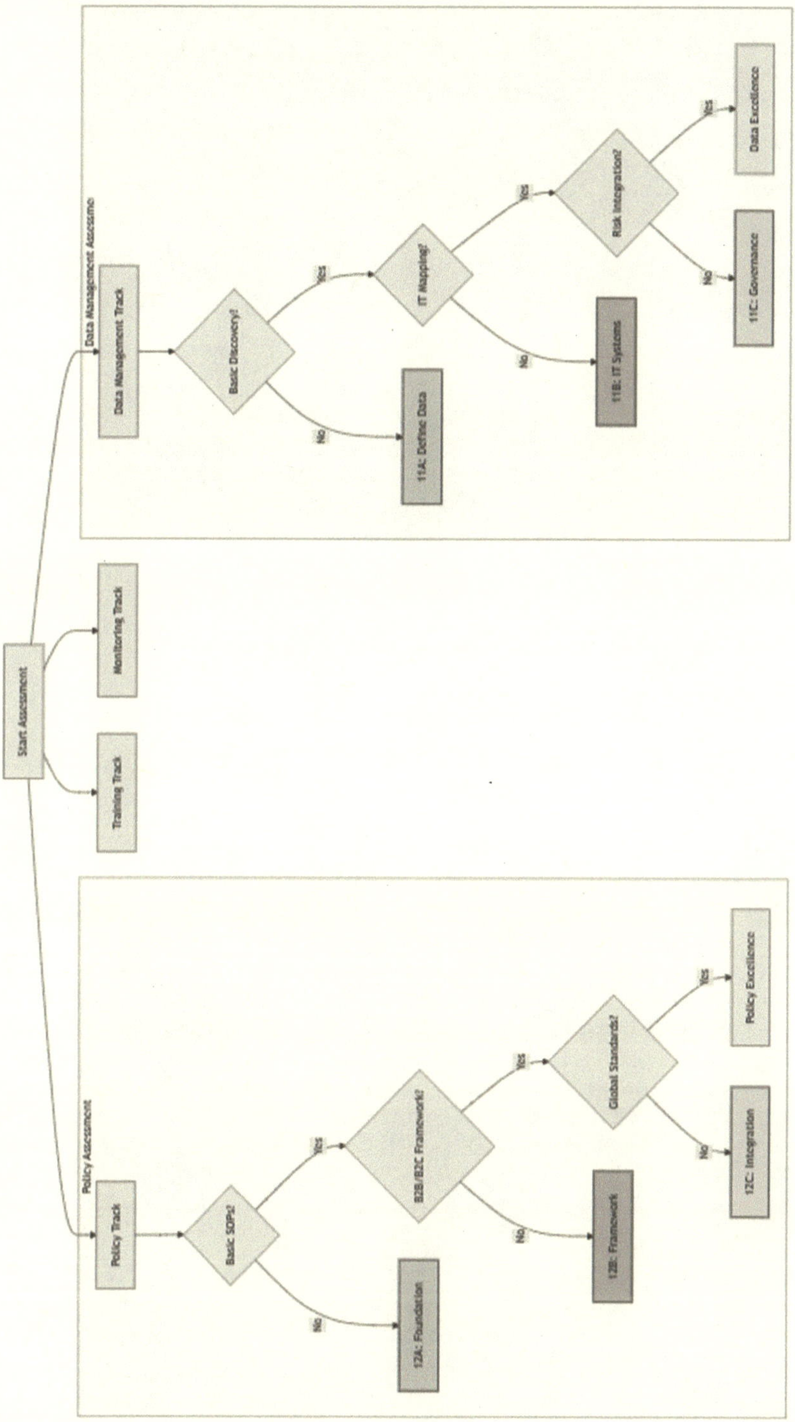

Start Assessment

Training Track

Monitoring Track

Data Management Assessme

Data Management Track

Basic Discovery?

No

11A: Define Data

Yes

IT Mapping?

No

11B: IT Systems

Yes

Risk Integration?

No

11C: Governance

Yes

Data Excellence

Policy Assessment

Policy Track

Basic SOPs?

No

12A: Foundation

Yes

B2B/B2C Framework?

No

12B: Framework

Yes

Global Standards?

No

12C: Integration

Yes

Policy Excellence

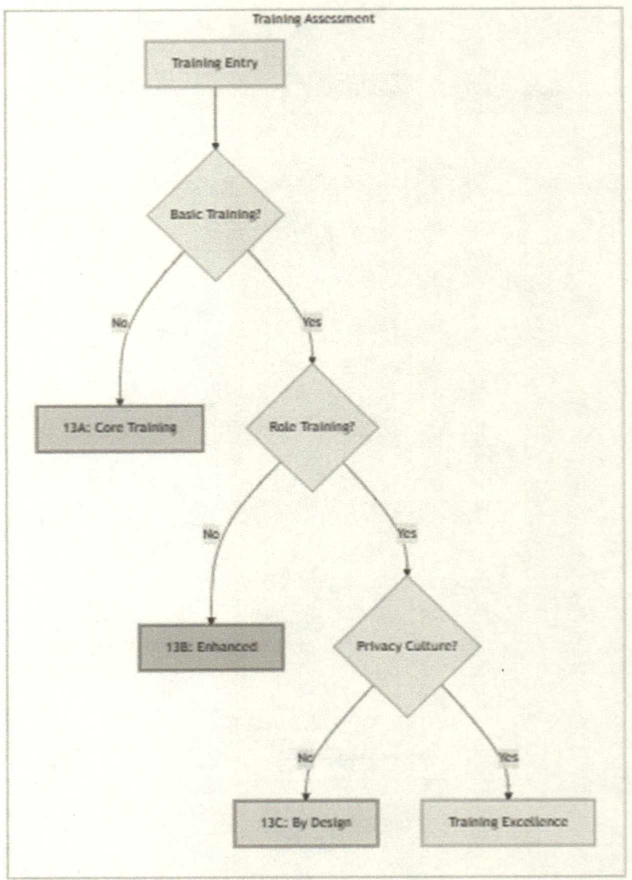
Training Assessment
Training Entry
Basic Training?
No
Yes
13A: Core Training
Role Training?
No
Yes
13B: Enhanced
Privacy Culture?
No
Yes
13C: By Design
Training Excellence

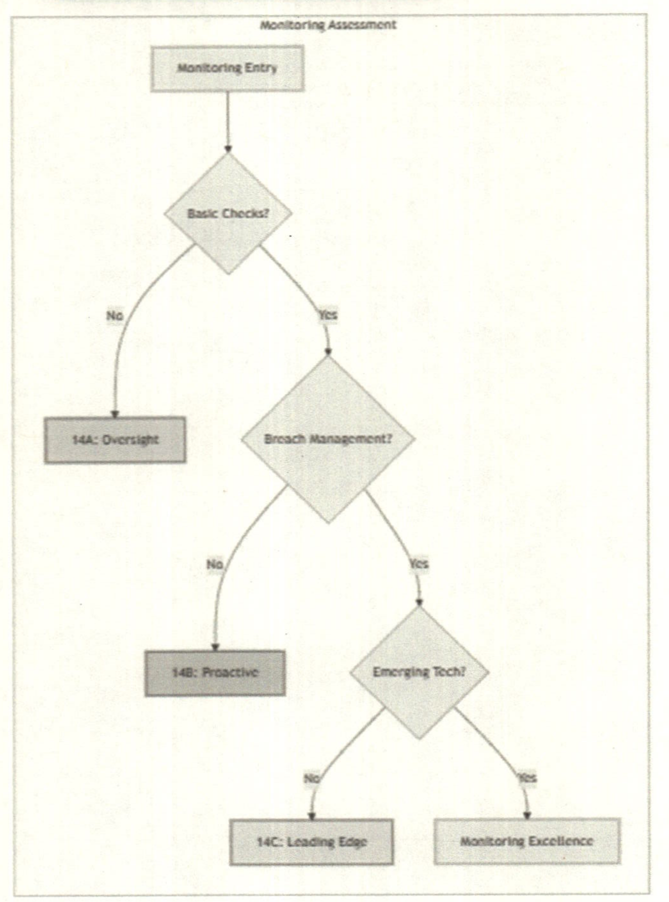
Monitoring Assessment
Monitoring Entry
Basic Checks?
No
Yes
14A: Oversight
Breach Management?
No
Yes
14B: Proactive
Emerging Tech?
No
Yes
14C: Leading Edge
Monitoring Excellence

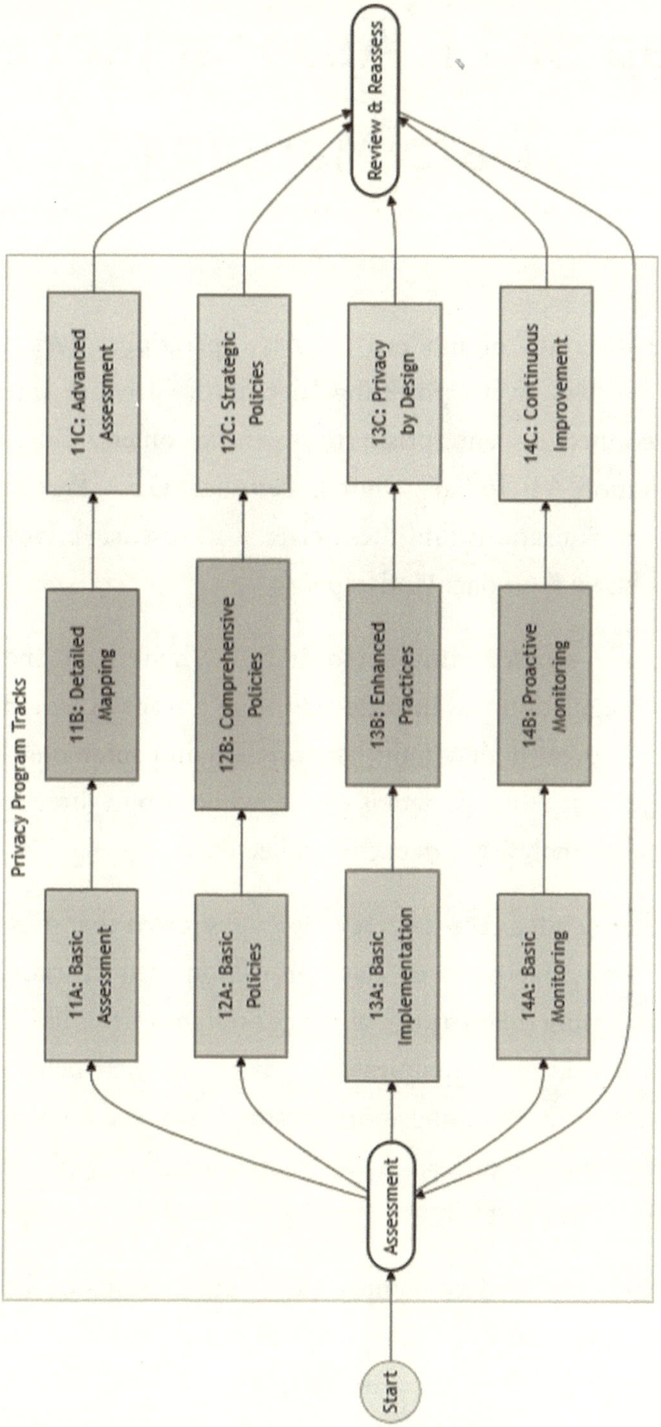

Start

Assessment

Privacy Program Tracks

11A: Basic Assessment → 11B: Detailed Mapping → 11C: Advanced Assessment

12A: Basic Policies → 12B: Comprehensive Policies → 12C: Strategic Policies

13A: Basic Implementation → 13B: Enhanced Practices → 13C: Privacy by Design

14A: Basic Monitoring → 14B: Proactive Monitoring → 14C: Continuous Improvement

Review & Reassess

Chapter 11: Assessment and Data Mapping

In the labyrinth of modern business operations, data flows like an invisible river, powering decisions, driving innovations, and connecting enterprises to their customers. But with the implementation of India's Digital Personal Data Protection Act (DPDPA), organizations find themselves at a crossroads: How well do they really know their data landscape?

This is not a problem unique to India. When the General Data Protection Regulation was introduced in the European Union, a study by Gemalto revealed that only half of the companies they surveyed knew where their sensitive data is stored, while two in three companies were unable to analyse the data they collected.[29]

On the other hand, a recent survey by PwC showed that 4 in 5 people in India think that personal data protection is a crucial factor in companies gaining their trust.[30] While consultancy firms like PwC have an interest in scaring companies into paying for their help, people in India are certainly becoming more aware of personal data – not least because of major ad campaigns by companies like Apple and Meta, both launched in 2024.[31]

With this growing need for companies to put in safeguards for personal data, not just to comply with regulations but to build trust with their users, it's important for companies to first understand where they even store their data. This is the foundation upon which all other data protection-related actions can be built.

This chapter will guide you through the critical process of data assessment and mapping, providing a roadmap from basic discovery to advanced data governance. Whether you're a startup taking your first steps in data protection or an established enterprise looking to enhance your practices, you'll find actionable strategies to navigate the complex terrain of data mapping.

Jargon Buster: Data Mapping

Data Mapping is the process of creating a comprehensive inventory of an organization's data assets, including what types of data are collected, where they are stored, how they flow through various systems, and who has access to them. In the context of data protection, it focuses particularly on personal data and sensitive personal data as defined by applicable laws like the DPDPA.

Key aspects include:

– Identifying data sources and repositories

– Tracking data flows within and outside the organization

– Categorizing data based on sensitivity and regulatory requirements

– Documenting data processing activities and purposes

Effective data mapping is crucial for compliance, risk management, and efficient data governance.

A. Basic Level: Getting Started

1. Defining Personal Data in Your Context

The journey of data mapping begins with a fundamental question: What constitutes personal data in your organization? The DPDPA defines personal data as any information about an identified or identifiable individual. However, the practical application of this definition can vary significantly across different business contexts.

For instance, an e-commerce platform might consider customer names, email addresses, and purchase histories as obvious personal data. But what about device identifiers, browsing patterns, or even the style of clothing frequently viewed? In the age of big data and advanced analytics, the line between personal and non-personal data often blurs.

This spectrum illustrates the range of data types, from clearly personal to potentially non-personal. Organizations must carefully consider where different data elements fall on this spectrum in their specific context.

To start defining personal data in your organization, this is what you must do:

1. List all customer touchpoints (website, app, customer service interactions)
2. Identify what information is collected at each point
3. Consider less obvious data (e.g., cookies, log files, derived or inferred data)

4. Determine which data can identify an individual, directly or indirectly

Remember, the DPDPA takes a broad view of personal data. When in doubt, it's safer to treat data as personal and subject to protection requirements.

DPDPA Insight: Personal Data Definition

The Digital Personal Data Protection Act (DPDPA) defines personal data as any data about an individual who is identifiable by or in relation to such data. This broad definition encompasses:

1. Direct identifiers (e.g., name, ID numbers)

2. Indirect identifiers (e.g., online identifiers, location data)

3. Any data that, when combined with other information, could identify an individual

Key points:

- The definition is technology-neutral, covering data that is born digital and non-digital data that is digitized in some way later on

- It includes both factual data and opinions about individuals

- The potential for identification is what matters, not whether identification actually occurs

Organizations should err on the side of caution and consider data as personal if there's any reasonable possibility of it being used to identify an individual.

As we progress through this chapter, we'll explore how to move from this basic understanding to a comprehensive data mapping strategy. Remember, in the world of data protection, knowledge is not just power—it's a fundamental responsibility.

2. Simple Data Discovery Techniques

Once you've established a basic understanding of what constitutes personal data in your organization, the next step is to discover where this data resides. At this basic level, sophisticated tools aren't necessary. Instead, focus on methodical, manual techniques to build your data inventory.

a. **Interviews and Workshops**

Start by talking to key personnel across different departments. These conversations can reveal surprising insights about data practices. For example, when a leading Indian healthcare provider conducted departmental interviews, they discovered that the marketing team had been collecting patients' family medical histories for targeted campaigns—a practice that raised significant privacy concerns.

Organize workshops with cross-functional teams to map out data flows. Use large whiteboards or digital collaboration tools to visualize how data moves through your organization. This collaborative approach not only uncovers hidden data processes but also raises awareness about data protection across the company.

b. **Document Review**

Examine existing documentation that can provide clues about data processing activities:

- Privacy policies and notices
- Data processing agreements with vendors
- Marketing materials and customer communications
- IT system documentation
- HR policies and employee handbooks

A thorough document review can often reveal discrepancies between stated practices and actual data handling. For instance, a review at an e-commerce company may find that their privacy policy hasn't been updated to reflect new data collection practices introduced in their mobile app.

c. **System Inventory**

Create a comprehensive list of all software applications, databases, and even physical filing systems used in your organization. Don't forget about these, if you have them:

- Cloud storage services
- Customer Relationship Management (CRM) systems
- Human Resources Information Systems (HRIS)
- Marketing automation tools
- Analytics platforms

Jargon Buster: Data Inventory

A Data Inventory, also known as a Data Register or Data Asset Register, is a comprehensive catalog of an organization's data assets. It typically includes:

- Types of data collected and stored
- Purposes for which the data is used
- Storage locations (both digital and physical)
- Data owners and stewards
- Retention periods
- Security measures applied

A well-maintained data inventory is crucial for effective data governance, compliance with data protection laws, and efficient data management. It serves as a foundation for more advanced data mapping and protection strategies.

d. **Physical Walk-through**

In the age of digital transformation, it's easy to overlook physical records. Conduct a walk-through of your offices, paying attention to:

- File cabinets and storage rooms
- Employee desks and common areas
- Reception and visitor logs
- CCTV cameras and access control systems

A physical walk-through could, for example, reveal a significant amount of customer data in paper forms (that have been digitized) stored in unlocked cabinets, highlighting a major security risk.

Data Discovery Checklist

- [ ] Schedule interviews with department heads
- [ ] Organize cross-functional data mapping workshops
- [ ] Review all customer-facing documents and policies
- [ ] Audit internal policies and procedures
- [ ] Create a comprehensive inventory of IT systems and applications
- [ ] Conduct a physical walk-through of all office spaces
- [ ] Document all findings in a centralized data inventory
- [ ] Cross-reference findings with legal requirements (e.g., DPDPA)
- [ ] Identify gaps and inconsistencies in data handling practices
- [ ] Prioritize high-risk areas for immediate attention

By systematically applying these simple data discovery techniques, organizations can build a solid foundation for their data mapping efforts. Remember, at this stage, the goal is to cast a wide net and capture as much information as possible about your data practices. The refinement and detailed analysis will come in later stages.

As you progress through this discovery process, you may uncover practices that don't align with data protection principles or legal requirements. This is a normal and valuable part of the process. Each discovery is an opportunity to improve your data handling practices and move towards better compliance and data governance.

In the next section, we'll explore how to use this discovered information to conduct an initial risk assessment, setting the stage for more advanced data protection strategies.

Deep Cuts: An Inventory of Purposes

Most companies in India have simply grown organically, without ever auditing how or why they have collected their vast treasure troves of data. In my experience, most senior executives and CXOs have little idea about what they do with personal data beyond a high-level understanding of the business context of their collection practices. This is always the first problem to tackle – reaching out to function or department heads to create an inventory of all the purposes for which personal data is collected, stored and processed. This inventory goes a long way towards giving every decision-maker and stakeholder in the company a fair idea of the how's, what's, where's, and why's of their personal data empire, and requires a minimal investment of time. This exercise could be conducted before, or perhaps in parallel to, creating a full record or summary of processing activities.

Depending on their progress towards a complete data governance framework, some companies may even choose to create an inventory of all the purposes for which they process data in general, and not just personal data.

3. Initial Risk Identification

With a basic inventory of your data practices in hand, the next crucial step is to identify potential risks associated with your data handling. This process not only helps in prioritizing your data protection efforts but also aligns with the DPDPA's requirement for organizations to implement reasonable security practices.

Common Risk Areas

1. **Overcollection of Data**: Many organizations collect more data than necessary, increasing both risk and liability.
2. **Inadequate Access Controls**: Ensure that only authorized personnel have access to personal data.
3. **Retention Beyond Necessity**: Holding onto personal data longer than required not only violates data minimization principles but also increases the risk of breaches.
4. **Insufficient Third-Party Oversight**: Many organizations struggle to maintain control over how their vendors and partners handle shared personal data.
5. **Cross-Border Data Transfers**: With India's growing role in global services, many companies transfer data internationally without adequate safeguards.

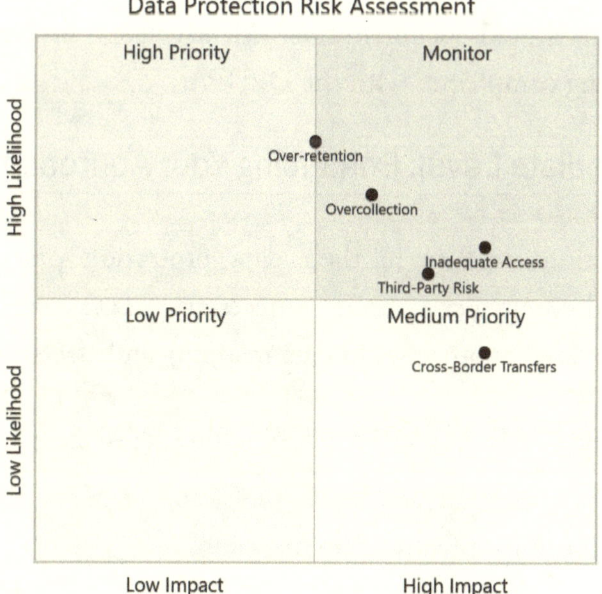

This risk assessment matrix helps visualize and prioritize identified risks based on their potential impact and likelihood of occurrence.

DPDPA Insight: Risk Assessment

The Digital Personal Data Protection Act (DPDPA) emphasizes a risk-based approach to data protection. Key points:

1. Organizations must implement reasonable security practices based on the nature and sensitivity of the personal data they handle.
2. The Act mandates the reporting of data breaches that are "likely to result in significant harm" to affected individuals, underscoring the importance of ongoing risk assessment.
3. While not explicitly required, conducting regular risk assessments is implicitly necessary to comply with the Act's principles of accountability and transparency.

Organizations should document their risk assessment process as part of demonstrating compliance with the DPDPA.

B. Intermediate Level: Enhancing Your Approach

As organizations mature in their data protection practices, more sophisticated strategies become necessary. Let's explore some intermediate-level approaches to data mapping and assessment.

1. Leveraging Existing IT Systems for Data Mapping

Many organizations already have tools and systems that can be repurposed for more effective data mapping:

a) **Database Schemas**: Analyze your database structures to understand data relationships and identify personal data fields. For example, an Indian fintech company used their database schema analysis to discover unnecessary duplication of sensitive financial data across multiple systems.

b) **Network Diagrams**: Existing network maps can help trace data flows between systems, highlighting potential vulnerabilities. A large Indian IT services provider used this method to identify unsecured data transfers between their development and production environments.

c) **Data Lineage Tools**: If available, these tools can track data from origin to destination, providing valuable insights into data transformations and usage.

Jargon Buster: Data Lineage

Data Lineage refers to the life-cycle of data, including its origins (or provenance), movements, transformations, and destinations. It provides a visual representation of how data flows through systems and processes within an organization.

Key aspects:

- Tracks data from its point of origin to its point of consumption
- Shows how data is transformed, aggregated, or combined at each step
- Helps in understanding data dependencies and impact analysis
- Crucial for ensuring data quality, regulatory compliance, and effective data governance

In the context of data protection, data lineage helps organizations understand how personal data is used, transformed, and shared throughout their systems, aiding in compliance efforts and risk management.

2. Conducting Effective Data Protection Impact Assessments (DPIAs)

While not explicitly mandated by the DPDPA for all processing activities, conducting Data Protection Impact Assessments (DPIAs) is a best practice adopted from global standards like the GDPR. DPIAs are particularly valuable for new projects or significant changes to existing data processing activities.

Steps in conducting a DPIA:

1. Describe the nature, scope, context, and purposes of the processing
2. Assess necessity, proportionality, and compliance measures
3. Identify and assess risks to individuals
4. Identify measures to mitigate those risks

An example outcome of a DPIA may look like this: perhaps a healthcare company may conduct a DPIA before launching a new predictive diagnosis tool. The assessment could reveal potential biases in their AI model that could lead to unfair treatment of certain patient groups. This discovery would allow them to refine their algorithms and implement additional safeguards before launch.

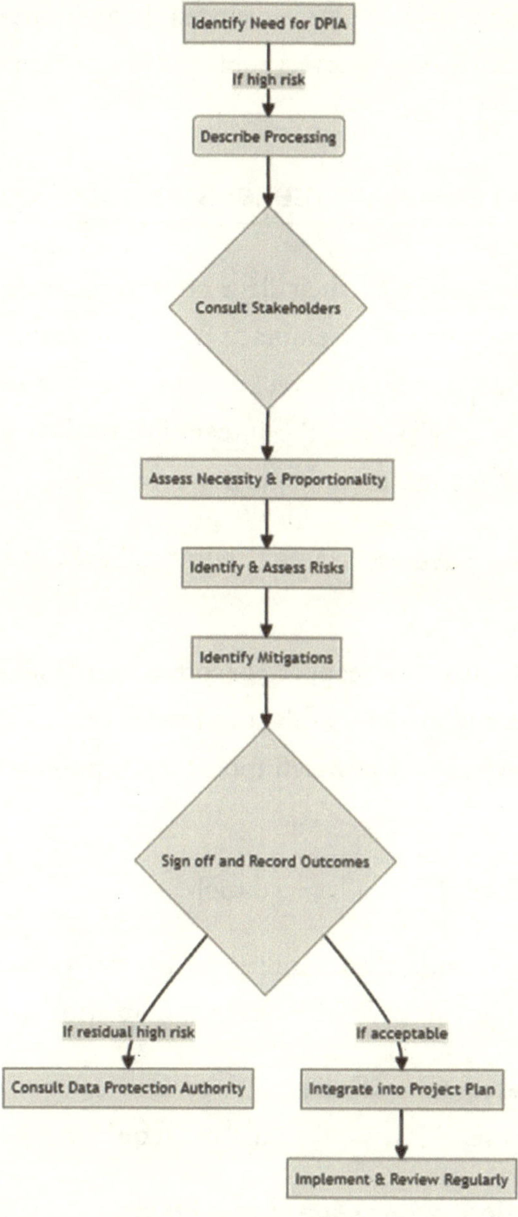

As we progress through these intermediate strategies, organizations can build a more comprehensive and nuanced understanding of their data landscape. This enhanced visibility not only supports compliance efforts but also enables more effective data-driven decision making.

In the next section, we'll explore advanced data governance strategies, including automated data discovery tools and integration with enterprise risk management frameworks.

C. Advanced Level: Comprehensive Data Governance

As organizations mature in their data protection journey, they move beyond mere compliance to embrace data governance as a strategic imperative. This advanced level focuses on sophisticated tools, comprehensive strategies, and the integration of data protection into the very fabric of organizational operations.

1. Implementing Advanced Data Discovery and Classification Tools

At this stage, manual data mapping becomes insufficient to handle the volume, variety, and velocity of data in modern enterprises. Advanced organizations leverage AI-powered tools for continuous data discovery and classification.

Key features to look for in advanced tools:

- **Pattern Recognition**: Ability to identify personal data using machine learning algorithms, even in unstructured formats.
- **Automated Classification**: Real-time categorization of data based on sensitivity and regulatory requirements.
- **Integration with Data Loss Prevention (DLP) Systems**: Seamless connection with existing security infrastructure.
- **Continuous Monitoring**: Ongoing scanning and alerting for new or changed data stores.

Jargon Buster: Data Loss Prevention (DLP)

Data Loss Prevention (DLP) refers to a set of tools and processes that ensure sensitive data is not lost, misused, or accessed by unauthorized users.

Key aspects:

- Identifies, monitors, and protects data in use, in motion, and at rest
- Uses content inspection and contextual analysis to detect potential data breaches
- Can prevent unauthorized actions such as uploads, file transfers, or sending emails containing sensitive data
- Often integrates with other security systems for comprehensive data protection

In the context of data mapping, DLP systems can provide valuable insights into data flows and potential exposure points, complementing other discovery and classification tools.

2. Cross-Border Data Flow Mapping

With India's position as a global IT hub, many organizations deal with complex international data transfers. Advanced data mapping at this stage involves a detailed understanding of cross-border data flows.

Steps in comprehensive cross-border data mapping:

1. Identify all instances of data leaving India
2. Understand the legal basis for each transfer (e.g., standard contractual clauses, adequacy decisions)

3. Assess the data protection regime in recipient countries

4. Implement appropriate safeguards for high-risk transfers

With the evolving global privacy landscape, some organizations are adopting "data localization by design" principles. This involves architecting systems to keep data within geographical boundaries unless absolutely necessary for processing elsewhere.

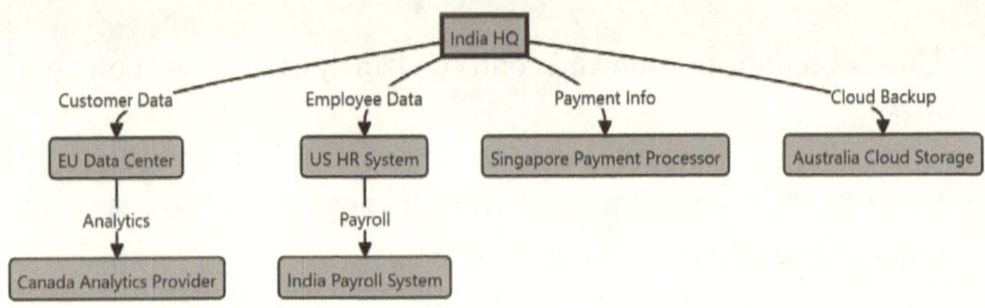

This diagram illustrates the complexity of cross-border data flows in a typical multinational organization. Each arrow represents a data flow that needs to be assessed for compliance with data protection regulations.

3. Integrating Data Protection into Enterprise Risk Management

At the most advanced level, data protection becomes an integral part of the organization's overall risk management framework.

Key aspects of this integration:

- **Risk Registers**: Include data protection risks in enterprise-wide risk registers.

- **Business Continuity Planning**: Incorporate data protection considerations into disaster recovery and business continuity plans.

- **Mergers and Acquisitions**: Make data protection due diligence a standard part of M&A processes.

- **Board-Level Reporting**: Regular updates to the board on data protection risks and mitigation efforts.

While the DPDPA doesn't explicitly mandate this level of integration, such comprehensive risk management aligns with the Act's principles of accountability and the requirement for organizations to implement reasonable security practices.

4. Leveraging Blockchain-like databases for Data Mapping and Audit Trails

Some cutting-edge organizations are exploring blockchain technology to enhance their data mapping and create immutable audit trails of data processing activities.

Potential applications of blockchain in data protection:

- **Consent Management**: Creating tamper-proof and non-repudiable records of user consent.

- **Data Processing Logs**: Maintaining an unalterable history of how and when data was accessed or modified.

- **Third-Party Audits**: Facilitating transparent and verifiable audits of data processing activities.

While blockchain can enhance transparency and trust, it's crucial to implement it in a way that doesn't conflict with data protection principles like the right to erasure.

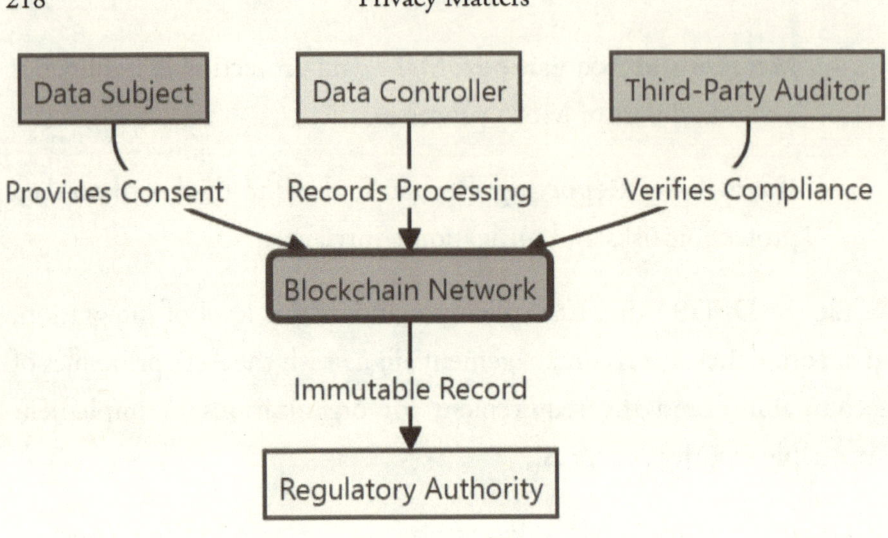

This diagram illustrates how blockchain technology can be used to create a transparent and verifiable record of data protection activities, enhancing trust and compliance.

It's important to note that reaching this level of sophistication is an ongoing journey. Organizations should continually assess new technologies and methodologies to enhance their data protection practices.

Conclusion: The Never-Ending Journey of Data Protection

As we conclude this chapter on data mapping and assessment, it's crucial to recognize that this is not a destination, but an ongoing journey. From the basic steps of identifying personal data to the advanced strategies of AI-powered data governance, each stage builds upon the last, creating a robust framework for responsible data handling.

In the Indian context, as we navigate the implementation of the DPDPA and position ourselves in the global digital economy, effective data mapping and assessment are not just compliance requirements—they're competitive advantages. They enable organizations to build trust, innovate responsibly, and unlock the true value of their data assets.

Remember:

- Start with the basics, but don't stop there.
- Regularly reassess and upgrade your strategies.
- Stay informed about regulatory changes and technological advancements.
- Foster a culture where every employee sees themselves as a guardian of data.

As you embark on or continue your data protection journey, keep in mind that every step towards better data mapping and assessment is a step towards a more trustworthy, efficient, and ethical digital future.

In the next chapter, we'll explore how to translate the insights gained from data mapping into effective policy and procedure development, ensuring that your newfound understanding of your data landscape translates into actionable, compliant practices across your organization.

Case Study: DataTech Solutions' Data Mapping Journey

**Note:* This is a fictional narrative created for illustrative purposes. Any resemblance to real companies or individuals is purely coincidental.*

In the heart of Bengaluru's tech corridor, DataTech Solutions faces a pivotal moment. Founded by Rajesh Kapoor in 2015, this cloud analytics firm has grown rapidly, but now grapples with a critical challenge: preparing for India's Digital Personal Data Protection Act (DPDPA).

One Monday morning, Rajesh receives an alarming email from his legal team. DataTech is unprepared for the new regulations, lacking even basic knowledge of its data practices. Determined to address this, Rajesh convenes his leadership team, including Ananya Desai, a sharp-minded product manager who volunteers to spearhead the data mapping initiative.

Ananya begins with a company-wide scoping exercise, aligning with the basic strategies outlined in Chapter 11.A.1. She moves from department to department, uncovering a maze of undocumented data processes. The marketing team's customer data collection, the engineering team's application data processing, and even HR's handling of employee information all lack proper cataloging and purpose definition.

Compiling this information, Ananya creates a preliminary data inventory, implementing the simple data discovery techniques described in Chapter 11.A.2. This inventory reveals the startling extent of DataTech's personal data processing, often without clear purpose or adequate safeguards.

Building on this foundation, Ananya leads the creation of a comprehensive Record of Processing Activities (ROPA), a key component of the manual data mapping process outlined in Chapter 11.A. This ROPA becomes DataTech's single source of truth for data-related activities.

Collaborating with the UX team and system architects, Ananya then develops a visual representation of data flows across the organization, completing the basic level strategies as described in Chapter 11.A.3.

Recognizing the need for more sophisticated approaches, Rajesh brings in Sanjay Mehra, an experienced IT consultant. Sanjay implements intermediate level strategies, starting with the validation of manual mapping using IT inventories and data schemas, as detailed in Chapter 11.B.1.

Sanjay also introduces a formal Data Protection Impact Assessment (DPIA) process, aligning with the strategies in Chapter 11.B.2. The first DPIA uncovers potential risks in DataTech's new machine learning project, leading to privacy-enhancing redesigns.

As DataTech's efforts mature, they expand existing security frameworks to encompass data protection principles, following the guidance in Chapter 11.B.3. This integration helps foster a culture of data responsibility among employees.

The final phase sees DataTech investing in advanced data discovery and classification tools, implementing the sophisticated strategies described in Chapter 11.C.1. These AI-powered solutions provide unprecedented detail in their data mapping, giving Rajesh a comprehensive view of DataTech's data ecosystem.

Addressing their growing international client base, DataTech tackles the complex task of mapping cross-border data flows, as outlined in Chapter 11.C.2. This exercise uncovers potential compliance issues with data transfers to countries lacking adequate data protection laws, leading to strategic decisions about data storage and processing locations.

Finally, DataTech integrates data protection into their enterprise risk management framework, following the advanced strategies in Chapter 11.C.3. This holistic approach ensures that data protection is considered in all business decisions.

As DataTech emerges from this transformative journey, they find themselves not just compliant, but at a competitive advantage. Clients, particularly those in regulated industries, are impressed by DataTech's robust data protection measures.

The story of DataTech Solutions illustrates the power of a systematic approach to data protection. From a company unaware of its data practices to one at the forefront of privacy-enhancing technologies, DataTech's journey demonstrates the transformative potential of comprehensive data mapping and protection strategies.

As Rajesh, Ananya, and Sanjay reflect on their achievements, they recognize that this is an ongoing process. In India's rapidly evolving data protection landscape, they stand ready to face future challenges, armed with knowledge, tools, and a deep respect for the power and responsibility of handling personal data in the digital age.

Chapter 12: Policy and SOP Development

In the rapidly evolving landscape of data protection in India, organizations face a critical challenge: translating their understanding of data flows into actionable policies and procedures. The Digital Personal Data Protection Act (DPDPA) 2023 has set new standards for how businesses handle personal data, making the development of robust data protection policies and Standard Operating Procedures (SOPs) not just a legal requirement, but a business imperative.

For many Indian companies, the journey from data awareness to comprehensive policy implementation can seem daunting. Whether you're a small startup in Bangalore or a multinational corporation in Mumbai, the task of creating policies that both comply with regulations and align with business objectives requires careful consideration and strategic planning.

This chapter will guide you through the process of developing and implementing data protection policies and SOPs, tailored to the Indian business context. We'll explore a maturity-based approach, allowing organizations at different stages of their data protection journey to find relevant strategies and actionable insights.

We'll begin by examining the essential foundations of policy creation, including basic data protection policies and key SOPs. As we progress, we'll delve into more advanced topics such as tailoring policies for different business models, establishing dedicated data protection offices, and integrating data protection principles into overall business strategy.

Throughout the chapter, we'll use real-world scenarios and practical examples to illustrate key concepts, helping you navigate common challenges in policy development. We'll also highlight global best practices and their relevance to the Indian regulatory landscape, ensuring your policies are both locally compliant and internationally competitive.

By the end of this chapter, you'll have a clear roadmap for developing policies and procedures that not only meet regulatory requirements but also foster a culture of data responsibility within your organization. Let's begin our exploration of how to transform data protection principles into effective organizational practices.

A. Basic Level: Essential Foundations

As organizations begin their journey towards comprehensive data protection compliance, establishing a solid foundation is crucial. This section will guide you through the essential first steps in developing policies and Standard Operating Procedures (SOPs) that align with the DPDPA 2023 requirements and set the stage for more advanced practices.

1. Creating a Basic Data Protection Policy

The cornerstone of any data protection program is a clear, concise policy that outlines your organization's approach to handling personal data. Here's how to develop this fundamental document:

a) **Scope and Purpose**: Begin by clearly defining the policy's scope and purpose. This should include a statement of commitment to data protection and an overview of the types of data your organization handles.

b) **Key Definitions**: Include definitions of important terms like 'personal data', 'processing', and 'data subject', ensuring alignment with DPDPA 2023 terminology.

c) **Data Protection Principles**: Outline the core principles your organization will follow, such as purpose limitation, data minimization, and storage limitation.

d) **Rights of Data Principals**: Clearly state the rights of individuals under the DPDPA 2023, including the right to access, correct, and erase personal data.

e) **Data Security Measures**: Provide an overview of the security measures in place to protect personal data from unauthorized access or breaches.

f) **Incident Response**: Include a brief section on how your organization will respond to data breaches or other security incidents.

g) **Review and Update Mechanism**: Establish a process for regularly reviewing and updating the policy.

Data Dilemma: The One-Size-Fits-All Policy

Rahul, the newly appointed Data Protection Officer at a mid-sized IT services company in Bangalore, is tasked with creating the company's first data protection policy. He finds a template online and decides to use it as-is, without customization. Is this approach sufficient? What potential issues might arise?

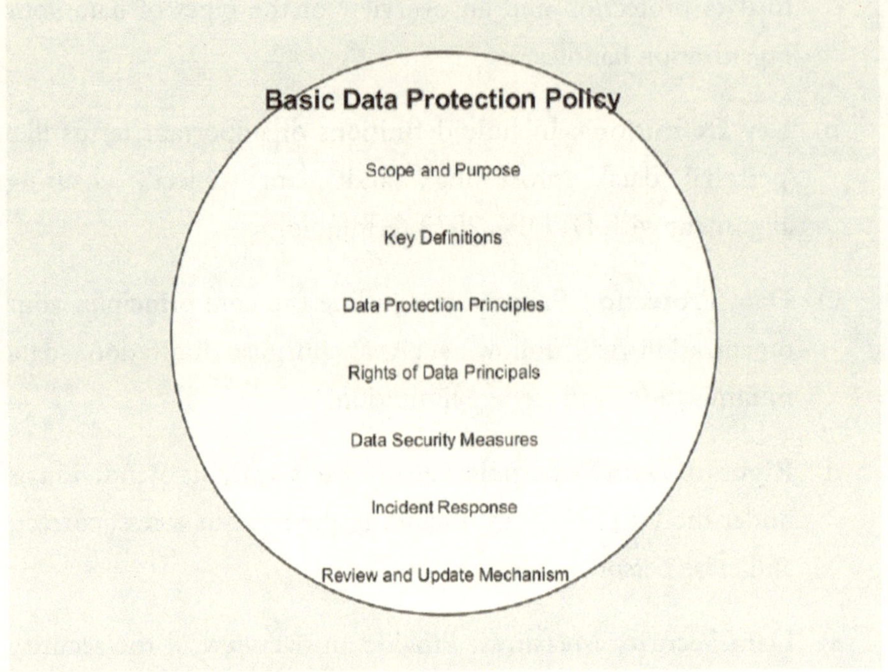

2. Developing Key Standard Operating Procedures (SOPs)

While a policy provides the overarching framework, SOPs translate these principles into actionable steps. Here are some essential SOPs to develop:

a) **Data Collection and Processing SOP**: Outline the procedures for collecting and processing personal data, ensuring compliance with consent requirements and purpose limitation.

b) **Data Subject Rights SOP**: Detail the steps for handling requests from individuals exercising their rights under the DPDPA 2023.

c) **Data Retention and Deletion SOP**: Establish procedures for retaining data only as long as necessary and securely deleting it when no longer needed.

d) **Data Breach Response SOP**: Create a step-by-step guide for identifying, containing, and reporting data breaches.

> **Quick Tip:** When developing SOPs, involve employees from relevant departments to ensure the procedures are practical and aligned with day-to-day operations.

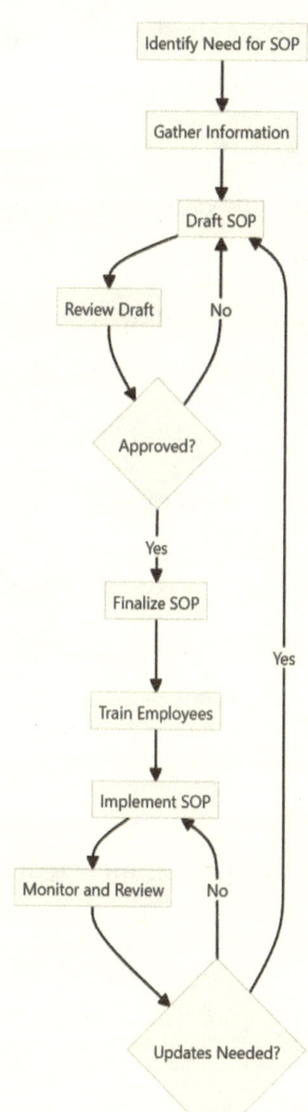

3. Designating Data Protection Responsibilities

Clear allocation of responsibilities is crucial for effective data protection. Consider the following steps:

a) **Appoint a Data Protection Officer (DPO)**: While not mandatory for all organizations under the DPDPA 2023, designating a DPO or a similar role can provide clear leadership on data protection matters.

b) **Define Departmental Responsibilities**: Outline the data protection responsibilities of different departments, such as IT, HR, and Marketing.

c) **Employee Training**: Develop a basic training program to ensure all employees understand their role in protecting personal data.

Jargon Buster: **Data Protection Officer (DPO)** A DPO is an enterprise security leadership role required by the GDPR and recommended by many data protection regulations. The DPO is responsible for overseeing data protection strategy and implementation to ensure compliance with regulatory requirements.

By implementing these basic elements, organizations can establish a solid foundation for their data protection practices. As we move forward, we'll explore how to build upon this foundation to create a more comprehensive and sophisticated approach to policy and SOP development.

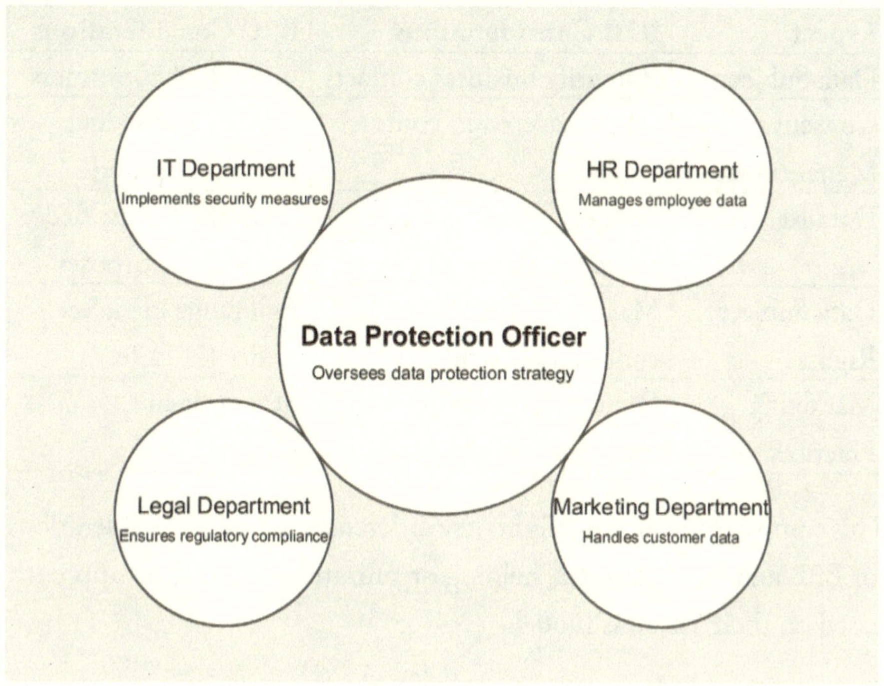

B. Intermediate Level: Comprehensive Framework

As organizations mature in their data protection practices, they need to develop a more comprehensive framework that addresses the nuances of their specific business context. This section explores how to tailor policies for different business models, expand SOPs to cover the entire data lifecycle, and establish a dedicated Data Protection Office.

1. Tailoring policies for B2B vs B2C contexts

Different business models require different approaches to data protection. Let's examine how to adapt policies for B2B (Business-to-Business) and B2C (Business-to-Consumer) contexts:

Aspect	B2B Considerations	B2C Considerations
Data Subjects	Primarily business contacts	Individual consumers
Consent Management	Often covered in contracts	Explicit individual consent required
Data Retention	Longer periods due to business relationships	Shorter periods, tied to specific purposes
Data Subject Rights	May be limited by contractual terms	Full range of rights under DPDPA
Marketing Practices	Focus on legitimate interests	Strict opt-in requirements

This comparison table highlights key differences in policy considerations for B2B and B2C contexts, helping organizations tailor their approach based on their business model.

2. Expanding SOPs to cover the entire data lifecycle

At the intermediate level, organizations should develop SOPs that address each stage of the data lifecycle. Let's visualize this process:

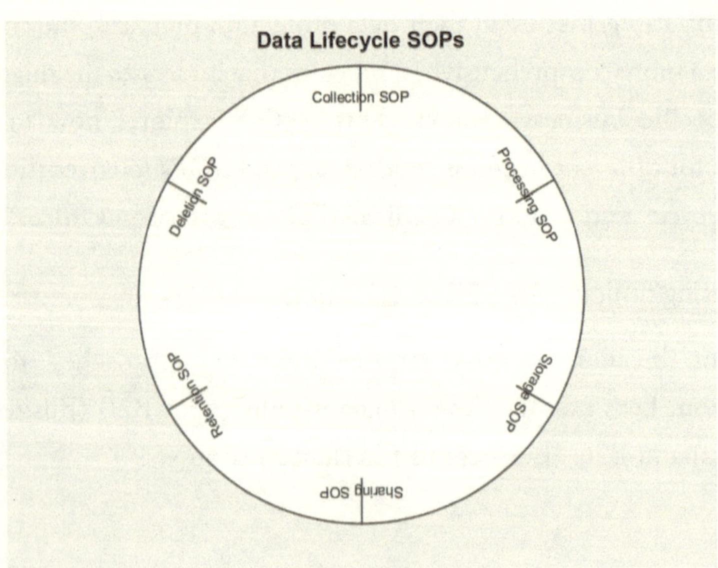

This circular diagram illustrates the various stages of the data lifecycle and the corresponding SOPs that organizations should develop to ensure comprehensive data protection.

3. Establishing a Data Protection Office

Creating a dedicated Data Protection Office (DPO) is a crucial step in maturing an organization's data protection practices. Let's visualize the structure and responsibilities of a DPO:

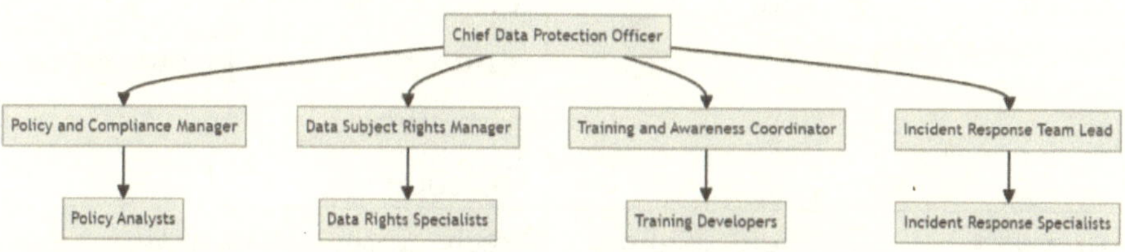

This organizational chart provides a visual representation of a typical Data Protection Office structure, helping organizations understand the key roles and reporting lines involved in establishing this function.

C. Advanced Level: Strategic Integration

At the advanced level, organizations aim to fully integrate data protection into their business strategy and operations. This section explores how to align policies with global standards, embed data protection into all business processes, and develop sophisticated governance structures.

1. Aligning policies with global data protection standards

As businesses expand globally, it's crucial to align data protection policies with international standards while maintaining compliance with local regulations.

Aspect	*DPDPA (India)*	*GDPR (EU)*	*CCPA (California, USA)*
Scope	Indian entities and foreign entities dealing with Indian data	EU entities and those offering goods/services to EU residents	For-profit entities doing business in California
Individual Rights	Access, correction, erasure	Access, rectification, erasure, portability, objection	Access, deletion, opt-out of sale
Consent Requirements	Explicit, specific, informed	Freely given, specific, informed, unambiguous	Opt-out for sale of personal information
Data Breach Notification	To Data Protection Board, timeline TBD	Within 72 hours to supervisory authority	Without unreasonable delay

This comparison table helps organizations understand key differences between major global data protection standards, facilitating the development of policies that can meet multiple regulatory requirements.

2. Integrating data protection into all business processes

At the advanced level, data protection should be seamlessly integrated into every aspect of business operations. Let's visualize this concept:

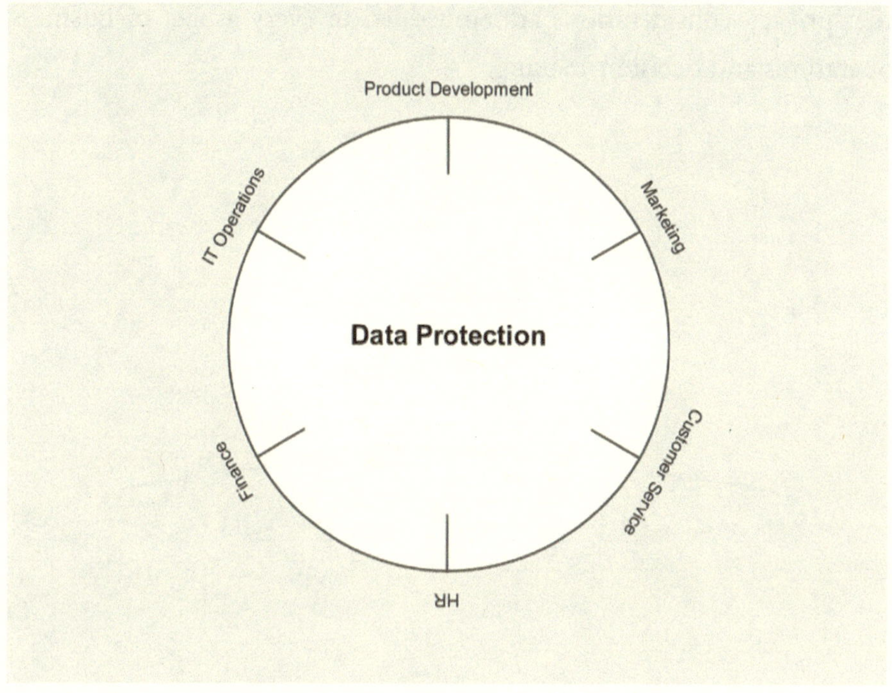

This diagram illustrates how data protection should be central to all business processes, emphasizing the need for a holistic approach to data protection integration.

3. Developing advanced governance structures

Advanced data protection requires sophisticated governance structures that ensure accountability and continuous improvement.

This flowchart illustrates an advanced governance structure for data protection, showing the relationships between various roles and committees involved in ensuring comprehensive data protection oversight.

By implementing these advanced strategies and structures, organizations can elevate their data protection practices to a strategic level, ensuring that privacy considerations are embedded in every aspect of business operations and decision-making.

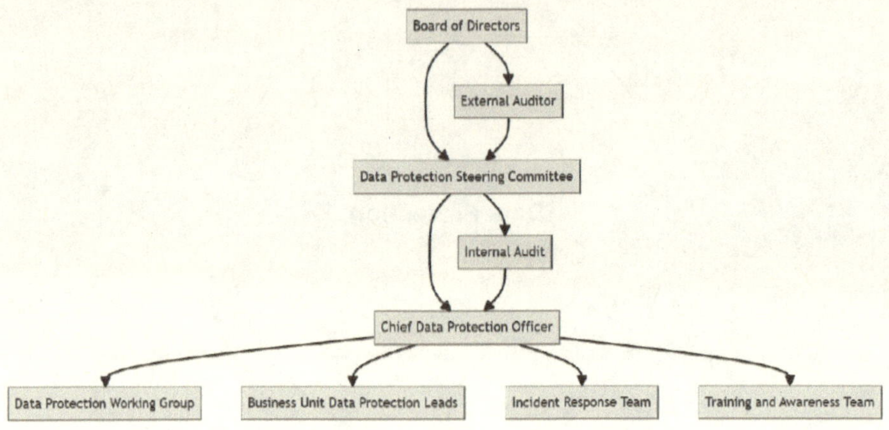

Case Study: HealthGuard Inc.'s Data Protection Policy Evolution

HealthGuard Inc., a mid-sized healthcare technology company based in Mumbai, found itself at a critical juncture when the Digital Personal Data Protection Act (DPDPA) 2023 was introduced. The company, known for its innovative patient management systems, realized it needed to rapidly evolve its approach to data protection.

CEO Vikram Mehta recognized the challenge ahead. "We've always prioritized patient data security, but this new regulation requires a complete overhaul of our policies and procedures," he explained during a board meeting.

To spearhead this initiative, HealthGuard Inc. brought in Anjali Desai, an experienced data protection consultant, as their new Chief Data Protection Officer. Anjali's first assessment of the company's data protection practices revealed significant gaps.

Anjali began by implementing the basic level strategies outlined in Section A of the chapter:

1. She developed a basic data protection policy (Section A.1), clearly defining the scope, purpose, and key data protection principles for HealthGuard Inc.

2. Anjali then created essential Standard Operating Procedures (SOPs) as described in Section A.2, focusing on data collection, processing, and breach response procedures.

3. Following the guidance in Section A.3, she designated data protection responsibilities across the organization, ensuring

each department understood its role in safeguarding patient data.

As HealthGuard Inc.'s data protection practices matured, Anjali moved on to implementing intermediate level strategies from Section B:

1. Recognizing the company's dual B2B and B2C operations, Anjali tailored policies for each context as outlined in Section B.1. This involved creating separate guidelines for handling healthcare provider data and individual patient data.

2. Following Section B.2, she expanded the SOPs to cover the entire data lifecycle, from collection to deletion, paying special attention to the sensitive nature of health data.

3. As described in Section B.3, Anjali established a dedicated Data Protection Office, with clear roles and responsibilities aligned with HealthGuard Inc.'s specific needs in the healthcare sector.

As the company planned for international expansion, Anjali recognized the need for advanced level strategies from Section C:

1. She began aligning HealthGuard Inc.'s policies with global data protection standards as detailed in Section C.1, ensuring compliance with GDPR and HIPAA while maintaining DPDPA compliance.

2. Following the guidance in Section C.2, Anjali worked to integrate data protection considerations into all of HealthGuard Inc.'s business processes, from product development to customer support.

3. As outlined in Section C.3, she developed an advanced governance structure, including board-level oversight of data protection matters and regular third-party audits.

Eighteen months after the start of their data protection journey, HealthGuard Inc. had transformed its approach to data protection. The company's policies and procedures not only ensured compliance with DPDPA and international regulations but also became a key selling point for their products.

"Data protection has become integral to our business strategy," Vikram reflected. "It's not just about compliance anymore; it's about building trust and driving innovation."

HealthGuard Inc.'s journey demonstrates the practical application of the policy and SOP development strategies outlined in this chapter. By systematically progressing through basic, intermediate, and advanced levels of data protection maturity, the company not only mitigated risks but also uncovered new opportunities for growth and innovation in the healthcare technology sector.

Chapter 13: Implementation Strategies

In the bustling tech hub of Bengaluru, Priya, the newly appointed Data Protection Officer at TechInnovate India, stares at her computer screen, a mix of determination and apprehension in her eyes. The company's data protection policies are in place, meticulously crafted to align with the Digital Personal Data Protection Act (DPDPA) 2023. But as Priya knows all too well, a policy is only as good as its implementation.

"How do we turn these words into action?" she wonders, echoing a sentiment shared by countless professionals across India's diverse business landscape.

Implementation – the bridge between theory and practice, between compliance on paper and protection in reality. It's here, in the realm of day-to-day operations, staff behaviors, and technological solutions, that the true test of data protection lies. As India steps into a new era of digital rights and responsibilities, organizations face the critical challenge of translating legal requirements and corporate policies into tangible, effective practices.

The task is particularly daunting in India's unique digital ecosystem. With over 700 million internet users and counting, India represents one of the world's largest and fastest-growing digital markets. However, this rapid digital adoption comes with its own set of challenges. According to a 2023 DSCI (Data Security Council of India) survey, only 45% of Indian organizations have fully implemented basic data protection measures. This statistic is alarming, considering the increasing sophistication of cyber threats and the stringent requirements of the DPDPA 2023.

The challenges are multifaceted:

1. **Diverse digital literacy levels**: From tech-savvy urban professionals to first-time internet users in rural areas, Indian businesses must cater to a wide spectrum of digital awareness.

2. **Resource constraints**: Many Indian SMEs struggle to allocate sufficient resources for data protection. A 2022 study by NASSCOM found that 60% of small businesses in India lack fundamental cybersecurity tools.

3. **Rapid technological adoption**: As India embraces emerging technologies like AI, IoT, and 5G, the data protection landscape becomes increasingly complex.

4. **Regulatory compliance**: The DPDPA 2023 introduces new compliance requirements, pushing organizations to reevaluate their data handling practices.

5. **Cultural factors**: Traditional attitudes towards privacy and data sharing in India are evolving, requiring a nuanced approach to data protection implementation.

This chapter is your guide to navigating these challenges and implementing robust data protection strategies. Whether you're a small startup taking your first steps towards compliance or a large corporation looking to enhance your existing practices, you'll find strategies tailored to your level of maturity and resources.

We'll explore a range of implementation strategies, from fundamental practices that form the bedrock of data protection, to advanced solutions that embed privacy into the very DNA of an organization. Along the way, we'll address common challenges faced by Indian businesses, highlight success stories from various sectors, and provide practical tips to help you navigate the implementation journey.

Remember, implementation is not a one-time effort but an ongoing process of improvement and adaptation. As we delve into these strategies, keep in mind that the goal is not just compliance, but the cultivation of a data protection culture that enhances trust, drives innovation, and creates value in our increasingly data-driven world.

Let's begin our exploration of how to turn data protection principles into practice, one step at a time, in the unique and vibrant context of Digital India.

A. Basic Level: Fundamental Practices

As organizations in India embark on their data protection journey, establishing a solid foundation is crucial. This section explores the fundamental practices that form the bedrock of effective data protection implementation, tailored to the unique challenges and opportunities in the Indian context.

1. Essential Data Protection Training for All Staff

At the heart of any successful data protection program lies a well-informed workforce. In India's diverse business landscape, where digital literacy levels vary widely, comprehensive and culturally sensitive training is paramount.

Key components of a basic data protection training program in the Indian context:

a) Overview of DPDPA 2023 and its implications for Indian businesses

b) Understanding personal data in the Indian context (e.g., Aadhaar numbers, caste information)

c) Basic data protection principles aligned with Indian cultural values

d) Common threats in the Indian cybersecurity landscape

e) Best practices for data handling in daily operations, considering local work cultures

f) Incident reporting procedures tailored to Indian organizational structures

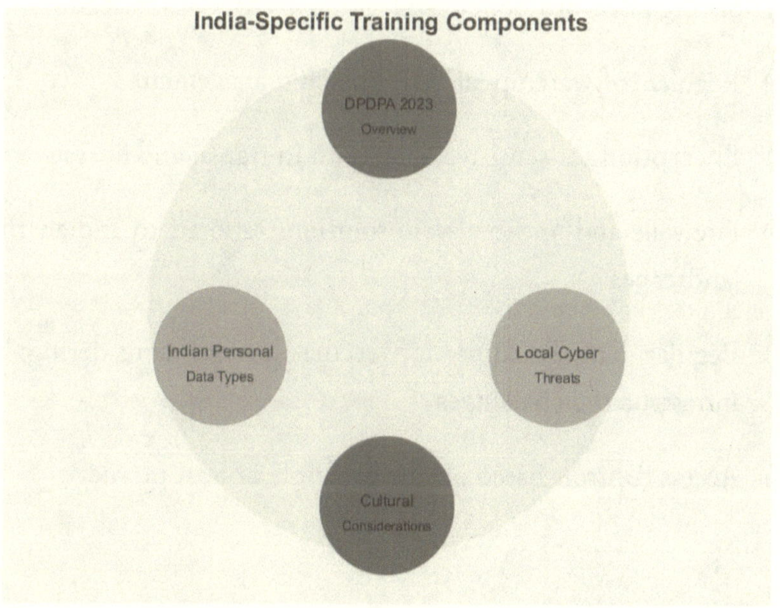

This infographic illustrates the key components of a data protection training program tailored to the Indian context, emphasizing local regulations, data types, threats, and cultural considerations.

Quick Tip: Incorporate local languages and culturally relevant scenarios in your training modules. A Mumbai-based fintech startup found that this approach increased employee engagement and retention of data protection concepts by 30%.

2. Implementing Basic Technical Security Measures

While comprehensive staff training is crucial, it must be complemented by robust technical measures. At the basic level, organizations should focus on implementing fundamental security controls that provide a strong first line of defense against common threats in the Indian cybersecurity landscape.

Essential technical security measures for Indian businesses:

a) Strong password policies and multi-factor authentication

b) Regular software updates and patch management

c) Encryption for sensitive data, both in transit and at rest

d) Firewalls and anti-malware solutions tailored to Indian threat landscapes

e) Regular data backups and secure storage, considering local infrastructure challenges

f) Access controls based on the principle of least privilege

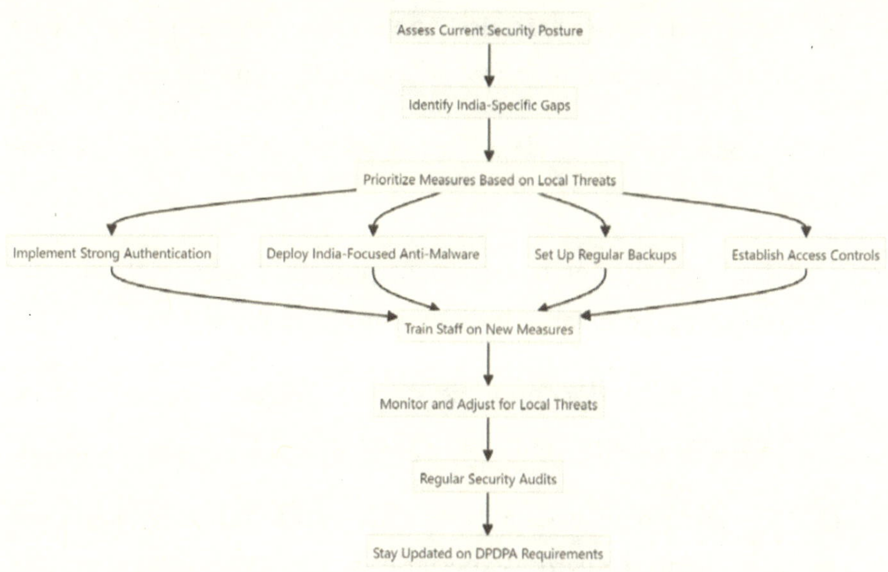

This flowchart outlines the process of implementing basic technical security measures, tailored to the Indian context, from initial assessment to ongoing monitoring and compliance with local regulations.

DPDPA Connection:

3. Key Operational Changes for Data Protection

Implementing data protection isn't just about technology – it often requires significant changes to day-to-day operations. These changes, while sometimes challenging to implement, are crucial for embedding data protection into the organization's DNA, especially in the Indian business environment where data practices may be deeply ingrained in traditional workflows.

Key operational changes to consider in the Indian context:

a) Introducing data protection impact assessments for new projects, considering local data sensitivity

b) Implementing a clear desk policy to prevent physical data breaches, adapted to shared office spaces common in India

c) Establishing a data classification system aligned with DPDPA 2023 categories

d) Creating a vendor management process to ensure third-party compliance, crucial in India's complex supply chains

e) Developing and communicating an incident response plan, considering local reporting requirements

f) Instituting regular data protection audits and reviews, aligned with Indian regulatory expectations

Regulatory Insight: The DPDPA 2023 emphasizes the principle of 'privacy by design'. This means basic data protection measures are not just best practice, but a legal requirement for businesses operating in India. Organizations must be prepared to demonstrate their implementation of these measures in case of regulatory scrutiny.

Data Dilemma: The Oversharing Salesperson in an Indian Context

Rahul, a star salesperson at TechInnovate India, is known for his charismatic personality and ability to close deals. He often shares detailed customer information with potential clients to demonstrate the company's impressive customer base, a practice common in India's relationship-driven business culture. However, Priya discovers that this clearly violates data protection principles under the DPDPA 2023.

How should Priya address this situation, considering both the legal requirements and the cultural context? What operational changes might prevent similar incidents in the future while maintaining the relationship-building aspect crucial in Indian business?

This scenario highlights the challenges of balancing traditional business practices with new data protection requirements in India, emphasizing the need for clear operational guidelines and culturally sensitive training.

As organizations implement these fundamental practices, they lay the groundwork for more advanced data protection strategies. In the next section, we'll explore intermediate-level implementation strategies that build upon this foundation to enhance an organization's overall data protection posture in the Indian business landscape.

Checklist for Basic Strategies

- [ ] Conducted basic DPDPA 2023 awareness training for all staff
- [ ] Implemented strong password policies and multi-factor authentication
- [ ] Established a clear desk policy adapted to your office layout
- [ ] Created a basic incident response plan aligned with DPDPA requirements
- [ ] Implemented regular software updates and patch management processes
- [ ] Developed a simple data classification system

- [ ] Conducted a basic data inventory to identify personal data storage locations

Score: ____ / 7

Practical Exercise for Basic Level: Conduct a "Data Discovery Day"

1. Organize a company-wide event where each department identifies and lists all the personal data they collect, use, or store.
2. Create a simple template for departments to fill out, including:
   - Types of personal data handled
   - Purpose of data collection
   - Storage location (physical and digital)
   - Retention period
   - Access controls
3. Compile the results into a central document.
4. Use this information to identify potential risk areas and prioritize next steps in your data protection journey.

B. Intermediate Level: Enhanced Protection

As organizations in India mature in their data protection practices, they need to adopt more sophisticated strategies to enhance their overall security posture. This section explores intermediate-level implementation strategies that go beyond the basics to provide more robust and tailored protection, considering India's unique digital landscape and regulatory environment.

1. Role-specific Training Programs

While basic training for all staff is essential, organizations at the intermediate level should implement role-specific training programs that address the unique data protection challenges and responsibilities of different positions within the Indian business context.

Key aspects of role-specific training programs in India:

a) **IT Staff**: Focus on advanced security measures, threat detection specific to Indian cyberspace, and incident response aligned with DPDPA requirements.

b) **Human Resources**: Emphasis on handling sensitive employee data (e.g., Aadhaar numbers, caste information) and ensuring compliant recruitment processes in India's diverse job market.

c) **Marketing**: Concentration on consent management in multi-lingual campaigns, data minimization in India's data-rich environment, and compliant use of customer data in a market with rapidly evolving privacy expectations.

d) **Customer Service**: Training on secure handling of customer inquiries and data subject rights requests, considering India's varied levels of digital literacy.

e) **Management**: Strategic overview of data protection risks in the Indian market, governance aligned with DPDPA, and decision-making that balances innovation with compliance.

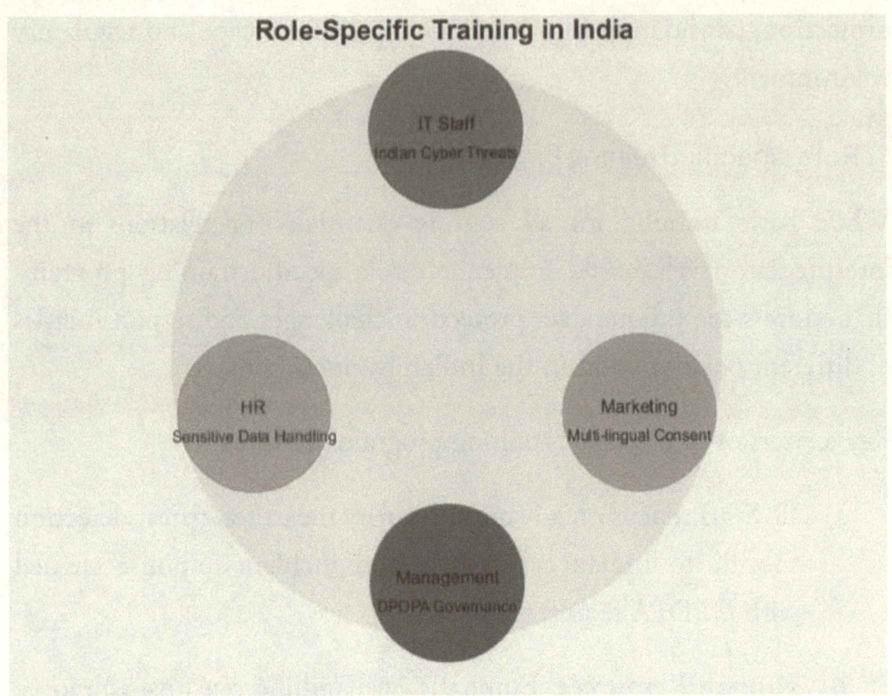

This infographic illustrates role-specific training focus areas tailored to the Indian context, highlighting the unique challenges and responsibilities for different roles in Indian organizations.

> **Quick Tip**: Develop a certification program for role-specific training completion. A Hyderabad-based IT services company found that gamifying their training program with "Data Protection Champion" badges increased voluntary participation by 40%.

2. Adopting Privacy-Enhancing Technologies (PETs)

At the intermediate level, organizations should explore and implement privacy-enhancing technologies that go beyond basic security measures to provide more sophisticated data protection. In India's rapidly evolving tech landscape, PETs are becoming increasingly crucial for maintaining competitiveness and building trust.

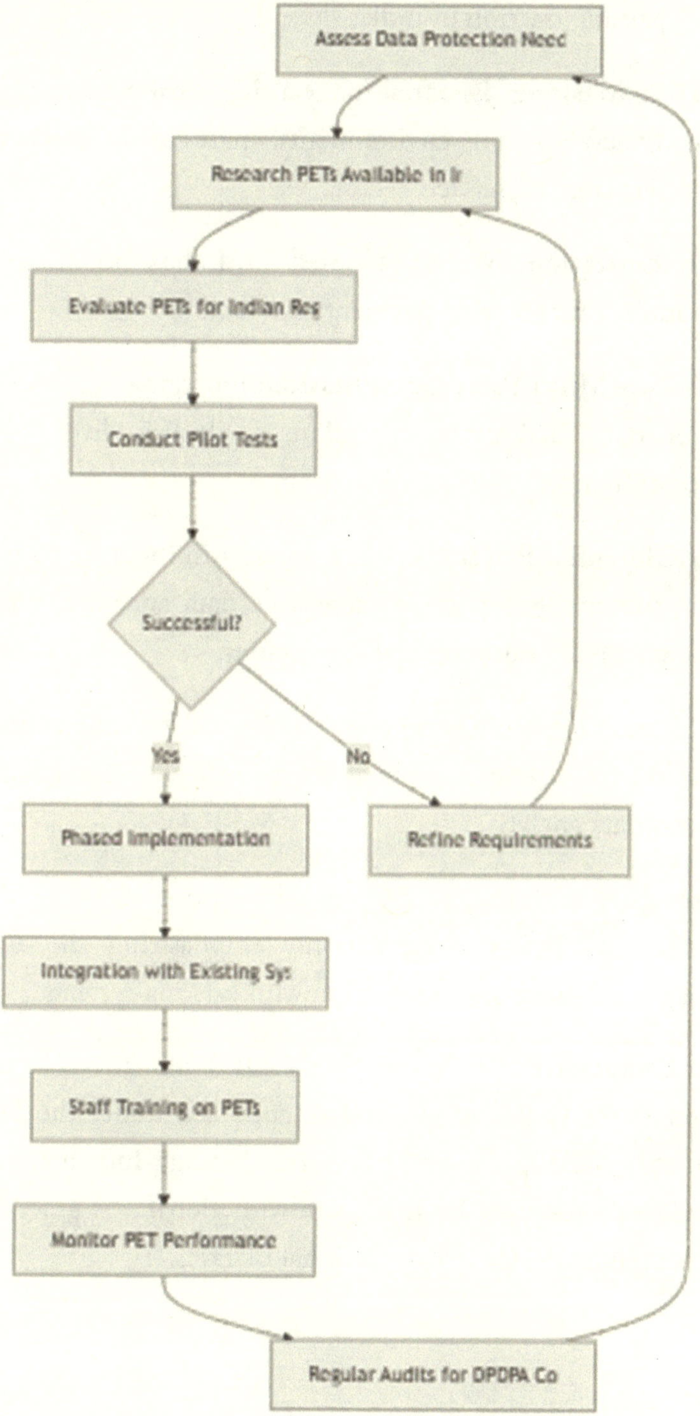

Assess Data Protection Neec

Research PETs Available in Ir

Evaluate PETs for Indian Reg

Conduct Pilot Tests

Successful?

Yes

No

Phased Implementation

Refine Requirements

Integration with Existing Sys

Staff Training on PETs

Monitor PET Performance

Regular Audits for DPDPA Co

Key PETs gaining traction in India:

a) **Data Masking**: Essential for securing sensitive data in testing and development environments, particularly important in India's large IT services sector.

b) **Tokenization**: Widely adopted in India's booming fintech industry for securing payment card data.

c) **Secure Multi-Party Computation**: Emerging as a valuable tool for data analysis collaborations in India's diverse business ecosystem.

d) **Differential Privacy**: Gaining interest in India for its potential in preserving privacy in large-scale data analytics, crucial for sectors like healthcare and smart cities.

e) **Homomorphic Encryption**: While still nascent in India, it's attracting attention for its potential in secure cloud computing and data analysis.

This flowchart outlines the process of adopting privacy-enhancing technologies in Indian organizations, emphasizing the need for regulatory compliance and integration with existing systems.

Global Perspective: While the EU's GDPR has driven significant adoption of PETs in Europe, India's approach under the DPDPA 2023 is still evolving. However, forward-thinking Indian companies are proactively adopting PETs to align with global best practices and gain a competitive edge in international markets.

3. Re-engineering Processes for Better Data Protection

As organizations mature, they often find that existing processes need to be redesigned to fully incorporate data protection principles. This re-engineering effort can lead to more efficient, secure, and compliant operations, particularly crucial in India's dynamic business environment.

Key areas for process re-engineering in the Indian context:

a) **Data collection**: Streamline data collection processes to align with data minimization principles, considering India's traditionally data-rich collection practices.

b) **Data storage**: Implement data lifecycle management to ensure timely deletion of unnecessary data, crucial in a country with rapidly growing data volumes.

c) **Access controls**: Refine access management processes based on the principle of least privilege, addressing challenges in India's often hierarchical organizational structures.

d) **Third-party management**: Enhance vendor assessment and ongoing monitoring processes, vital in India's complex and diverse supply chains.

e) **Data subject rights fulfillment**: Develop efficient processes for handling data access, correction, and deletion requests, considering varying levels of digital literacy among Indian consumers.

f) **Data breach response**: Refine and regularly test incident response procedures, aligning with DPDPA reporting requirements and considering India's unique threat landscape.

Ethical Consideration: When re-engineering processes, organizations must balance efficiency with ethical data use. For instance, while AI can streamline customer service, over-reliance on automated decision-making can raise fairness concerns, especially in a diverse market like India where algorithms may not account for all socio-economic factors.

Data Dilemma: The Legacy System Conundrum in an Indian Bank

A large public sector bank in India relies on a legacy core banking system that doesn't support easy data extraction or deletion. This makes it challenging to fulfill data subject rights requests within the timeframes specified by the DPDPA. The system also lacks robust access controls, potentially exposing customer data to unauthorized internal access - a significant risk given the sensitive financial information involved.

How should the bank approach this situation, considering the substantial costs and operational challenges of system overhaul? What interim measures can be implemented to enhance data protection while long-term solutions are developed?

This scenario highlights the unique challenges faced by traditional Indian institutions in adapting to new data protection requirements, emphasizing the need for careful planning and potentially significant investments in technology and process re-engineering.

As we conclude this section on intermediate-level implementation strategies, it should be clear that enhancing data protection often requires a multi-faceted approach involving specialized training, advanced technologies, and process improvements. In the next section, we'll explore advanced strategies that take data protection to the next level by embedding it into the very core of organizational culture and product development, with a specific focus on the Indian business landscape.

Intermediate Level Implementation Checklist

- [ ] Implemented role-specific data protection training programs
- [ ] Adopted privacy-enhancing technologies (e.g., data masking, tokenization)
- [ ] Re-engineered data collection processes to align with data minimization principles
- [ ] Established a comprehensive vendor management process for data protection
- [ ] Developed efficient processes for handling data subject rights requests
- [ ] Implemented data protection impact assessment (DPIA) processes for new projects
- [ ] Created a data protection audit program

Score: ____ / 7

Practical Exercise for Intermediate Level: Conduct a "Privacy Impact Assessment (PIA) Workshop"

1. Choose a new or existing product/service your company offers.

2. Gather a cross-functional team (e.g., Product, IT, Legal, Customer Service).
3. Use a PIA template (aligned with DPDPA requirements) to assess:
   - Types of personal data collected
   - Purpose and necessity of data collection
   - Data flows and storage
   - Potential risks to individuals' privacy
   - Existing and required safeguards
4. Document findings and action items.
5. Create a plan to address identified risks and implement necessary safeguards.

C. Advanced Level: Privacy by Design

At the advanced level, organizations move beyond reactive compliance to proactively embedding privacy considerations into every aspect of their operations and culture. This approach, often referred to as "Privacy by Design," ensures that data protection is not an afterthought but a fundamental aspect of business strategy and product development. In India's rapidly evolving digital landscape, this advanced approach can be a key differentiator and driver of innovation.

1. Fostering a Privacy-First Organizational Culture

Creating a privacy-first culture goes beyond training and policies; it involves instilling a deep respect for personal data at every level of the organization. This cultural shift can lead to more innovative, trustworthy, and resilient business practices, particularly valuable in India's competitive and fast-paced business environment.

Strategies for fostering a privacy-first culture in Indian organizations:

a) **Leadership commitment**: Ensure top management visibly champions privacy initiatives, crucial in India's often hierarchical corporate structures.

b) **Continuous education**: Implement ongoing privacy awareness programs, adapting to India's evolving data protection landscape.

c) **Transparent practices**: Openly communicate data practices to build trust with employees and customers, addressing growing privacy concerns among Indian consumers.

d) **Employee empowerment**: Encourage employees to raise privacy concerns and suggest improvements, fostering a culture of responsibility.

e) **Privacy champions**: Designate privacy advocates across different departments, creating a network of expertise throughout the organization.

f) **Ethical decision-making**: Incorporate privacy considerations into business decision frameworks, balancing innovation with responsible data use.

g) **Reward and recognition**: Acknowledge and reward privacy-conscious behaviours and initiatives, motivating employees to prioritize data protection.

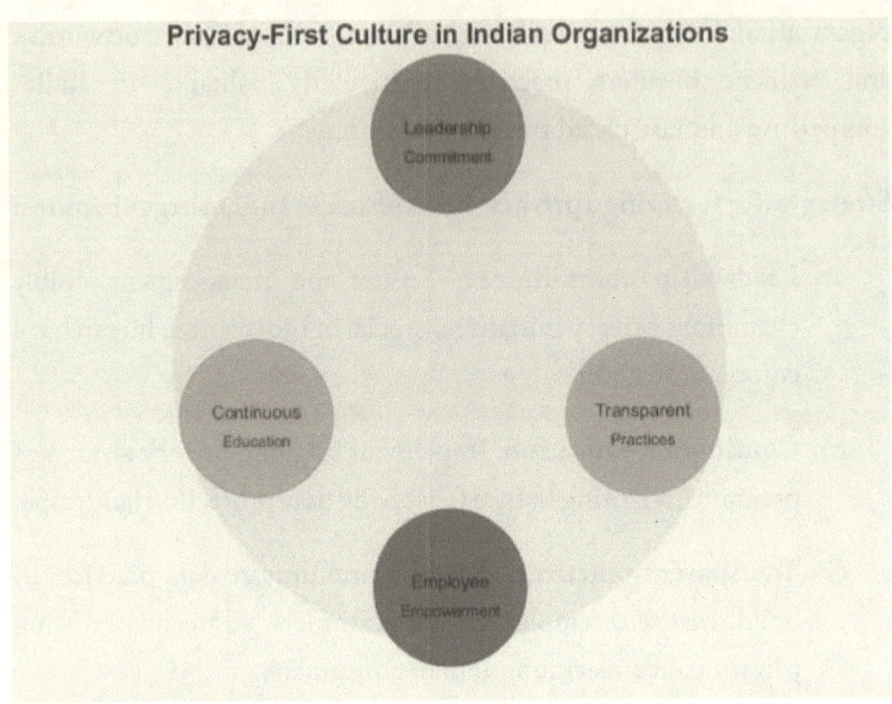

Ethical Consideration: In fostering a privacy-first culture, organizations must navigate the balance between transparency and privacy. For instance, while open communication about data practices is important, care must be taken not to expose sensitive information or vulnerabilities, especially in India's complex socio-economic environment.

2. Implementing Advanced Data Protection Solutions

Organizations at the advanced level should leverage cutting-edge technologies and methodologies to enhance their data protection capabilities. In India's rapidly advancing tech ecosystem, these advanced solutions can provide a significant competitive advantage.

Advanced data protection solutions gaining traction in India:

a) **AI-powered anomaly detection systems**: Leveraging machine learning to identify unusual patterns in data access and usage, crucial in India's large and complex IT environments.

b) **Quantum-resistant encryption algorithms**: Preparing for the future of cryptography, particularly relevant as India invests in quantum computing research.

c) **Homomorphic encryption**: Enabling secure computation on encrypted data, with potential applications in India's growing cloud services sector.

d) **Blockchain-based consent management**: Providing transparent and immutable records of user consent, addressing trust issues in data handling.

e) **Zero-trust architecture**: Enhancing access control and network security, particularly valuable in India's increasingly distributed work environments.

f) **Federated learning**: Allowing machine learning models to be trained across decentralized devices, preserving data privacy in India's diverse and geographically spread markets.

Global Perspective: While homomorphic encryption is still in early adoption stages globally, India's strong IT sector and growing focus on data protection position it well to become a leader in implementing these advanced technologies. Countries like the United States and Israel are currently at the forefront of homomorphic encryption research and development, providing valuable insights for Indian organizations looking to adopt this technology.

Deep Cuts: A Balanced Approach Towards Implementing Advanced Data Protection Solutions

While cutting-edge technologies can enhance data protection capabilities, it's crucial for organizations to approach advanced solutions with caution and pragmatism. In India's diverse business landscape, where companies range from tech giants to traditional SMEs, the rush to adopt the latest solutions can sometimes lead to unnecessary complexity and resource drain.

Consider the following balanced approach:

a) **Assess Current Needs**: Before implementing advanced solutions, thoroughly evaluate whether existing measures are being fully utilized and if they meet current requirements.

b) **Cost-Benefit Analysis**: Carefully weigh the costs of advanced solutions against the tangible benefits they provide. In many cases, optimizing current systems may offer better returns.

c) **Scalability and Integration**: Ensure that any advanced solution can integrate seamlessly with existing systems and scale with the organization's growth.

d) **User Adoption**: Consider the learning curve and potential resistance from employees. Advanced solutions are only effective if they're properly implemented and used.

e) **Regulatory Compliance**: While advanced solutions may offer enhanced capabilities, ensure they align with DPDPA requirements and other relevant Indian regulations.

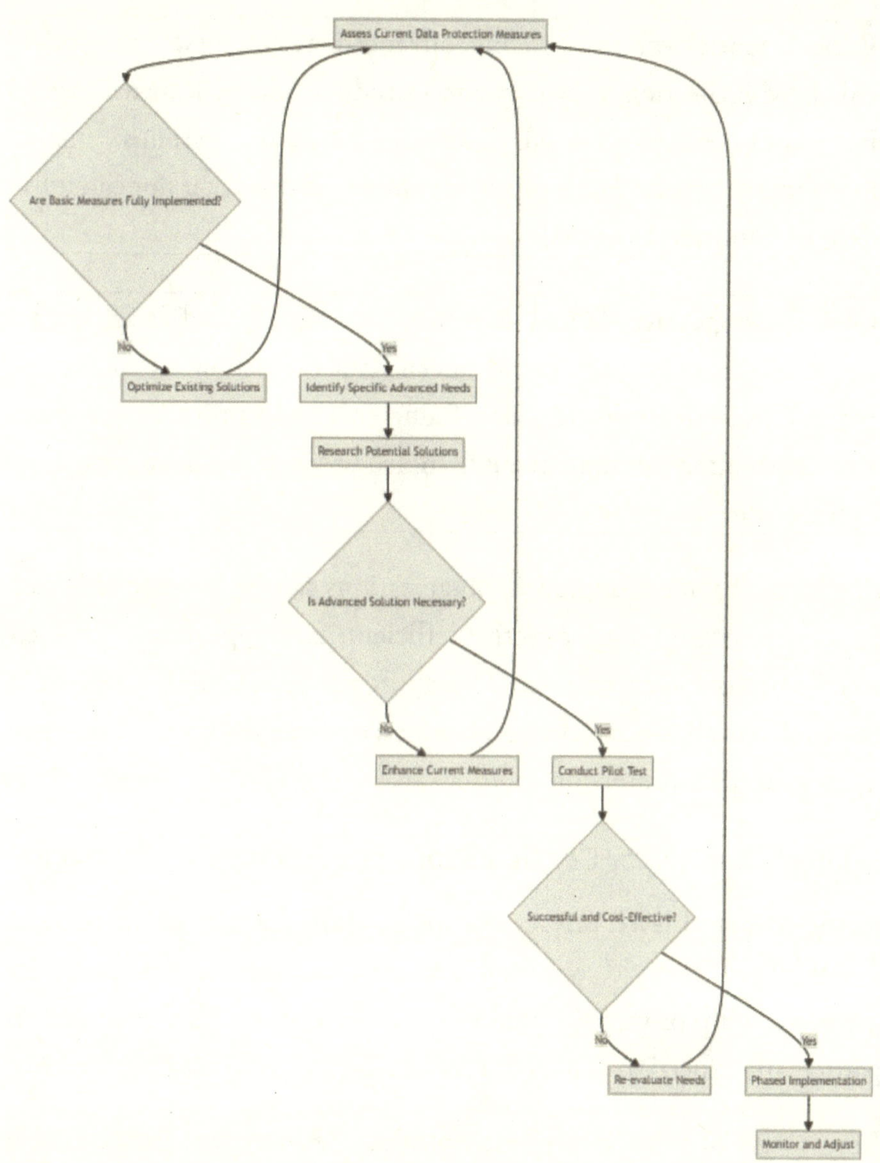

Quick Tip: Before investing in advanced solutions, conduct a thorough audit of your current data protection measures. Often, optimizing existing tools and processes can yield significant improvements without the need for complex new technologies.

Ethical Consideration: While advanced technologies can offer enhanced protection, they may also introduce new ethical challenges. For instance, AI-powered anomaly detection systems might inadvertently create biases or invade employee privacy if not carefully designed and implemented.

Global Perspective: While countries like the US and Israel are at the forefront of developing advanced data protection technologies, many European companies have found success in prioritizing robust implementation of fundamental measures over rapid adoption of cutting-edge solutions.

By taking a balanced approach, organizations can ensure that their data protection strategies are effective, efficient, and appropriate for their specific needs and capabilities. This approach is particularly relevant in India's diverse business ecosystem, where one size does not fit all when it comes to data protection solutions.

3. Integrating Privacy Considerations into Product Development

At the advanced level, privacy becomes an integral part of the product development lifecycle, ensuring that new products and features are designed with privacy in mind from the outset. This approach is particularly crucial in India's innovation-driven tech sector.

Key aspects of privacy-integrated product development in the Indian context:

a) Privacy impact assessments at the conceptualization stage, considering India-specific data sensitivity concerns.

b) Privacy-enhancing features as product differentiators, appealing to India's increasingly privacy-conscious consumer base.

c) Default privacy-protective settings in all products, addressing varying levels of tech-savviness among Indian users.

d) Regular privacy reviews throughout the development process, aligned with evolving DPDPA requirements.

e) Privacy-focused user experience design, ensuring accessibility across India's diverse linguistic and cultural landscape.

f) Transparent communication of privacy features to users, building trust in a market often skeptical of data collection practices.

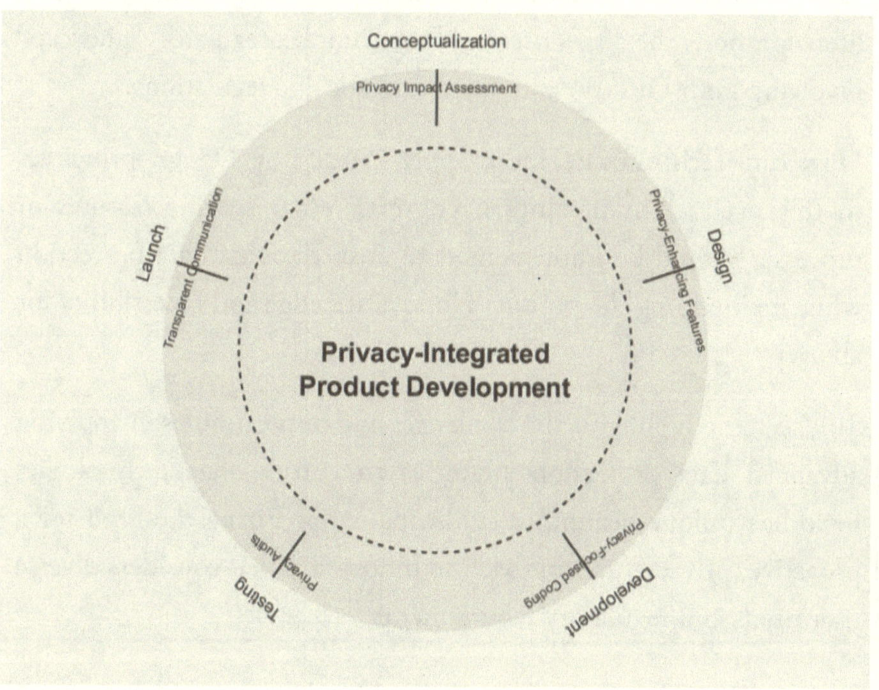

This diagram illustrates how privacy considerations are integrated throughout the product development lifecycle in the Indian context, from conceptualization to launch.

Data Dilemma: The Innovative IoT Device in India's Healthcare Sector

TechInnovate India is developing a groundbreaking IoT device for home health monitoring, targeting India's growing elderly population. The device can collect a wide range of health data, from heart rate to sleep patterns, and is designed to integrate with various third-party health apps and government health initiatives. While the product team is excited about its potential to revolutionize home healthcare in India, Priya is concerned about the privacy implications of collecting such sensitive data, especially given the varying levels of digital literacy among the target users and the complex regulatory landscape involving both DPDPA and healthcare-specific regulations.

How can TechInnovate India apply Privacy by Design principles to this product in the Indian context? What specific features or processes should be implemented to ensure robust data protection while maintaining the product's innovative edge and accessibility for all users?

This scenario highlights the challenges and opportunities in applying advanced data protection strategies to cutting-edge technologies in India's unique healthcare landscape, emphasizing the need for a proactive, privacy-first approach to innovation that considers diverse user needs and regulatory requirements.

As we conclude this section on advanced implementation strategies, it's clear that at this level, data protection becomes more than just a compliance exercise—it's a core business value that drives innovation, builds trust, and creates competitive advantage in India's dynamic digital ecosystem. In our next and final section, we'll explore a case study that brings these concepts to life, demonstrating how an Indian organization can evolve its data protection practices from basic to advanced levels.

Advanced Level Implementation Checklist

- [ ] Established a privacy-first organizational culture
- [ ] Implemented advanced data protection solutions after careful assessment
- [ ] Integrated privacy considerations into the product development lifecycle
- [ ] Developed a comprehensive data ethics framework
- [ ] Implemented a privacy by design approach in all new initiatives
- [ ] Established a data protection governance structure with board-level oversight
- [ ] Developed privacy-enhancing features as product differentiators

Score: _____ / 7

Practical Exercise for Advanced Level: Conduct a "Privacy Innovation Challenge"

1. Organize a company-wide challenge to develop privacy-enhancing features for your products/services.

2. Form cross-functional teams including members from Product, IT, Legal, and Customer Service.

3. Each team should:

   - Identify a privacy pain point in your current offerings
   - Develop an innovative solution that enhances privacy while maintaining or improving functionality
   - Consider the unique needs of the Indian market (e.g., language diversity, varying digital literacy)
   - Present their ideas to a panel of judges (including senior management and external privacy experts if possible)

4. Implement the winning idea(s) in your product development pipeline.

Case Study: Secure Shop - Transforming Operations with Evolving Implementation Strategies

SecureShop, an up-and-coming e-commerce platform based in Pune, serves as a compelling example of how organizations can progressively enhance their data protection practices in the Indian context. Let's follow their journey from basic compliance to advanced, privacy-centric operations.

Phase 1: Basic Level Implementation

When SecureShop first launched in 2020, its founders were more focused on growth than data protection. However, the announcement of the Digital Personal Data Protection Act (DPDPA) 2023 served as a wake-up call.

1. Essential Training: SecureShop started with a company-wide training program. All employees, from customer service representatives to developers, underwent basic data protection training. This included an overview of the DPDPA, the importance of personal data in the Indian context, and basic security practices.

2. Basic Technical Measures: The IT team implemented fundamental security measures, including:

   - Strong password policies and multi-factor authentication

   - Regular software updates and patch management

   - Basic firewalls and anti-malware solutions tailored to Indian cyber threats

3. Operational Changes: SecureShop made key operational changes, including:

   – Implementing a clear desk policy, adapted for their open-office layout

   – Establishing a basic incident response plan aligned with DPDPA requirements

   – Creating a simple data classification system

At this stage, SecureShop discovered that 30% of their customer data was unnecessarily duplicated across different systems, highlighting the importance of data minimization.

Phase 2: Intermediate Level Implementation

As SecureShop's customer base grew, particularly in tier-2 and tier-3 Indian cities, so did the complexity of its data protection needs. The company decided to invest in more sophisticated strategies.

1. Role-specific Training: SecureShop developed tailored training programs. For instance:

   – The marketing team received specialized training on consent management in multi-lingual campaigns.

   – Customer service representatives were trained on securely handling customer inquiries in various Indian languages.

2. Privacy-Enhancing Technologies: SecureShop adopted several PETs, including:

   – Data masking for development and testing environments

   - Tokenization for payment data, crucial for compliance with RBI guidelines

3. Process Re-engineering: The company overhauled several processes, including:

   - Streamlining data collection to align with data minimization principles

   - Implementing a comprehensive vendor management process to ensure third-party compliance, crucial in India's complex e-commerce ecosystem

Ethical Consideration: During this phase, SecureShop grappled with balancing personalized user experiences (highly valued in the Indian market) with data minimization principles. They ultimately decided to offer tiered personalization options, allowing users to choose their comfort level.

Phase 3: Advanced Level Implementation

Recognizing that data protection could be a key differentiator in India's competitive e-commerce landscape, SecureShop decided to embrace a "Privacy by Design" approach.

1. Privacy-First Culture: SecureShop took several steps to foster a privacy-first culture:

   - The CEO became a vocal privacy advocate, regularly discussing its importance in company meetings and public forums.

   - A "Privacy Champion" program was established, with representatives from each department.

2. Advanced Solutions: SecureShop considered implementing cutting-edge data protection solutions but took a balanced approach:

   – After careful assessment, they decided against implementing AI-powered anomaly detection, realizing their current SIEM solution, when properly optimized, could meet their needs.

   – They did, however, implement a blockchain-based consent management platform, seeing significant value in transparent and immutable consent records for their diverse user base.

3. Privacy in Product Development: Privacy became a core consideration in SecureShop's product development process:

   – Privacy impact assessments became mandatory at the conceptualization stage of all new features.

   – The UX team focused on creating privacy-friendly interfaces, ensuring accessibility for users with varying levels of digital literacy.

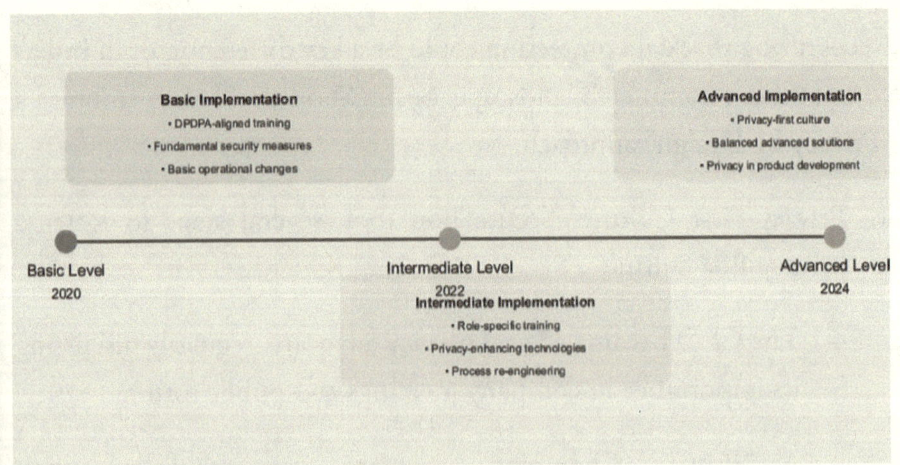

This timeline illustrates SecureShop's progression through the different levels of data protection implementation, highlighting key strategies at each stage.

The results of SecureShop's data protection journey were significant:

- Customer trust increased, leading to a 25% improvement in customer retention rates, particularly notable in a price-sensitive market like India.

- SecureShop's advanced data protection practices became a key selling point, attracting privacy-conscious consumers from metro cities.

- The company's privacy-centric approach to product development led to innovative features, such as a "Privacy Health Score" for users, which was well-received in the market.

- SecureShop was well-prepared for regulatory audits, avoiding potential fines and reputational damage.

- The company became recognized as a leader in data protection within India's e-commerce sector, frequently being invited to speak at industry conferences on privacy best practices.

Secure Shop's journey mirrors similar transformations seen in companies across the EU following GDPR implementation. However, their approach was uniquely tailored to the Indian market, considering factors like linguistic diversity and varying levels of digital literacy.

SecureShop's journey demonstrates that implementing robust data protection strategies is not just about compliance—it's a pathway to building trust, driving innovation, and creating competitive advantage in India's dynamic digital landscape. By progressively enhancing their data protection practices and taking a balanced approach to advanced solutions, organizations can not only meet regulatory requirements but also position themselves as responsible stewards of personal data in the digital age.

As we conclude this chapter, remember that every organization's data protection journey is unique. The key is to start with a solid foundation, continuously evolve your practices, and thoughtfully consider the appropriateness of advanced solutions for your specific context and needs.

Chapter 14: Continuous Monitoring and Improvement

In the bustling tech hub of Bengaluru, Priya, the newly appointed Data Protection Officer at TechInnovate India, stares at her computer screen with a mix of pride and concern. The company has just successfully implemented a comprehensive data protection program, aligning with the Digital Personal Data Protection Act (DPDPA) 2023. Yet, Priya knows that in the dynamic world of data protection, today's solutions can quickly become tomorrow's vulnerabilities.

"How do we ensure our data protection measures remain effective in the face of evolving threats and regulations?" she wonders, echoing a sentiment shared by countless professionals across India's diverse business landscape.

Continuous monitoring and improvement – the often-overlooked final frontier of data protection. It's here, in the realm of ongoing vigilance and adaptive strategies, that the true test of an organization's commitment to data protection lies. As India steps into a new era of digital rights and responsibilities, the ability to not just implement but continuously enhance data protection measures becomes paramount.

The task is particularly crucial in India's unique digital ecosystem. With over 800 million internet users and counting, India represents one of the world's largest and fastest-growing digital markets. This rapid digital adoption, coupled with a complex regulatory landscape, creates a perfect storm of challenges and opportunities for data protection.

Consider these startling statistics:

- According to a 2023 DSCI (Data Security Council of India) survey, while 75% of Indian organizations have implemented basic data protection measures, only 30% have robust continuous monitoring systems in place.
- The Indian Computer Emergency Response Team (CERT-In) reported a 300% increase in cybersecurity incidents in 2023 compared to the previous year, highlighting the ever-evolving nature of threats.
- A 2024 study by NASSCOM found that organizations with mature continuous improvement processes in data protection were 60% less likely to experience significant data breaches.

These figures underscore a critical reality: in the realm of data protection, standing still is akin to moving backwards.

This chapter is your guide to navigating the complex landscape of continuous monitoring and improvement in data protection. Whether you're a small startup taking your first steps towards a mature data protection program or a large corporation looking to stay ahead of the curve, you'll find strategies tailored to your level of maturity and resources.

We'll explore a range of approaches, from essential oversight practices that form the bedrock of ongoing compliance, to advanced, AI-driven solutions that anticipate and mitigate risks before they materialize. Along the way, we'll address common challenges faced by Indian businesses, highlight success stories from various sectors, and provide practical tips to help you navigate this critical aspect of data protection.

Remember, continuous monitoring and improvement is not a one-time effort but an ongoing journey of adaptation and enhancement. As we delve into these strategies, keep in mind that the goal is not just maintaining compliance, but fostering a culture of proactive data protection that enhances trust, drives innovation, and creates lasting value in our increasingly data-driven world.

Let's begin our exploration of how to turn data protection from a static set of policies into a dynamic, evolving practice that keeps pace with the rapid changes in India's digital landscape.

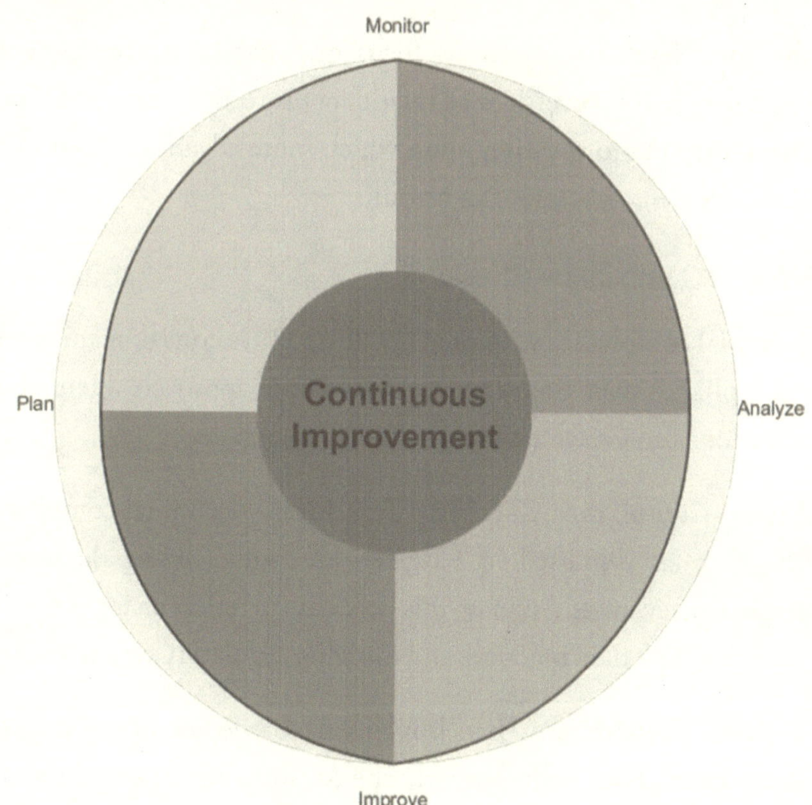

This infographic illustrates the cyclical nature of continuous monitoring and improvement in data protection. The four key stages - Monitor, Analyze, Improve, and Plan - form a continuous loop, emphasizing the ongoing nature of this process. The central "Continuous Improvement" text reinforces the core concept.

As we progress through this chapter, we'll explore each of these stages in detail, providing strategies and insights for organizations at different levels of data protection maturity. Let's begin with the foundational practices that form the bedrock of continuous monitoring and improvement.

A. Basic Level: Essential Oversight

At the basic level, organizations focus on establishing fundamental practices for ongoing oversight of their data protection measures. These practices form the foundation upon which more advanced monitoring and improvement strategies can be built.

1. Evolving Compliance Checks

While initial compliance with the DPDPA 2023 is crucial, maintaining that compliance over time requires a dynamic approach. Here's how organizations can evolve their compliance checks:

a) **Living Compliance Checklist**: Transform your initial compliance checklist (as discussed in Chapter 12) into a living document. Regularly review and update this checklist to reflect changes in your organization's data practices and evolving regulatory requirements.

b) **Periodic Self-Assessments**: Implement a schedule of regular self-assessments. Start with quarterly checks, focusing on key areas such as data collection practices, consent management, and data subject rights fulfillment.

c) **Non-Conformity Tracking**: Develop a simple system to track and address non-conformities identified during self-assessments. This could be as basic as a spreadsheet listing issues, responsible parties, and target resolution dates.

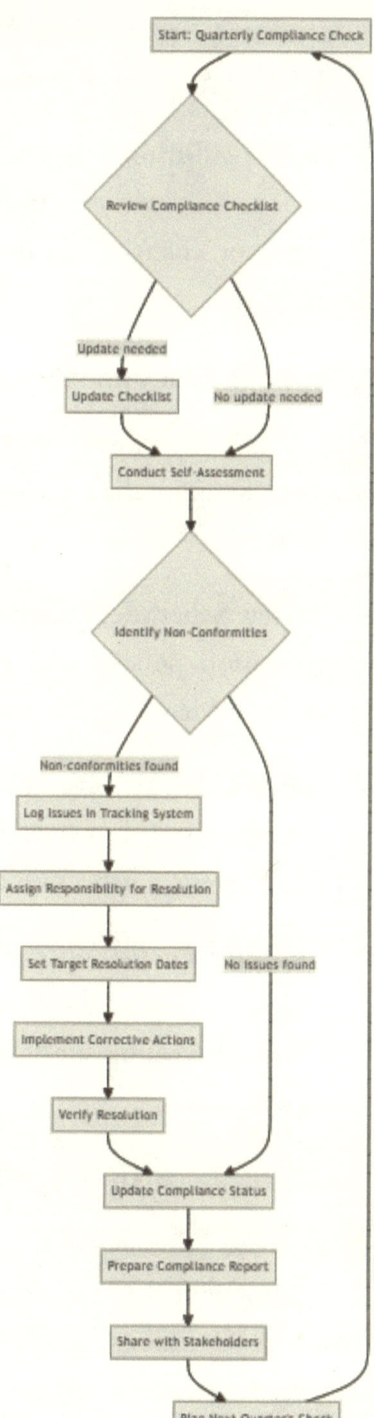

2. Maturing Incident Response Capabilities

An incident response plan is not a static document but a dynamic framework that should evolve based on experience and changing threats. Here's how organizations can mature their incident response capabilities:

a) **Regular Testing**: Conduct periodic tabletop exercises to test your incident response plan. Start with annual exercises, simulating common scenarios such as data breaches or ransomware attacks.

b) **Lessons Learned**: After each real incident or simulated exercise, conduct a "lessons learned" session. Use insights from these sessions to refine your response procedures.

c) **Role Evolution**: Regularly review and update the roles and responsibilities in your incident response team. As your organization grows or changes, ensure your response team structure remains effective.

3. Dynamic Policy and Procedure Reviews

Policies and procedures form the backbone of your data protection program. Keeping them current is crucial for ongoing compliance and effectiveness.

a) **Review Schedule**: Establish a regular schedule for reviewing all data protection policies and procedures. For most organizations, an annual review is a good starting point.

b) **Stakeholder Involvement**: Involve representatives from various departments (IT, Legal, HR, Marketing) in the review process. Their diverse perspectives can help identify gaps and improvements.

c) **Usability Focus**: With each review, assess the usability of your policies and procedures. Are they easy to understand and follow? Consider creating simplified versions or visual guides for complex procedures.

Data Dilemma: The Stagnant Security Measure

Vihan, the IT manager at a mid-sized fintech startup in Mumbai, is dealing with the aftermath of a data breach. During the incident response, he realizes that their data classification policy, last updated two years ago, doesn't account for a new category of sensitive financial data they've been collecting over the past year. This oversight led to inadequate protection measures for this data, contributing to the breach.

As Vihan explains the situation to the board, he's asked a tough question: "Why wasn't this policy updated when we started collecting this new data?"

This scenario highlights the critical importance of regular, dynamic policy reviews. How could Vihan's company have prevented this situation? What processes should they implement to ensure their policies evolve with their data practices?

This "Data Dilemma" underscores the need for dynamic policy reviews and illustrates the potential consequences of neglecting this aspect of continuous improvement in data protection.

As organizations master these basic oversight practices, they lay the groundwork for more proactive and sophisticated approaches to continuous monitoring and improvement. In the next section, we'll explore intermediate-level strategies that take these foundational practices to the next level, enabling organizations to stay ahead of emerging risks and compliance challenges in India's evolving data protection landscape.

B. Intermediate Level: Proactive Management

As organizations mature in their data protection practices, they move beyond basic oversight to more proactive and comprehensive approaches. This section explores strategies that enable organizations to anticipate challenges, respond more effectively to incidents, and stay ahead of regulatory changes.

1. Evolving Data Protection Audit Programs

While basic compliance checks are essential, a more structured audit program can provide deeper insights and drive continuous improvement. Here's how to evolve your audit approach:

a) **Systematic Internal Audits**: Transition from ad-hoc checks to a formal internal audit program. Develop an annual audit plan that covers all key areas of your data protection program.

b) **Risk-Based Scheduling**: Prioritize audit areas based on risk. For instance, departments handling large volumes of sensitive data or new data processing activities should be audited more frequently.

c) **Continuous Improvement Cycle**: Use audit findings to drive a cycle of continuous improvement. Implement a formal process for tracking audit recommendations, assigning responsibilities, and following up on corrective actions.

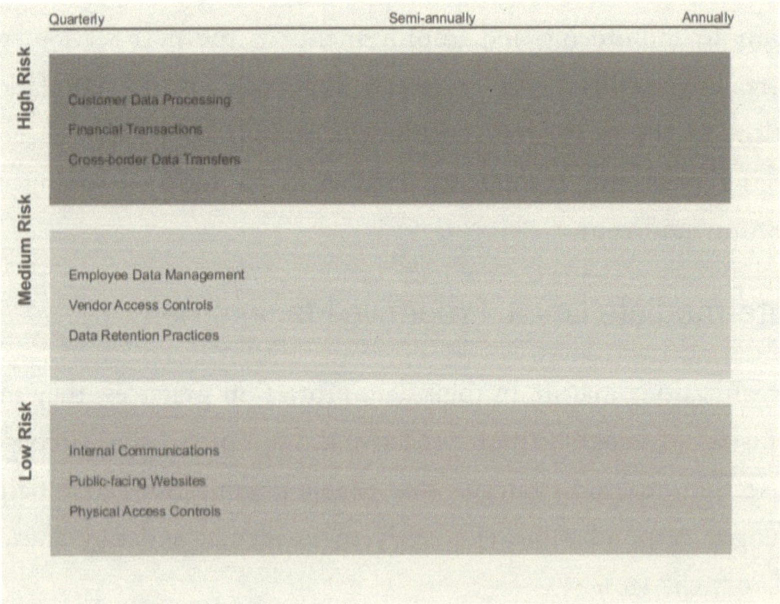

Quarterly
Semi-annually
Annually
High Risk
Customer Data Processing
Financial Transactions
Cross-border Data Transfers
Medium Risk
Employee Data Management
Vendor Access Controls
Data Retention Practices
Low Risk
Internal Communications
Public-facing Websites
Physical Access Controls

High-risk areas are audited more frequently (quarterly), while medium-risk areas are checked semi-annually, and low-risk areas annually. This approach ensures that resources are allocated efficiently, focusing on the areas of greatest potential impact.

2. Adaptive Breach Management and Notification

As cyber threats evolve, so too must an organization's approach to breach management. Here's how to create a more adaptive system:

a) **Evolving Response Workflow**: Regularly update your breach response workflows based on new threats and lessons learned from past incidents or simulations. For example, if you notice an increase in supply chain attacks in your industry, update your workflows to include specific steps for this scenario.

b) **Enhanced Detection and Analysis**: Implement more sophisticated tools for breach detection and analysis. This might include Security Information and Event Management (SIEM) systems or User and Entity Behaviour Analytics (UEBA) tools, for example.

c) **Streamlined Notification Procedures**: Refine your notification procedures to ensure timely compliance with DPDPA requirements. Develop templates for different types of breaches and establish clear decision-making protocols for determining when and how to notify affected individuals and authorities. Once response timeframes are announced, these will be of immediate assistance.

Quick Tip: Leveraging Technology for Effective Breach Response

Consider implementing a dedicated breach management platform that integrates with your existing security tools. Look for features such as:

- Automated incident logging and tracking
- Built-in notification templates aligned with DPDPA requirements
- Integration with threat intelligence feeds for real-time risk assessment
- Collaboration tools for coordinating response across teams
- Analytics for post-incident review and continuous improvement

Remember, the goal is not just to respond faster, but to respond smarter. Choose tools that enhance your team's decision-making capabilities in high-pressure situations.

3. Systematic Regulatory Tracking and Adaptation

In India's dynamic regulatory environment, staying compliant requires a proactive approach to tracking and adapting to changes. Here's how to develop a more systematic approach:

a) **Regulatory Monitoring System**: Establish a robust system for monitoring regulatory changes. This could involve subscribing to updates from legal firms, joining industry associations, and assigning team members to follow key regulatory bodies.

b) **Impact Assessment Process**: Develop a formal process for assessing the impact of new regulations on your existing practices. This should include a cross-functional team to evaluate changes from various perspectives (legal, IT, operations, etc.).

c) **Efficient Policy Updates**: Create a streamlined process for updating policies and procedures in response to regulatory changes. This might include maintaining modular policy documents that can be quickly updated and a change management process for communicating updates across the organization.

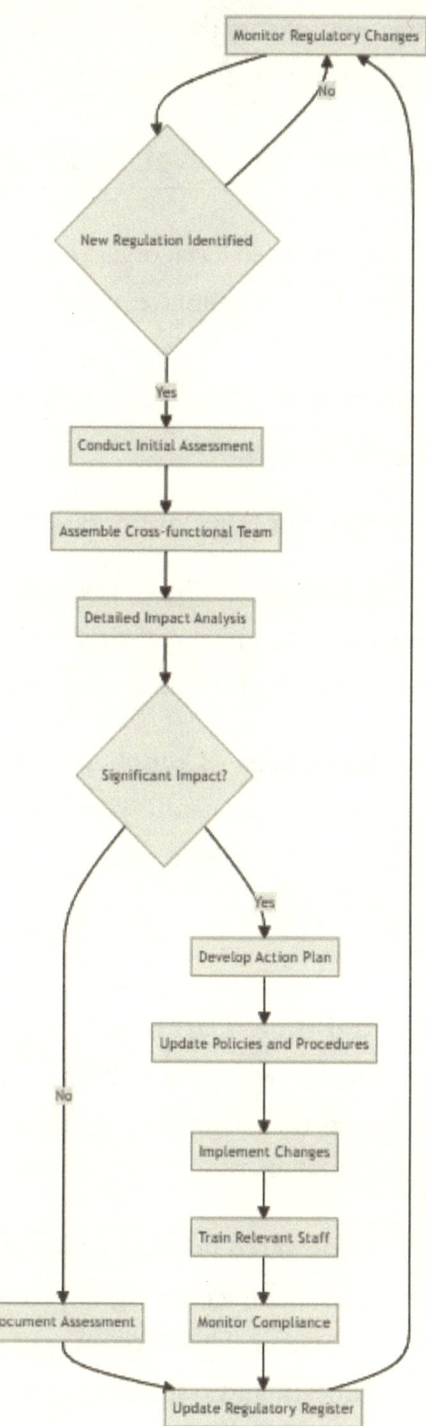

This flowchart outlines a systematic process for adapting to regulatory changes. It starts with continuous monitoring, moves through assessment and planning stages, and concludes with implementation and ongoing compliance monitoring. This cyclical process ensures that organizations can efficiently respond to the evolving regulatory landscape in India.

As organizations implement these intermediate-level strategies, they significantly enhance their ability to proactively manage data protection risks and compliance requirements. However, true leadership in data protection requires even more advanced approaches. In the next section, we'll explore cutting-edge practices that can position organizations at the forefront of data protection excellence in India's competitive business landscape.

C. Advanced Level: Leading Edge Practices

At the advanced level, organizations move beyond reactive and proactive approaches to embrace predictive and innovative strategies for data protection. This section explores cutting-edge practices that can position companies as leaders in data protection within India's rapidly evolving digital landscape.

1. Implementing Continuous Compliance Monitoring

While periodic audits and assessments are valuable, true data protection excellence requires real-time visibility into compliance status. Here's how organizations can implement continuous compliance monitoring:

a) **Automated Compliance Scanning**: Implement tools that continuously scan your systems and processes for compliance violations. These tools can check configurations, access controls, data flows, and other parameters against predefined compliance rules.

b) **Real-time Dashboards and Alerts**: Develop dashboards that provide real-time visibility into your compliance posture. Set up alerts for potential compliance issues, allowing for rapid response to emerging risks.

c) **AI-powered Predictive Compliance**: Leverage artificial intelligence and machine learning to predict potential compliance issues before they occur. These systems can analyze patterns in data usage, access requests, and system changes to flag potential risks.

2. Evolving Risk Management Strategies

Advanced organizations move beyond traditional risk management to embrace more dynamic and comprehensive approaches:

a) **Adaptive Risk Assessment Framework**: Develop a risk assessment framework that automatically adjusts based on changing internal and external factors. This could include real-time threat intelligence feeds, changes in data processing activities, and shifts in the regulatory landscape.

b) **Continuous Risk Monitoring**: Implement tools for continuous risk monitoring across your entire data ecosystem. This includes monitoring of third-party risks, emerging threats, and changes in data flows or processing activities.

c) **Integration with Business Strategy**: Elevate data protection risk management to a strategic level by integrating it with overall business planning. This ensures that data protection considerations are factored into all major business decisions, from new product development to market expansion.

Jargon Buster: Quantitative Risk Assessment

A term borrowed from engineering, Quantitative Risk Assessment (QRA) is an advanced approach to evaluating data protection risks using numerical and statistical methods. Unlike qualitative assessments that use broad categories like "high," "medium," and "low," QRA assigns specific numerical values to:

1. The probability of a risk occurring

2. The potential impact of the risk

3. The effectiveness of controls

This allows for more precise risk calculations, enabling organizations to:

– Prioritize risks based on expected loss

– Conduct cost-benefit analyses of risk mitigation measures

– Make data-driven decisions about risk acceptance or transfer

In the context of data protection, QRA can help Indian organizations make more informed decisions about where to allocate resources for maximum risk reduction. Having said that, this is far more advanced than most Indian organizations require at this point; it is certainly not an essential requirement for data protection regulations in the country.

3. Embracing Emerging Technologies and Practices

To stay at the forefront of data protection, organizations must continuously explore and adopt emerging technologies and practices:

a) **Privacy-Enhancing Technologies (PETs)**: Investigate and implement PETs that are particularly relevant to Indian businesses. This might include:

   - Homomorphic encryption for secure data processing
   - Federated learning for privacy-preserving AI development
   - Blockchain for immutable audit trails

b) **Zero Trust Architecture**: Adopt a zero trust approach to security, which assumes no user, device, or network should be trusted by default, even if they're inside the organization's network perimeter.

c) **Data Ethics Framework:** Develop a comprehensive data ethics framework that goes beyond compliance to address ethical considerations in data use. This is particularly important in India's diverse social and cultural context.

Ethical Consideration: Balancing Innovation with Privacy in the Indian Market

As Indian companies embrace advanced data analytics and AI, they face a unique ethical challenge: How to balance the drive for innovation with the need to protect individual privacy in a society with diverse levels of digital literacy?

Consider a fintech startup developing an AI-powered credit scoring system. The system could potentially provide access to credit for millions of underserved Indians by analyzing alternative data sources. However, it also raises concerns about data privacy, potential bias, and the right to financial privacy.

Questions to consider:

1. How can the company ensure informed consent when many users may not fully understand the implications of data sharing?

2. What safeguards should be in place to prevent misuse of the data or discriminatory outcomes?

3. How can the company balance the societal benefit of financial inclusion with individual privacy rights?

These ethical considerations underscore the need for a robust data ethics framework that goes beyond mere compliance, taking into account the unique social and economic context of India.

As we conclude this advanced section, it's clear that leading-edge data protection practices require a combination of technological innovation, strategic thinking, and ethical consideration. Organizations that successfully implement these advanced strategies will not only ensure robust data protection but also position themselves as trusted leaders in India's digital economy.

In our final section, we'll explore a case study that brings these concepts to life, demonstrating how an Indian organization successfully implemented continuous monitoring and improvement strategies across all levels of maturity.

Case Study: FutureTech Corp - Building an Adaptive, Future-proof Monitoring System

FutureTech Corp, a rapidly growing technology company based in Pune, India, provides cloud-based solutions for businesses across South Asia. As the company expanded its operations and customer base, it recognized the need for a robust, adaptive approach to data protection. This case study follows FutureTech's journey from basic compliance to advanced, AI-driven monitoring over a span of three years.

Phase 1: Establishing the Basics (Year 1)

When Amita Sharma joined FutureTech as its first Data Protection Officer in 2023, she found a company struggling with the basics of data protection. "We had policies in place, but they were gathering dust," Amita recalls. "Our first task was to bring our practices to life."

Amita began by implementing the essential oversight practices outlined in Section A:

1. **Evolving Compliance Checks**: She developed a living compliance checklist, updating it quarterly to reflect changes in FutureTech's data practices and the evolving interpretations of the DPDPA 2023.
2. **Maturing Incident Response**: Amita organized the company's first tabletop exercise, simulating a data breach. The exercise revealed significant gaps in their response capabilities, leading to a comprehensive review and update of their incident response plan.
3. **Dynamic Policy Reviews**: She established an annual policy review cycle, involving stakeholders from across the organization. This

process uncovered several outdated procedures, particularly in the rapidly evolving area of cross-border data transfers.

Challenge Overcome: Resistance to Change Amita faced initial resistance from some department heads who viewed regular compliance checks as a burden. She overcame this by demonstrating how these checks could prevent costly incidents and by integrating the checks into existing business processes to minimize disruption.

Phase 2: Proactive Management (Year 2)

As FutureTech's data protection practices matured, Amita pushed for more proactive approaches, implementing strategies from Section B:

1. **Data Protection Audit Program**: Amita developed a risk-based audit program, prioritizing high-risk areas such as customer data processing and financial transactions for quarterly audits.
2. **Adaptive Breach Management**: FutureTech invested in a Security Information and Event Management (SIEM) system, significantly enhancing their ability to detect and respond to potential breaches.
3. **Regulatory Tracking**: Amita established a cross-functional regulatory working group that met monthly to review changes in the data protection landscape across FutureTech's operating regions.

Success Story: Averting a Major Incident The new SIEM system detected an unusual pattern of data access that turned out to be an attempted insider threat. Thanks to the improved detection and response capabilities, FutureTech was able to prevent a potentially major data breach, saving the company from significant financial and reputational damage.

Phase 3: Leading Edge Practices (Year 3)

With basic and intermediate practices well established, FutureTech was ready to implement advanced strategies from Section C:

1. **Continuous Compliance Monitoring**: FutureTech implemented an AI-powered compliance monitoring tool that provided real-time visibility into their compliance posture across all systems and processes.

2. **Advanced Risk Management**: Amita led the development of an adaptive risk assessment framework that incorporated real-time threat intelligence and automated risk scoring.

3. **Emerging Technologies**: FutureTech began exploring privacy-enhancing technologies, implementing homomorphic encryption to enable secure analysis of sensitive data.

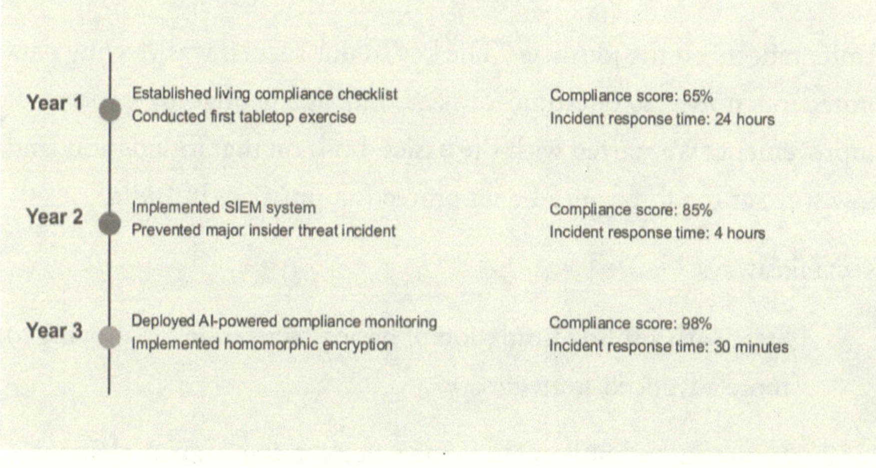

This timeline illustrates FutureTech's progression in data protection practices over three years, highlighting key milestones and improvements in metrics such as compliance scores and incident response times.

Results and Lessons Learned

By the end of the third year, FutureTech's approach to data protection had transformed dramatically:

1. **Improved Compliance**: FutureTech's overall compliance score improved from 65% to 98%, as measured by their continuous monitoring tools.

2. **Enhanced Incident Response**: Average incident response time decreased from 24 hours to just 30 minutes.

3. **Competitive Advantage**: FutureTech's advanced data protection practices became a key differentiator, helping them win contracts with privacy-conscious clients in regulated industries.

4. **Culture Shift**: Data protection became ingrained in the company culture, with employees at all levels actively contributing to privacy and security initiatives.

Amita reflects on the journey: "The key to our success was viewing data protection not as a one-time project, but as an ongoing process of improvement. We started with the basics, built on that foundation, and now we're at the forefront of data protection practices in India."

Key Takeaways:

1. Start with a solid foundation of basic practices before moving to more advanced strategies.

2. Invest in technology, but don't neglect the human element – training and culture are crucial.

3. Stay adaptable – the data protection landscape is constantly evolving, especially in a dynamic market like India.

4. Use data protection as a business enabler, not just a compliance requirement.

FutureTech's journey demonstrates that with commitment, strategic planning, and continuous improvement, organizations can build a robust, adaptive data protection program that not only ensures compliance but also drives business success in India's competitive digital economy.

Conclusion: Sustaining Your Data Protection Program

As we conclude Part 3 of our exploration into implementing effective data protection practices in the Indian context, it's clear that the journey from initial compliance to data protection excellence is both challenging and rewarding. Through our examination of data mapping and assessment, policy development, implementation strategies, and continuous monitoring and improvement, we've uncovered a roadmap for organizations at every stage of data protection maturity.

Recap: Key Strategies Across Maturity Levels

Our journey through data protection implementation has revealed a progression of strategies that organizations can adopt as they mature:

1. **Foundation Building**:
   - Conducting thorough data mapping exercises to understand your data landscape
   - Developing essential policies and standard operating procedures
   - Implementing basic oversight and compliance checks
2. **Proactive Management**:
   - Creating comprehensive data protection audit programs
   - Implementing robust breach management and notification systems
   - Tailoring policies for different business contexts (B2B vs. B2C)

3. **Advanced Practices**:
   - Deploying continuous compliance monitoring tools
   - Implementing privacy by design principles in all business processes
   - Leveraging emerging technologies like AI and privacy-enhancing technologies (PETs)

This progression underscores a crucial truth: data protection is not a destination, but an ongoing journey of improvement and adaptation.

Next Steps: Planning Your Ongoing Progression

As you reflect on your organization's current position in the data protection maturity spectrum, consider a comprehensive approach to continued progress. Begin by honestly assessing your current state using the frameworks and checklists provided in these chapters. Based on this evaluation, set clear, specific, and measurable goals for improving your data protection program, ranging from implementing basic processes to deploying advanced technologies. Develop a phased roadmap to reach these goals, taking into account your resources, risk profile, and business priorities.

Foster a culture of continuous improvement by encouraging ongoing learning, regular policy reviews, and proactive identification of areas for enhancement. Stay informed about evolving regulations, emerging threats, and new technologies that could impact your data protection strategies. Remember, progression doesn't always have to be linear; implementing certain advanced practices in specific high-risk areas while still developing your overall program can often yield significant benefits.

The Bigger Picture: Data Protection as a Business Enabler

As we've seen throughout these chapters, effective data protection is far more than just a compliance exercise. In India's rapidly evolving digital landscape, it can be a powerful business enabler. Robust data protection practices build trust with customers, partners, and regulators, offering a significant competitive advantage in an era where data breaches regularly make headlines. When properly implemented, privacy by design principles can drive innovation, challenging us to think creatively about delivering value while respecting individual privacy.

Proactive data protection strategies not only help avoid costly breaches and regulatory fines but also position your organization to respond swiftly and effectively when incidents occur. As global data protection standards evolve, organizations with mature practices are better positioned to enter new markets and forge international partnerships.

Moreover, the process of mapping data flows, streamlining policies, and implementing monitoring tools often uncovers opportunities for broader operational improvements. In essence, effective data protection can transform from a regulatory requirement into a strategic asset, driving trust, innovation, and growth in India's dynamic digital ecosystem.

As we conclude this exploration of data protection implementation strategies, we stand at an exciting juncture in India's digital journey. The unique challenges and opportunities presented by India's diverse and rapidly evolving digital ecosystem make the pursuit of data protection excellence both complex and rewarding.

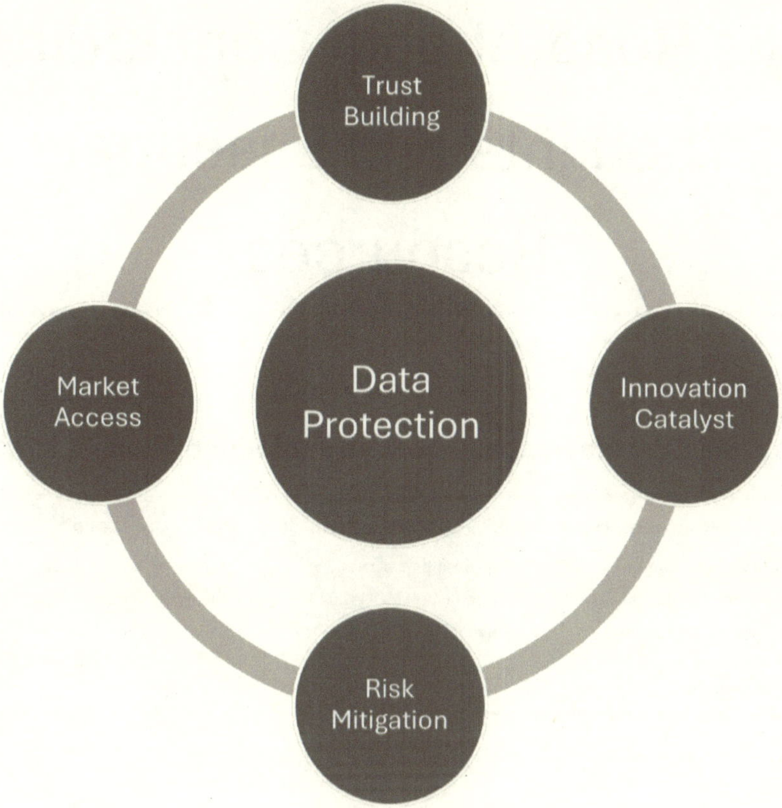

Trust Building

Market Access

Data Protection

Innovation Catalyst

Risk Mitigation

We encourage you to take the insights and strategies presented here and apply them to your organization's unique context. Start today: assess your current state, set a goal for the next stage of your data protection journey, and take concrete steps towards achieving it. Remember, in the dynamic landscape of Indian data protection, the organizations that act proactively and view data protection as a strategic asset will be the ones that thrive in the digital age.

The Road Ahead: Concluding Thoughts and Essential Resources

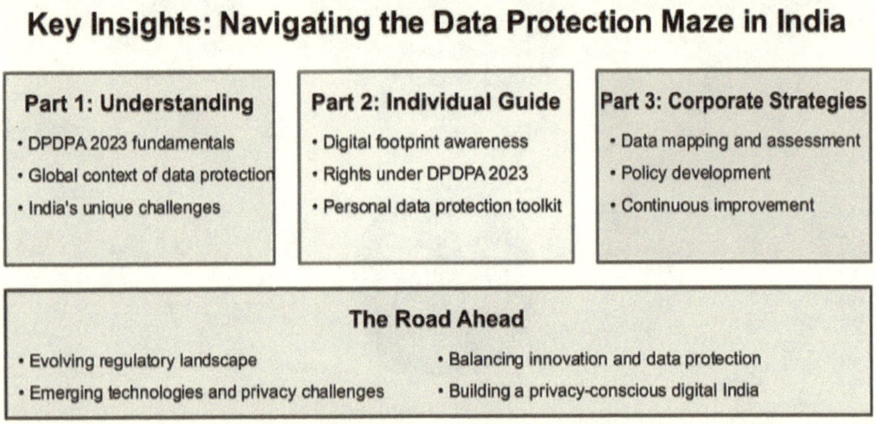

Key Insights: Navigating the Data Protection Maze in India

Part 1: Understanding
- DPDPA 2023 fundamentals
- Global context of data protectio
- India's unique challenges

Part 2: Individual Guide
- Digital footprint awareness
- Rights under DPDPA 2023
- Personal data protection toolkit

Part 3: Corporate Strategies
- Data mapping and assessment
- Policy development
- Continuous improvement

The Road Ahead
- Evolving regulatory landscape
- Emerging technologies and privacy challenges
- Balancing innovation and data protection
- Building a privacy-conscious digital India

As we reach the end of our journey through India's data protection landscape, it's time to reflect on the key insights we've gained and look towards the future. Our exploration has taken us from the fundamentals of data protection to the intricacies of implementing robust privacy practices, both as individuals and organizations.

Let's recap the key insights from each part of our journey:

Part 1: Understanding Data Protection in India

– We delved into the foundations of the Digital Personal Data Protection Act (DPDPA) 2023, understanding its implications for individuals and businesses alike.

- We explored the global context of data protection, seeing how India's approach aligns with and differs from international standards.
- We recognized the unique challenges and opportunities presented by India's diverse and rapidly digitalizing society.

Part 2: The Individual's Guide to Data Protection

- We learned the importance of understanding our digital footprint and the data trails we leave in our increasingly connected lives.
- We explored the rights granted to individuals under the DPDPA 2023, empowering ourselves to take control of our personal data.
- We built a personal data protection toolkit, equipping ourselves with practical strategies to safeguard our privacy in the digital age.

Part 3: Corporate Strategies for Data Protection Compliance

- We navigated the complex process of data mapping and assessment, laying the groundwork for robust data protection practices.
- We developed comprehensive policies and standard operating procedures, translating legal requirements into actionable guidelines.
- We embraced the concept of continuous improvement, recognizing that data protection is an ongoing journey rather than a destination.

As we look to the future, it's clear that the landscape of data protection in India will continue to evolve. The implementation of the DPDPA 2023 marks not an end, but a beginning – the start of a new era in which privacy and data protection become integral to India's digital growth story.

We stand at a crucial juncture where emerging technologies like artificial intelligence, the Internet of Things, and 5G networks promise to revolutionize our lives and businesses. Yet, these same technologies present new and complex challenges to data protection. As we embrace innovation, we must remain vigilant in safeguarding individual privacy and data rights.

The path ahead requires a delicate balance between fostering innovation and ensuring robust data protection. It calls for a collaborative effort from policymakers, businesses, technologists, and individuals. We must work together to create a digital ecosystem that respects privacy, builds trust, and drives sustainable growth.

As we conclude, remember that your role in shaping India's data protection future is crucial. Whether you're an individual making informed choices about your personal data or a business leader implementing privacy-first strategies, your actions contribute to building a more privacy-conscious digital India.

Stay curious, stay informed, and stay engaged in the ongoing conversation about data protection. The journey we've embarked upon in this book is just the beginning. As India's data protection landscape continues to evolve, so too must our understanding and practices.

In the following sections, we'll provide you with essential resources to continue your data protection journey. From a glossary of key terms to practical templates and self-assessment tools, these resources will help you navigate the ever-changing data protection maze with confidence.

Remember, in the world of data protection, knowledge is not just power – it's the key to preserving our digital dignity and building a trustworthy digital future for India.

Personal Reflection from the Author

As I reflect on the journey of writing this book, I'm struck by the rapid evolution data protection has made in India after years of languishing in the background. When I first began this project, the Digital Personal Data Protection Act (DPDPA) 2023 had just been passed into law by the President of India. By the time I penned the final chapters, it has played a major part in fundamentally reshaping India's data protection landscape.

This experience has reinforced my belief in the dynamic nature of data protection. It's not just a set of rules or best practices, but a living, breathing aspect of our digital lives that continually adapts to new technologies, societal changes, and emerging challenges.

One of the most profound insights I've gained is the unique position India occupies in the global data protection discourse. Our country's diversity – in languages, cultures, and levels of digital literacy – presents both challenges and opportunities. We have the chance to craft a data protection framework that's not only robust but also inclusive, one that works for the tech-savvy urbanite and the first-time smartphone user in a rural village alike.

I've always appreciated the critical role of education and awareness in fostering a privacy-conscious society; I would be a terrible academic otherwise! Throughout the writing process, I've tried to bridge the gap between complex legal concepts and everyday digital experiences. My hope is that this book serves not just as a guide, but as a catalyst for broader conversations about privacy and data protection across India.

Looking ahead, I envision a future where data protection is not seen as a burden or an afterthought, but as a fundamental aspect of digital citizenship and responsible business practice. I see India not just keeping pace with global standards, but setting new benchmarks for how a diverse, rapidly digitalizing society can protect its citizens' data while fostering innovation.

This book is not the end of a journey, but the beginning of one. As you, the reader, take these insights and apply them in your personal and professional lives, you become part of a larger movement towards a more privacy-conscious digital India. Your actions, no matter how small, contribute to shaping this future.

I invite you to stay curious, to keep questioning, and to remain engaged in the ongoing dialogue about data protection. The digital landscape will continue to evolve, and with it, our approaches to protecting personal data. Let's navigate this future together, with awareness, empathy, and a commitment to preserving our digital dignity.

Glossary of Key Terms

To help you navigate the complex landscape of data protection, I've compiled a glossary of key terms used throughout this book. This list includes both technical and legal terminology, with a focus on concepts relevant to the Indian context.

Glossary of Key Data Protection Terms

A

Anonymization: The process of irreversibly transforming personal data in such a way that an individual can no longer be identified directly or indirectly.

Accountability: The principle that organizations are responsible for complying with data protection principles and must be able to demonstrate their compliance.

B

Breach Notification: The requirement to inform authorities and affected individuals about a data breach within a specified timeframe. The timeframe typically starts as soon as an organization becomes aware of the breach.

Biometric Data: Personal data resulting from specific technical processing relating to the physical, physiological, or behavioural characteristics of a natural person.

C

Consent: Freely given, specific, informed, and unambiguous indication (through an affirmative action) of the data subject's agreement to the processing of their personal data.

Controller: The entity that determines the purposes and means of processing personal data. In India, this is the Data Fiduciary.

D

Data Protection Impact Assessment (DPIA): A process to help identify and minimize the data protection risks of a project.

Data Subject: An identified or identifiable natural person to whom personal data relates. In India, this is the Data Principal.

Digital Personal Data Protection Act 2023 (DPDPA): The primary data protection law in India, enacted in 2023.

E

Encryption: The process of converting information or data into a code to prevent unauthorized access. Encryption can be one-way (where the original data can never be recovered – for example, hashes and checksums) and two-way (where the original data can be recovered using a key – for example, symmetric and asymmetric key encryption).

F

Fair Processing: The principle that personal data must be processed lawfully, fairly, and in a transparent manner.

G

General Data Protection Regulation (GDPR): A regulation in EU law on data protection and privacy for all individuals within the European Union and the European Economic Area. It has played a major role in defining data protection laws around the world.

H

Harm: In the context of the DPDPA, any injury, loss, damage, or violation of rights caused to a data principal as a result of a breach of the provisions of the Act.

I

Information Security: The practice of protecting information by mitigating information risks.

K

Know Your Customer (KYC): The process of verifying the identity of customers and assessing potential risks of illegal intentions in business relationships. It has also become a catch-all term used for identity authentication.

L

Lawful Basis: The specific reason, as defined in data protection law, that justifies the processing of personal data.

M

Metadata: Data that provides information about other data, often used in the context of understanding data processing activities. It may also be considered personal data based on the context.

P

Personal Data: Any information relating to an identified or identifiable natural person ('data subject').

Processor: An entity which processes personal data on behalf of the controller.

Privacy by Design: An approach to systems engineering which takes privacy into account throughout the whole engineering process.

R

Right to be Forgotten: The right of individuals to have their personal data erased under certain circumstances.

Right to Data Portability: The right for individuals to receive their personal data in a structured, commonly used, and machine-readable format.

S

Sensitive Personal Data: Under the GDPR, this refers to personal data revealing racial or ethnic origin, political opinions, religious or philosophical beliefs, trade union membership, genetic data, biometric data, data concerning health or sex life and sexual orientation. The definition used to exist in India as well under the Information Technology (Reasonable Security Practices and Procedures and Sensitive Personal Data or Information) Rules, 2011, which stands omitted upon the enactment of the DPDPA.

T

Transparency: The principle that data subjects should be informed about the collection and use of their personal data.

V

Valid Consent: Consent that is freely given, specific, informed, and unambiguous, often requiring a clear affirmative action.

Resources for Further Learning

To support your ongoing journey in data protection, I have compiled a list of valuable resources. These will help you stay informed about the latest developments, deepen your understanding of key concepts, and access practical tools for implementing data protection measures.

Government Resources

1. Data Protection Board of India (DPBI) website – whenever it releases
   - Official source for DPDPA 2023 updates, guidelines, and compliance information
2. Ministry of Electronics and Information Technology (MeitY)
   - Provides policy updates and digital initiatives related to data protection
   - [https://www.meity.gov.in/]
3. Indian Computer Emergency Response Team (CERT-In)
   - Offers cybersecurity guidelines and incident reporting mechanisms
   - [https://www.cert-in.org.in/]

Non-Governmental Organizations

1. Internet Freedom Foundation (IFF)
   - Advocates for digital rights and privacy in India
   - [https://internetfreedom.in/]

2. Centre for Communication Governance at NLU Delhi
   - Interdisciplinary research on internet and digital technologies
   - [https://ccgdelhi.org/]
3. Data Security Council of India (DSCI)
   - Industry body focused on data protection and cybersecurity
   - [https://www.dsci.in/]

Recommended Books and Articles

1. "Data and Goliath" by Bruce Schneier
   - Explores the hidden battles to collect your data and control your world
2. "The Privacy Engineer's Manifesto" by Michelle Finneran Dennedy, Jonathan Fox, and Thomas R. Finneran
   - Practical guide to integrating privacy into products and services
3. "Privacy's Blueprint: The Battle to Control the Design of New Technologies" by Woodrow Hartzog
   - Examines the role of design in shaping privacy and data protection

Useful Tools and Apps for Personal Data Protection

1. Privacy Badger
   - Browser extension that blocks invisible trackers
   - [https://privacybadger.org/]

2. DuckDuckGo

   - Privacy-focused search engine

   - [https://duckduckgo.com/]

3. Bitwarden

   - Open-source password manager

   - [https://bitwarden.com/]

This curated list of resources provides a starting point for further exploration of data protection topics. Whether you're looking to stay updated on regulatory changes, deepen your technical knowledge, or enhance your personal data protection practices, these resources offer valuable insights and tools.

Remember to critically evaluate any information you encounter and consider how it applies to your specific context, especially given the evolving nature of data protection in India.

This concludes our book on Navigating the Data Protection Maze in India. We hope this resource serves as a valuable guide in your data protection journey, empowering you to make informed decisions and implement effective practices in this critical area.

Appendices

These appendices provide practical tools and templates to help you implement data protection practices in your organization or personal life. They are based on the principles and requirements discussed throughout the book, with a specific focus on compliance with the DPDPA 2023 in the Indian context.

A. Quick Reference Guides

Summary of Individual Rights under DPDPA 2023

1. Right to Information: You have the right to be informed about the collection and use of your personal data.
2. Right to Access: You can request access to your personal data held by organizations.
3. Right to Correction: You can request the correction of inaccurate or incomplete personal data.
4. Right to Erasure: Under certain circumstances, you can request the deletion of your personal data.
5. Right to Grievance Redressal: You have the right to file complaints about data protection violations.
6. Right to Nominate: You can nominate another person to exercise your rights in case of incapacity or death.

Corporate Compliance Checklist for DPDPA 2023

- [ ] Conduct a comprehensive data inventory and mapping exercise
- [ ] Develop and maintain a Record of Processing Activities (ROPA)
- [ ] Implement appropriate technical and organizational security measures
- [ ] Establish procedures for honouring data principal rights
- [ ] Create and publish clear, concise privacy notices
- [ ] Implement a consent management system
- [ ] Conduct Data Protection Impact Assessments (DPIAs) for high-risk processing
- [ ] Establish a data breach response and notification procedure
- [ ] Implement data retention and deletion policies
- [ ] Ensure proper safeguards for cross-border data transfers
- [ ] Appoint a Data Protection Officer (if applicable)
- [ ] Provide regular data protection training to employees
- [ ] Establish a process for ongoing compliance monitoring and review

Data Breach Response Flowchart

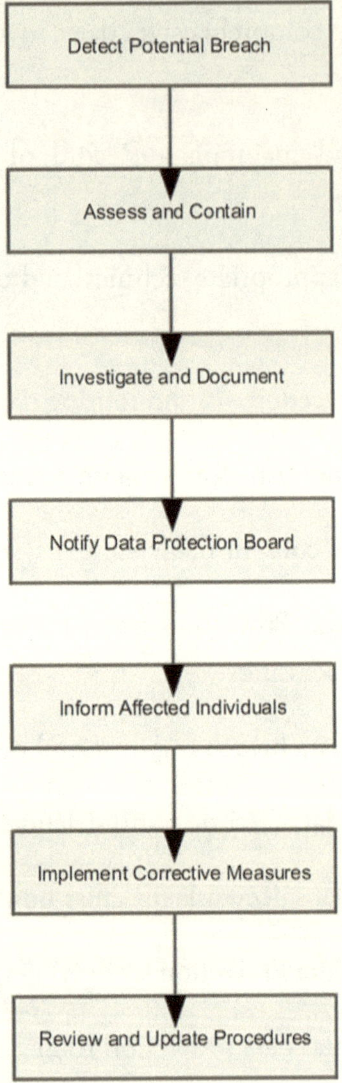

B. Templates and Sample Letters

1. Data Access Request Letter Template

   [Your Name]

   [Your Address]

[City, State, PIN Code]

[Date]

[Company Name]

[Company Address]

[City, State, PIN Code]

Subject: Request for Access to Personal Data under DPDPA 2023

Dear Sir/Madam,

I am writing to request access to personal data that [Company Name] holds about me, as per my rights under the Digital Personal Data Protection Act (DPDPA) 2023.

Please provide me with:

1. Confirmation of whether you are processing my personal data
2. A copy of my personal data that you hold
3. The purposes for which my data is being processed
4. The categories of personal data concerned
5. The recipients or categories of recipients to whom the data has been or will be disclosed
6. The retention period for storing my personal data or the criteria used to determine this period
7. Information about the source of the data, if not collected directly from me

If you need any further information from me to identify my records without placing an undue burden on me, please let me know as soon as possible.

I look forward to receiving the requested information within the timeframe specified by the DPDPA 2023. If you are unable to respond within this time, please inform me of the reasons for the delay.

Thank you for your assistance.

Yours sincerely,

[Your Name]"

2. Consent Withdrawal Template

'[Your Name]

[Your Address]

[City, State, PIN Code]

[Date]

[Company Name]

[Company Address]

[City, State, PIN Code]

Subject: Withdrawal of Consent for Processing Personal Data

Dear Sir/Madam,

I am writing to withdraw my consent for the processing of my personal data by [Company Name] for [specific purpose, e.g., marketing communications].

As per my rights under the Digital Personal Data Protection Act (DPDPA) 2023, I request that you:

1. Stop processing my personal data for the purpose(s) mentioned above

2. Confirm in writing that you have complied with this request

3. Notify any third parties with whom you have shared my data about this withdrawal of consent

If you require any further information to process this request without placing an undue burden on me, please contact me at [your email or phone number].

I look forward to receiving confirmation of the actions you have taken in response to this request within the timeframe specified by the DPDPA 2023.

Thank you for your prompt attention to this matter.

Yours sincerely,

[Your Name]'

3. Data Protection Policy Outline for Small Businesses

    1. Introduction

        – Purpose of the policy

        – Scope of application

    2. Definitions

        – Key terms (e.g., personal data, processing, data principal)

3. Data Protection Principles
   - Lawfulness, fairness, and transparency
   - Purpose limitation
   - Data minimization
   - Accuracy
   - Storage limitation
   - Integrity and confidentiality
4. Rights of Data Principals
   - List of rights under DPDPA 2023
   - Procedures for exercising these rights
5. Data Collection and Processing
   - Types of data collected
   - Purposes of processing
   - Legal basis for processing
6. Data Security Measures
   - Technical safeguards
   - Organizational safeguards
7. Data Breach Response
   - Detection and reporting procedures
   - Notification requirements

8. Third-Party Data Processors

   - Due diligence and selection criteria

   - Contractual obligations

9. Cross-Border Data Transfers

   - Conditions for transfers

   - Safeguards in place

10. Employee Training and Awareness

   - Training program outline

   - Frequency of training

11. Monitoring and Review

   - Compliance audits

   - Policy review schedule

12. Contact Information

   - Data Protection Officer (if applicable)

   - Grievance redressal mechanism

C. Self-Assessment Tools

1. Personal Data Protection Habits Quiz

   Answer Yes or No to the following questions:

1. Do you use unique, strong passwords for each of your online accounts?

2. Have you enabled two-factor authentication on your important accounts?
3. Do you regularly update your devices and applications?
4. Do you read privacy policies before agreeing to them?
5. Have you customized the privacy settings on your social media accounts?
6. Do you use a VPN when connecting to public Wi-Fi networks?
7. Have you ever conducted a personal data audit to know what information is available about you online?
8. Do you regularly clear your browser history and cookies?
9. Have you set up alerts for your name on search engines?
10. Do you avoid sharing sensitive personal information on social media?

Scoring:

- 8-10 Yes: Excellent data protection habits
- 5-7 Yes: Good habits, but room for improvement
- 0-4 Yes: Significant improvements needed in data protection practices

2. Company Data Protection Readiness Assessment

   Rate your organization's readiness on a scale of 1 (Not Started) to 5 (Fully Implemented):

1. Data Inventory and Mapping
   - We have a comprehensive inventory of all personal data we process
   - We maintain an up-to-date Record of Processing Activities (ROPA)
2. Policies and Procedures
   - We have a clear, publicly available privacy policy
   - We have internal data protection policies and procedures
3. Data Subject Rights
   - We have processes in place to handle data subject rights requests
   - Our staff is trained to recognize and respond to such requests
4. Consent Management
   - We obtain and record consent where required
   - We have a process for managing consent withdrawal
5. Data Security
   - We have implemented appropriate technical and organizational security measures
   - We have a data breach response plan
6. Third-Party Management
   - We have data processing agreements with all our data processors
   - We conduct due diligence on third parties who handle personal data

7. Cross-Border Transfers
   - We have identified all cross-border data flows
   - We have appropriate safeguards in place for international transfers
8. Training and Awareness
   - We provide regular data protection training to all staff
   - We have a program to maintain ongoing awareness of data protection issues
9. Governance and Accountability
   - We have appointed a Data Protection Officer (if applicable)
   - We maintain documentation to demonstrate DPDPA compliance
10. Continuous Improvement
    - We regularly review and update our data protection practices
    - We stay informed about changes in data protection laws and regulations

Scoring:

- 40-50: High level of readiness
- 25-39: Good progress, but improvements needed
- 0-24: Significant work required to achieve compliance

About the Author

Dr. **Ketan Modh** is an experienced data protection and privacy professional, with over a decade of experience in the field. He holds a double doctorate in Law and an LLM in Law and Digital Technologies, providing him with a unique perspective on the intersection of technology and legal frameworks.

As a privacy advisory professional at a Big 4 consulting firm, Ketan has led numerous data protection initiatives for major Indian companies, helping them navigate the complex landscape of global privacy regulations. His experience spans various sectors, including finance, healthcare, and technology, giving him a comprehensive understanding of industry-specific challenges.

Ketan's academic background is complemented by his practical experience in the field. He has served as a lecturer at the University of Malta, developing and delivering courses on information law, data protection, and big data. This experience has honed his ability to explain complex concepts in an accessible manner, a skill that shines through in this book.

In addition to his corporate and academic roles, Ketan has contributed significantly to the global privacy discourse. He has assisted the United Nations Special Rapporteur on the Right to Privacy, providing valuable insights on international privacy issues. His work has been presented at prestigious forums such as the European Parliament's Committee on Civil Liberties, Justice and Home Affairs (LIBE) and the Council of Europe.

Ketan is passionate about empowering individuals and organizations to navigate the evolving data protection landscape. He believes that effective data protection is not just about compliance, but about fostering a culture of respect for privacy that can drive innovation and build trust in the digital economy.

Through this book, Ketan aims to demystify data protection for Indian readers, providing practical guidance for both individuals and businesses. His vision is to contribute to the development of a robust, ethical, and innovative data protection ecosystem in India that can serve as a model for other emerging digital economies.

Acknowledgments

The creation of this book has been a collaborative effort, and I am deeply grateful to the many individuals and organizations who have contributed to its development.

First and foremost, I would like to thank my colleagues, whose insights and experiences have greatly informed the practical aspects of this book. Their dedication to navigating the complex world of data protection has been truly inspiring.

I am indebted to the academic community, particularly my mentors and colleagues at the University of Malta, the University of Groningen, the Leiden University, and the National Law University, Jodhpur. Their rigorous approach to legal and technological research has significantly shaped my understanding of data protection principles.

My sincere gratitude goes to the team at the Office of the UN Special Rapporteur on the Right to Privacy, whose global perspective on privacy issues has been invaluable in shaping this book's approach.

I would like to acknowledge the contributions of various Indian privacy advocates and organizations. Their tireless efforts to promote digital rights in India have been a constant source of inspiration.

A special thanks to the team at Notion Press for their support and guidance throughout the publishing process. Their commitment to producing high-quality, accessible content on complex topics has been crucial in bringing this book to fruition.

I am grateful to the numerous privacy professionals, legal experts, and technology specialists who reviewed early drafts of this book and provided valuable feedback. Their diverse perspectives have greatly enhanced the depth and breadth of the content.

On a personal note, I would like to express my heartfelt thanks to my family for their unwavering support and patience during the writing process. Their encouragement has been a constant source of motivation.

Finally, I would like to thank you, the reader, for your interest in this crucial topic. Your commitment to understanding and implementing strong data protection practices is vital for building a privacy-respecting digital future for India.

While many have contributed to this book, any errors or omissions are entirely my own.

Connect with the Author

For professional inquiries or to invite the author for speaking engagements on data protection topics, please contact:

[ketan@legalcircuits.com]

You may also reach him via LinkedIn (/in/ketanmodh).

End Notes

1. For a deeper examination privacy within ancient Indian texts, read the excellent white paper titled "Locating Constructs of Privacy within Classical Hindu Law" written by Ashna Ashesh and Bhairav Acharya and published on The Centre for Internet & Society.
2. This was the judgment of Justice K.S. Puttaswamy v. Union of India delivered on August 24, 2017. For further reading from the venerable court, the judgement on the constitutional validity of the Aadhaar Act is absolutely worth perusing. Fair warning – these judgements, when printed out, could probably fill a library on their own. Supreme Court judges tend to wax loquacious, but every bit of it is worth reading.
3. https://economictimes.indiatimes.com/industry/banking/finance/india-found-cybersecurity-lapses-at-national-payments-corporation-in-2019-govt-document/articleshow/77254889.cms
4. https://www.npci.org.in/what-we-do/upi/product-statistics
5. For reference, see RBI's Circular DPSS.CO.OD.No 2785/06.08.005/2017-18 dated April 06, 2018, or in regular English, "Storage of Payment System Data"
6. You can visit their homepage at https://abdm.gov.in/
7. Also called eSanjeevani, released on 25th March, 2020
8. https://www.ibef.org/news/e-commerce-market-to-hit-us-325-billion-by-2030-rural-india-to-lead-growth
9. https://www.cci.gov.in/images/marketstudie/en/market-study-on-e-commerce-in-india-key-findings-and-observations1653547672.pdf
10. https://www.cci.gov.in/economics-research/market-studies/details/20/1
11. https://zeotap.com/blog/data-clean-room-cdp/
12. https://www.airtel.in/b2b/secure-internet
13. https://www.defindia.org/national-digital-literacy-mission/
14. https://www.pmgdisha.in/about-pmgdisha/
15. https://www.gsma.com/asia-pacific/wp-content/uploads/2022/09/India-report-FINAL-WEB.pdf

16. https://www.wired.com/story/whatsapp-instagram-facebook-data/
17. https://health.economictimes.indiatimes.com/news/health-it/from-aiims-delhi-to-icmr-data-breaches-haunt-crores-of-indians/105173060
18. I'd encourage all my readers to explore this further. A great place to start may be "The Individual and Privacy", a series of essays edited by ex-UN Special Rapporteur on the right to privacy, Prof. Joe Cannataci (who also happened to be one of my doctoral supervisors), and published by Routledge. Cannataci, J.A. (Ed.). (2015). The Individual and Privacy: Volume I (1st ed.). Routledge. https://doi.org/10.4324/9781315239002
19. Here's a study discussed by Linklaters on British respondents (https://www.linklaters.com/en/insights/blogs/digilinks/does-anyone-read-privacy-notices-the-facts) and another by Pew Research on American respondents (https://www.pewresearch.org/internet/2019/11/15/americans-attitudes-and-experiences-with-privacy-policies-and-laws/). It's interesting that similar studies have not been conducted on an Indian sample population; food for thought for a researcher for their next paper, perhaps.
20. https://www.airvistara.com/in/en/privacy-policy
21. https://www.airtel.in/privacy-policy
22. https://www.jio.com/jcms/en-in/privacy-policy/
23. This case, *Karmanya Singh Sareen* v *Union of India*, is still pending in court as of this writing. You can follow it on the Supreme Court Observer for more details (https://www.scobserver.in/cases/karmanya-singh-sareen-union-of-india-whatsapp-facebook-privacy-case-background/)
24. Specifically, this was brought about via the 2014 case of *Google Spain* v *AEPD and Mario Costeja González* (Case C-131/12) before the European Court of Justice's Grand Chamber.
25. You may want to follow campaigns by organizations such as the Electronic Frontier Foundation (https://www.eff.org/) or the Privacy Rights Clearinghouse (https://privacyrights.org/) to see how individuals can contribute to such efforts.
26. You can find more about this action here (https://www.beuc.eu/tiktok)
27. The original press release can be found here (https://pib.gov.in/PressReleseDetailm.aspx?PRID=1635206®=3&lang=1)
28. You can read more about it here (https://developer.apple.com/documentation/apptrackingtransparency)

29. You can read more about it here (https://www.thalesgroup.com/en/markets/digital-identity-and-security/press-release/businesses-collect-more-data-than-they-can-handle-reveals-gemalto). While it's important to take this with a pinch of salt, as Thales has a vested interest in selling their products, this finding seems reasonable – perhaps even underestimated.

30. https://www.pwc.in/press-releases/2024/82-of-indian-consumers-consider-protection-of-personal-data-as-most-crucial-factor-in-building-trust-pwcs-voice-of-the-consumer-survey-2024.html

31. More details about Meta's campaign can be found here: https://about.fb.com/news/2024/07/whatsapps-privacy-campaign-is-an-ode-to-the-resilience-of-people-living-away-from-home/; For Apple's campaign, see here: https://businessworld.in/article/apple-unveils-privacy-focused-safari-ad-campaign-in-india-526275

www.ingramcontent.com/pod-product-compliance
Lightning Source LLC
LaVergne TN
LVHW091249150826
845673LV00006B/1370

* 9 7 9 8 8 9 6 3 2 3 0 6 8 *